CW00350973

Paddy Miller

Mission Critical Leadership

Getting you and your business up to
speed in the new economy

McGraw-Hill Publishing Company

London · Burr Ridge IL · New York · St Louis · San Francisco · Auckland
Bogotá · Caracas · Lisbon · Madrid · Mexico · Milan
Montreal · New Delhi · Panama · Paris · San Juan · São Paulo
Singapore · Sydney · Tokyo · Toronto

Published by

McGraw-Hill Publishing Company

Shoppenhangers Road, Maidenhead, Berkshire SL6 2QL, England

Telephone +44 (0)1628 502500

Facsimile +44 (0)1628 770224

British Library Cataloguing-in-Publication Data

A catalogue record for this book is available from the British Library

Library of Congress Cataloging-in-Publication Data

The LOC data for this book has been applied for and may be obtained from the
Library of Congress, Washington, D.C.

Further information on this and other McGraw-Hill titles is to be found at
http://www.mcgraw-hill.co.uk

McGraw-Hill

A Division of The McGraw·Hill Companies

ISBN 007 709808 0

Sponsoring editor: Elizabeth Robinson
Desk Editor: Alastair Lindsay
Produced by: Steven Gardiner Ltd
Cover design: Simon Levy
Text design: Barker/Hilsdon, Dorset, D17 3TT.
Typeset by David Gregson Associates, Beccles, Suffolk
Printed in Great Britain by Bell & Bain Ltd., Glasgow

To my wife, Sara

Contents

Preface   *xi*

Acknowledgements   *xv*

1 Introduction to Mission Critical Leadership   1

A New Set of Principles   7
  The 1,000-Day Imperative   7
  Simultaneous Implementation   8
  Short-Term Measurement   8
  Clearly Articulated Leadership Architecture   8
  Hewlett Packard and Carly Fiorina   8
The 1,000 Day Imperative   10
  So What Happened to the Time?   11
  1000 Days in the Business Model   13
Simultaneous Implementation   13
Short-Term Measurement   14
  Case-Study: ABC Computer Company   15
Clearly Articulated Leadership Architecture   17
Where Do They Fail?   20
Conclusion   20

2 Mission Critical Leadership in Action   23

The Implications of a New Time-frame   23
  Organizations Are in a Permanent State of Flux   25
  Leadership Tenure is Extremely Restricted   25
  Electronic Communications Dominate   26
  Globalization in Changing the Nature of Teamwork   26
  The Company Stakeholder Model Has Become Increasingly
    Complex   27
The Window of Effectiveness   27

The Challenges   30
The Tasks of the Window of Effectiveness   34
Building a Coalition of Stakeholders   35
Managing Oneself During Transition   36
Window of Efficiency   36
Maintaining Momentum   42
Measures Assessing the Consequences of the Window of
      Effectiveness   42
Redefining the Business Model   42
Relationship Capital   44
Reassess Key People   44
Conclusion   45

3 Reassessment and Alignment of the Business Models   47

The Virtual Corporation   55
Core Competency   57
First Movers versus Slow Movers   58
Business Models and the Internet   58
Conclusion   60

4 Relationship Capital   63

Three Components of Relationship Capital   66
A Rogue's Gallery?   67
Virtual Networks   68
Network Management   71
On Internal Networks   71
On External Networks   72
Building the Network   73
Communication Networks   74
Advice Networks   74
Trust Networks   75
Mapping the Communications Networks   76
Structure, Roles and Membership   76
Density and Holes   77
International Relationship Capital   78
The Power of Globally Distributed Teams   80
Conclusion   81

5 Winning Teams — 83

The TMT is Not a Team! — 85
A New Culture? — 87
What Makes a Mission Critical Team? — 90
  Upward Influence — 91
  Mission — 92
Measures and Rewards — 93
From Team Leader to Mission Critical Leadership — 94
Selecting Potentially Outstanding Team Leaders — 95
Recognizing Potential Winners — 96
Spread the Risk — 97
Reinforcing the Team Culture — 98
Protect the Mavericks — 99
The Problem of Globally Distributed Teams — 99
Conclusion — 102

6 Teams, Task Forces and Tantrums: Getting Mission Critical Teams Working — 103

Design of the Support Structure — 105
The Design of Mission Critical Teams — 107
  Team Composition — 108
  Team Roles — 110
  Training — 111
  Team-Development Process — 113
The Constructive Cycle — 113
  The Kick-off Cycle — 116
  The Operational Cycle and the Destructive Cycle — 117
  The Review Cycle — 119
Conclusion — 120

7 Performance Measurement – Balancing the Scorecard — 121

Out of the Industrial Age and into the Twenty-first Century — 121
Resolving Two Perspectives: The Company and the Mission Critical Leader — 122
A Shift in Pace — 124
The Balanced Scorecard — 125

BT Worldwide: Building Speed into the Scorecard   127
Analysis of Linkages   130
Implementing the Scorecard   131
EVA (economic value added)   133
Problems for the Top-Management Team   138
West Friburg Regional Bank   139
Conclusion   142

8 Leadership Architecture   143

The Shift from Centrality of Control   145
Think Global, Sink Local   146
Social Architecture   148
Scaffolding a Social Architecture   149
Facilitation at Work   149
So What Happened to Culture?   150
Vision   152
Fear of Complexity   152
A Guide to Vision Creation   153
Creating a Passion for the Vision   153
Power   154
Power of Transformation   156
Patronage   156
Understanding Product Architecture   159
Process Architecture   161
Conclusion   164

9 A Concluding Achievement   165

Relationship Capital   165
Successor   166
The Measures   167
Are Careers Dead?   167
Career Prisoners   168
Career Management   169
Personal Mission   169
Staying Too Long   171
Career Strategy   172
Career Scaffolding   172
Learning and Knowledge Acquisition   173

The Stretched Assignment Equals Burn-out   175
Exit Strategies   178
The Next Assignment   178
The Hunted Head   180
Headhunting   180
The Pressure for Creative Destruction   182
Conclusion   183

10 Concluding Observations   **185**

Notes   *189*
Bibliography   *195*
Index   *205*

Preface

After many years of working in the area of leadership writing this book should have been a straightforward undertaking. Everything I had observed and knew about leadership pointed towards an easy journey. Leadership, however, once labelled an illusive phenomenon, continues to be deceptive. What I had 'observed' was couched in terms of well-worn leadership clichés and what was 'known' was little more than common sense. Worse still it was 'known' by everybody else; thus raising the question of whether there was anything new that could be added to the discussion of leadership.

Like most people in the field my observations had been influenced by Gabarro, Covey, Hersey, O'Toole, Drucker and the like. During my student days I was even more strongly influenced by great men such as Bob Boland, Meyer Feldberg and Juan Antonio Pérez-López. They taught me about leaders and leadership and even practised it more often than not. One starts to question one's own ability to add to what had already been done.

Yet all of their models of leadership seemed to be baked in a slow oven at moderate temperatures in villas surrounded by the leafy glades of academe. When one entered the kitchens of business the popular cry was 'if you can't stand the heat, get out of the kitchen!' The intensity of action, the speed of decision making, the transience of new organizations seemed far distant from what was written and taught. The role models of Churchill, Patton, Welch and Carlson seemed to be remote from the types of the middle managers I was talking to – the locus of responsibility had descended in the organization, the level of authority had become very limited and most of them were, well, ordinary people. It's alright banging on about the finer points of Pelé's game as a great footballer but for most people, playing on a Saturday afternoon, they seldom lift their game to similar heights.

It is terribly clichéd to say that the business world is in rapid transition, but it is. Everything we knew about organizational life 10 years ago, maybe even 5, has changed. It is inevitable that we should go back to fundamental principles and start again. With regard to leadership we need to ask: 'With ongoing consolidation in so many industries is organizational stability the norm or the exception?', 'Slack time has all but disappeared in the system with technology accelerating decision making and feedback, how does this influence the existing models of leadership?' 'As demographic profiles shift in organizations, has leadership itself changed?. These were some of the issues that needed to be addressed if any new model of leadership was to prove robust and useful.

Personal experience and researching business leaders in action suggested that speed had become a common factor. Things seemed to be speeding up in most businesses. This new time element had even been labelled by Michael Cusumano as 'Internet time'. Not only were leaders' personal stories reflecting this, the stock markets during the late 1990s confirmed it and everyone's sensation was that 'things' were happening faster. So time, I thought, was the new factor, the new element that had been ignored in other leadership models.

It was the discovery of the story of the jeep that brought me to an abrupt stop. The jeep was the famous all-purpose American military vehicle used during the Second World War. From a design and manufacturing point of view Willys-Overland (the company with which the jeep is always associated) and Ford (the military's fallback supplier) had been amazingly successful. Together they built 700,000 vehicles. But there was a darker side to the jeep story.

In July 1940 the US Army's Quartermaster Corps issued the specification for a quarter-ton cross-country vehicle and called for bids. Bids with prototypes had to submitted within 49 days. All of the larger automobile manufacturers declined and only two bids were received – one from Willys and the other from a small struggling company, the Bantam Car Company. Bantam engineers had tackled the project as a last-ditch attempt to save the company. They had been highly innovative (even scouring the local garbage dump for likely materials to be adapted into their design) and delivered their prototype within the Army's specification and on time. From the point of view of leadership, here appeared to be demonstrated the defining elements of what I was to call mission-critical leadership – high-velocity decision making, teamwork, networking and ability to deliver. As the jeep project was in fact closely aligned to the survival of the business its success was truly mission critical.

Willys, on the hand, simply showed up. They were on time. That was about all they got right – organizationally they showed many of the symptoms of modern 1990s multinationals. Their vehicle was grossly over-weight, in a 7-week test practically every major component failed – the clutch, transmission, springs, steering pin, windshield, frame. Its engine design had been hyped up by the management but was weak (it was replaced three times during the test phase). Management also lobbied extensively in Washington to get the deal.

Bantam got the order for the first seventy vehicles but before too long its plan was handed over to Willys and Ford who then produced all of the Army's vehicles. Bantam had missed an important point – the project was only the first step; it needed to have developed a much broader view on how to link the success of the project to the success of the firm. And this was a problem that leadership had failed to address. In effect, the Bantam management had been great project managers but had failed to be mission-critical leaders – they had won the battle but had lost the war. Admittedly Willys were lucky to get the deal. In fact, showing up on the submission date with whatever they had proved to be vital.

There has been a great similarity between the start-ups and dotcoms of the 1990s – many have great ideas but an inability to deliver sustainable strategies. In the long run many of them would be little more than a Bantam Car Company. The problem for the larger established organization is really: Can it afford to be a Willys? There is little question that understanding and applying the principles of mission critical leadership could have saved Bantam. I came to believe that the same principles could have made Willys a lot more competitive at the outset. It seemed to me that the early success of the dotcoms and start-ups during the late 1990s could be turned to the advantage of managers in large organizations if they could learn the lessons of the Bantam-versus-Willys story – that understanding mission-critical leadership could make a difference.

Articulating those concepts proved to be a challenge because I have found working with managers that there is a need to always search for the practical. For every theory there must be an application and for every application there must be a theory. Outlining pure theory would probably not go down well with most of them. I have tried to apply that idea to this book. When theory is discussed I constantly try to link it to a company example. Most of these examples are based on my case research done over several years. Furthermore, the structure of each chapter facilitates application of the concepts to the reader's own business situation. The reader will find guidelines in each chapter that serve the purpose of focusing on his or her own business.

Acknowledgements

In writing this book I have benefited from the ongoing support of my colleagues at IESE – in them I have found a unique group of people, intellectually stimulating, kind, patient, always tolerant and endlessly entertaining. In particular, this book would not have been written without the encouragement of Dean Carlos Cavallé who more than anyone understood what it takes to get a project such as this to the finishing line. Professor Earl Sasser also played no small part in its completion. He invited me to Harvard Business School to write it. His sponsorship went beyond the call of duty and his generosity together with that of the Harvard faculty is greatly appreciated.

There are so many other people who have contributed to this book that it is inevitable that I will miss some of them. To them I apologize. Others have offered insights that have helped me to formulate the concepts of mission critical leadership over several years: José Luis Alvarez, Pablo Cardona, Bob Christofferson, John Deighton, Ken Dovey, Harry Howell, Eric Joachimstahler, Jaume Ribera, Alan Robinson, Bernard Taylor, Josep Valor and Paul Verdun. Many general managers were interviewed and shared their ideas with me. Though they might not be quoted in the book their time and efforts to clarity the real meaning of mission critical leadership are appreciated. There is also a group of general managers who have generously allowed me into their lives: Gianluca Brozzetti, Alois Linder, Juha Korppi Tommola, Bernard Merric, Tony Phillips, Martin Rafferty, Rich Raimundi and Juan Vila. They have given me insights to their leadership and their organizations and have helped me find the application of the theories espoused herein.

Finally a thank-you to a group of special people. Clare Demarest, my editor, who never rested until every line of this book had been questioned, clarified and rewritten. Clare brought to me an appreciation of writing that I had never had before. Then Sabina Ciminero, the chimney sweep, who cheerfully spent many hours in Baker Library making sure that no stone was left unturned in the search for accurate data for this book. A special thanks to Sabina for contributing in many ways to the writing, editing and presentation of the final manuscript. Finally to Sara (my wife) and Georgina (my daughter) both of whom have had to endure my moments of being a writer. Sara supported this project from the outset, moved to Boston to make it happen and provided every type of support imaginable.

Boston
November 2000

Introduction to Mission Critical Leadership

The new economy has become a big problem. Not for Napster founder Shawn Fanning of course, he stands to make millions basically for showing kids how to pirate music on the Internet. Nor for Timothy Koogle founder of Yahoo! who leveraged up a deal with Ford that won't give him many sleepless nights. These young turks are making their fortunes almost exclusively *because* of the new economy. For some, however, the new economy is decidedly not a windfall, but a tangle of thorns. These folks are managers in old-economy businesses who have to lead, drag or kick their businesses into the new world. To accomplish this, they need to become strong, savvy, fast-stepping leaders. Their salvation lies in mission critical leadership.

Jon van Heck is a perfect example of a leader of an old economy division trying to drag his part of the business into the new economy. Van Heck is a division leader at the Windmill, a global corporation specializing in fast-moving consumer goods (fmcg). He has a traditional marketing background – he progressed through basic training up through the ranks of a large German electronics firm. Then he joined Windmill – where he rose to general manager of Windmill's Mercasur Division. He has almost 20 years marketing experience in South America, and has built a solid career by any standards. Not so long ago, the story would have ended there, happily. But it doesn't.

In recent years, Windmill has had to respond aggressively to its competitors, companies such as Procter & Gamble and Unilever, all of them global and present in every market that Windmill would like to dominate. After helping to facilitate a company-wide restructure and strategy refocus, Van Heck realized that his own job, as well as his role as general manager, had been caught in the maelstrom. As the company implemented ecommerce initiatives on a global scale, the job disappeared before his eyes into a global matrix structure. The company responded by redefining Van Heck's responsibilities and giving him much broader global responsibilities. Now, he was to run both South American and Chinese operations.

Van Heck now found himself in an unsettling situation. He had left behind a regional structure in which, as a successful manager, he had clear and direct impact on bottom-line results. He was entering a much more ambiguous role. In the new structure, regional sections reported directly to the head office and he had little or no impact on the bottom line. Complicating matters was the fact that the regions he managed were on different sides of the globe. Now Van Heck was challenged to find new ways to communicate. Email and videoconferencing, once peripheral technology, became primary communications tools. Managing the technologies became another task for his workload. He began to divide his time between overseeing the region in which he was physically present, and where he spent most of the day, and the region on the other side of the world, which he managed remotely, before dawn and/or after dark.

The story might have ended there, but it didn't. In the time it took Windmill to revamp, the competition had moved on, and ratcheted the pace up another notch. Just as Van Heck was coming to terms with the new role he had taken on, he was given another region – this time, the Iberian peninsula.

Three years ago, Van Heck had a team with whom he could meet on a face-to-face basis almost daily. Today his team is spread around the world, and he is working to learn new global leadership skills on the job. Three years ago he could think in terms of teambuilding. Now he thinks in terms of teambuilders. Then, his leadership role was traditional, face to face, transactional and transforming. Now it is electronic, brief and intermittent. A few years ago Van Heck was one of the best marketing brains in South America. Today, he's working (albeit, overtime) to become one of its best global managers.

Bear in mind that Windmill is neither a start-up nor a dotcom. Its products are traditional fast-moving consumer goods. However, it's been caught up in a process in which competition has speeded up; markets have become increasingly global and a whole host of technologies have combined to change the world in which it operates. Windmill will either learn to move quickly in this new world or become extinct. Moreover, it will find small consolation in the fact that one of its principal competitors, Procter & Gamble, has in recent times also been struggling, and had to replace Durk Jager, its CEO (chief executive officer), with a leader who is equal to the current challenges.

It's not that managers don't understand what the Internet revolution is about. They've read the books. They've taken courses. As the popular expression goes – they have the T-shirt and the keyring – now what? They know that they have to progress from email to ecommerce, from new business models into EB models, to B2B models, to B2C models – and they must do it at warp speed. Most managers know they would steamroller over the new economy upstarts, if only – and this is a big if – they could get their businesses facing the right direction and ready to roll. But the convergence of sheer size, locked-in decisions from the past, the challenges of an ongoing technological revolution, and the bottom line need to maintain cash flow and profitability, conspires to make their efforts sluggish and non-reactive. Like aged prizefighters, managers are waiting in the corner for the next round. They wonder what it will take to get spring back into the legs and to whip the new young challenger.

This book will help managers get up to speed through the principles of mission-critical leadership.

The term 'mission critical' goes back to the early days of the NASA space programme; it signifies any activities that are essential to the success of the mission. It was adopted, then adapted, by business – primarily IT – to describe any technology, supplier or service provider that must function virtually constantly in real time in order for the business to be viable.

In the old economy we joined companies that had many activities but few that were mission critical – companies tried to do everything in house regardless of whether they were profitable or not. To join a company like Royal Dutch/Shell, ICI or IBM was to enter into a perfect world in which there was a department for handling everything from customer complaints to the size of the carpet in your office. How quaint that now seems. Most of

---

Step 1   Guidelines to Assessing Mission Critical Leadership*

(rank and proceed to Step 2)

1.   How fast is your company's sector changing?
     ① Very slowly   ② Slow   ③ Moderate   ④ Fast   ⑤ Very fast

2.   Your company's measurement system measures things that are important?
     ① Mostly   ② Often   ③ Sometimes   ④ Seldom   ⑤ Never

---

*Note: In several chapters, you will find three boxes similar to this that serve as guidelines for practical application of the theory. You may wish to stop and make notes during the reading of the chapter or come back to them after completing each chapter.

business is now mission critical, which means that it is happening now, that we are operating in real time.

Currently, as businesses pare down to become leaner and more adaptive, they are cleaving ever more tightly to the mission-critical principle. Nearly every area of operations in a new-economy company must prove itself to be mission critical to survive. Superfluous activities have generally been pushed aside, outsourced and/or divested. Once a company recognizes its direction, and begins to make operations mission critical, it must set about to find leaders who can effectively lead in this new environment.

Thus, more and more companies will be looking for leaders who can function in very specific ways. The new economy manager must be able to focus on speed of execution in situations where many different things are happening simultaneously and quickly. She must understand that to operate successfully in a fast-paced environment, she must develop and rely on a cohesive, collaborative workforce. She must clearly emphasize short-term execution over long-term planning, but be prepared to investigate myriad scenarios as they develop over time. Her time is restricted – much more so in the new economy than the old. As a consequence, the mission critical leader will need to create urgency around a vision of a new business model that will change thinking and behaviour within a very restricted time-frame and ultimately achieve results.

The mission critical managers who appear in these pages are leaders who are successfully transforming their businesses to bring them up to speed in the new economy. Their cases speak directly to old-economy managers who want to lead their new organizations into the new economy while still maintaining, even improving profitability. This company has no desire, no possibility of becoming a new start-up or a dotcom, they say. What, then, do I need to learn about the new economy that will help me revamp this business and get it into fighting shape? Most of the managers interviewed for this book saw these as the challenges and questions they faced:

- Providing leadership in a traditional organization that is only haltingly adapting to the new-economy market place. Do the traditional leadership models still apply? Are there new rules for leadership?

- Dealing with new and shifting business models. Does 'business model' currently have a common definition? If so, what is it? How do we evaluate business models in a climate where most seem to consist of no more than a good marketing idea?

- Coping with teams that are geographically broadly dispersed. Should we continue to offer teambuilding training for widely dispersed teams whose members rotate often? If so, what kind of training will produce constancy in this environment?

- Keeping talent, and motivating team members. Are we using the right measures to evaluate performance? Are the rewards right for that performance? Can we marshal a response to the start-ups who offer stock options and sophisticated incentive schemes and seem to be able to steal talented people at will?

- Developing a career path now that the organization has given up on the task. How do I think about my own future? What do I tell my people about their future? How can we talk about career paths when the company is evolving so quickly that no path is discernible?

These challenges and questions are complexly interwoven into the problems facing large old-economy businesses. In early 2000, I sat through a strategy presentation by senior managers of a large European bank. Now nearly a century old, the bank has a real drive to go global by increasing its online banking services. Most presenters had been with the bank for 10 to 15 years; they knew banking. They knew the major strategy of every competitor in their sector, traditional European rivals like Deutschebank, Fortis, Amro ABN and Barclays and newer global arrivals like Citibank. Aware that the number of online-banking accounts in Europe were forecast to skyrocket from nearly 10 million accounts in 1999 (17 per cent of Internet users) to 34 million in 2003 (30 per cent of Internet users),[1] they also knew that the riches of online banking are deceptive. Though the number of users of online-banking services in the US (Figure 1.1) has been on the increase as well, no bank has yet shown a profit out of these services.[2]

As I observed the meeting, I became aware that these bankers could develop dynamic and effective strategies to deal with any of their external problems – competitors included. They could not deal as effectively with their internal problems, which in-cluded: their own history; a recent merger, the consequences of which had not yet fully filtered down; and a majority of employees locked into doing things in the old-economy way. More than anything, I sensed, they felt constrained by a feeling of impotence about whether they, as individuals, or even as a group, could effectively do much to change these things.

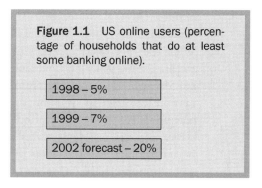

Figure 1.1 US online users (percentage of households that do at least some banking online).

1998 – 5%

1999 – 7%

2002 forecast – 20%

Combine the problems of changing the organization with the uncertainty of online banking and you have a recipe for paralysis. As one senior member of the management board ruefully commented: 'We know we have to move. We have known it for a long time, but when we move, we have to bring the whole bank with us. There's no other way for us.'

The rapid shift to the new economy has caught these managers in the headlights. New entrants providing specialized services are restructuring their market place. Trade-union agreements made with their own employees in another age have forced them to remain entrenched in the old structure. (One of the presenters warned those present not to divulge a single word of the content of his presentation because it might cause a strike among employees.) Their performance measures are not effective. As careers drift toward stalemate, each member faces a personal challenge – to try to survive the next 15 to 20 years until retirement. These managers do not need to be frightened into action. Fear has already created panic and indecision among them. To deal effectively with this situation, they need another perspective.

This book suggests another perspective, and, in presenting it, takes a look at another group of managers, a group that is successfully making the jump from old to new. CEOs like John Chambers at Cisco, Jorma Ollila at Nokia and Carly Fiorina at Hewlett Packard provide us with cogent insight on how to turn challenges into successes. To do so, they are using skills developed in the old economy that will give them a major advantage over start-up leaders – the engineers, inventors and entrepreneurs who have pioneered start-ups – they have proven leadership ability.[3] Start-up leaders must learn those skills, and quickly, before being able to ensure long-term viability of their operations. The managers we will look at have demonstrated their leadership abilities in the old economy, and are adapting them for the new. They have became mission critical leaders, creating real solutions to real problems.

But they've brought more than retooled skills to the table. They have also brought a willingness to think in more complex terms than was required in the old economy. Often, solutions are as complex as the problems they solve. Managers like simple answers to tangled problems. What they are likely to get is more complex. 'It depends on x number of factors' rather than an 'It definitely is'. New-economy solutions are often paradoxical, and cannot be outlined with a laundry list of checkpoints. They may be couched in unfamiliar terminology, another product of the new economy. Terms such as 'intuition', 'belief' and 'feel' may insinuate themselves into the problem-solving dialogue, and transitional managers have begun to think in those terms.

In July 2000, Comstellar, a Chicago-based telecommunications start-up, raised $140 million in investment capital with a description of its *'unique business model based on the belief that if you combine the agility of a start-up with the resources of a large organization, you can launch and build new companies at an accelerated pace and with a higher success rate'.*[4] This was not a preamble to a long description of a business model – this was the business model!

The point is that mission critical leaders (MCLs) must learn to balance the hard and rational with the soft and intuitive. Functioning at high speed does not leave much room for double-checking. A shorter time-frame of execution means that MCLs have a one-time chance of getting strategy right before it goes into the market place to be judged and measured. The new economy has removed slack time from the business model. More importantly for managers, it has challenged them to round-the-clock performance. Some will meet these challenges; others, not.

A New Set of Principles

Humans have worried about not having enough time for ages. The Greek historian Herodotus reported one ancient's complaint – no doubt correct – that the introduction of the sundial had increased the pressure of time for him. Over the centuries, timekeeping technology has brought structure and, with it, strain into the everyday. Internet time, however, is like nothing we've ever seen before. Its pressure is spread across entire sectors, industries and countries. With Internet time, the old ways of planning, making decisions, developing strategy and giving feedback became obsolete almost immediately. Formalized reporting and reward structures are too stiff to accommodate the flexibility needed in the current fast-paced world. The new world required a new set of principles, and it was not long in arriving.

The new principles were initially seen as exceptions to the old rules, a common response to any significant shift in business. Time has tested and proven them, however, and they have gradually become the new rules for success in business. Four guiding principles shape the way MCLs manage. I'll elaborate on each of them in subsequent chapters of this book, but briefly, they are:

The 1,000-Day Imperative
Major strategic shifts of a business succeed or fail within 1,000 days or less. Within that period, various windows of opportunity arise. These I call the *Windows of Effectiveness, Efficiency* and *Achievement*.

Simultaneous Implementation
The processes required in strategic shifts are implemented simultaneously, and in parallel. There is no longer enough time to do things in sequence.

Short-Term Measurement
Process deadlines are measured in days and weeks, not months. Definable landmarks – such as strategy development, deployment and change processes – are constrained by the 1,000-day rule and limited by the ticking of the clock. Long-range planning has all but disappeared.

Clearly Articulated Leadership Architecture
Today's leader faces the dual challenge of having to create an overall vision of where the division is going – of its mission – and at the same time to build in real time the organization that will realize the vision. Since she has a restricted time-frame in which to achieve those conflicting goals, she must constantly balance creativity and practicality.

Hewlett Packard and Carly Fiorina

For 50 years, Hewlett Packard (HP) was considered a major technological leader. Between 1993 and 1997, revenues had doubled, HP had cornered a major slice of the PC market, and was the world's number one seller of printers. But by the end of the 1990s, it was a company with problems. Though its 1999 revenues equalled $42 billion, HP had been watching its growth in sales decline since 1995 – from 26 per cent to 22 per cent to 12 per cent and finally to 10 per cent. HP's stock price had not moved significantly in over a year. CEO Lewis Platt was discovering that drastic change was difficult to impose, though he had split HP into two divisions (HP and Agilent) in order to achieve agility. At Platt's proposal, HP brought in an outsider, Carly Fiorina, to take over the top job.

Fiorina moved quickly. She immediately developed a new brand-building programme, and made sure that all employees understood it and consequently associated it with her arrival. She then moved to cut back on the number of employees – keeping those who bought into her programme and dismissing those who resisted the renewal process. She created a new, more aggressive salary structure that rewarded employees cooperative with her new plan. At the same time, she promised Wall Street new growth – 15 per cent in the first year.

In order to implement her early decisions and actions, Fiorina had to build an internal support structure with the help of division heads, some of whom she had bypassed in her race for the top. She met with each of them, gaining buy-ins from most of them for a fast restructuring of the business, and for a proposal for how HP should handle its branding. In the process she shifted a major portion of the promotional budget out of product marketing and into corporate marketing.

To energize the organization, Fiorina introduced the company to Internet time, emphasizing that time itself was changing. 'Time does not mean what it used to mean,' she told Forbes Magazine. 'In the Internet age things move very, very quickly. And we have to move quickly enough to catch up with that pace.'[5]

Having staked out and articulated her path during her first 100 days, she set up a system whereby her achievements could be judged, then started the Internet clock ticking. At the same time, she began to consider options for the next stage wherein she would be given the opportunity to fine-tune results and consequences of earlier moves.

Fiorina's early victories were many. By the 200th day of her tenure, HP's stock price had doubled. The company had developed a plethora of new customer-focused products – including Espeak, a buying agent that searches the Web for inventories and brokers deals. She had successfully launched a new marketing campaign that focused on HP's corporate-brand image.

Inside and outside the company, the experts struggled to catch up with the changes, and measure the new CEO's performance. There were the usual sceptics. The Financial Times reported that several analysts had downrated their expectations of the company's performance. Others at Merrill Lynch charged that HP printers were 'not the best in class, but benefit from strong brand recognition'.[6] Ironically, that criticism seemed at least in part the result of her success at marketing the brand.

Fiorina's tenure at HP is still playing out. But from her first 200 days, we can extrapolate that she will achieve some measurable success at HP. Fiorina is a good example of mission critical leadership for several reasons. First, she has a strong foundation of experience and values, a characteristic she shares with many of the managers interviewed for the book. Prior to joining HP, she had established an estimable track record at Lucent Technologies. Her track record, as well as her strong personal values, afforded her a warm welcome at HP, a firm that has prided itself on high principles since its founding in 1939.

Step 2   Guidelines to Assessing Mission Critical Leadership

(rank and proceed to Step 3)

3. How many changes have you introduced while in your present job?

① two   ② four   ③ six   ④ eight   ⑤ ten+

4. What has your company's approach to ecommerce been?

① No interest   ② Some interest   ③ Planning   ④ Implementing

⑤ Implemented

Second, because she came well prepared, she was able to hit the ground running, quickly launching a strategy that took full advantage of her Windows of Effectiveness and Efficiency. A manager must initiate an effective strategy during the Window of Effectiveness, since this 180-day period may be the last opportunity to affect dramatic change that arises during her tenure. Many would believe that leaders such as Bob Horton at British Petroleum, Doug Ivestor at Coca-Cola and Bob Ayling at British Airways all made strategic errors at this early stage and were unable to recover speed later. Unlike the old economy, the new rarely affords a second chance for a leader to implement corrective strategy. Once out of Window of Effectiveness and into a Window of Efficiency, a leader's focus must move to fine-tuning the initial strategy, reinforcing momentum and measuring the impact of her early decisions.

Third, Fiorina invested in relationship capital, developing a network of stakeholders to whom she communicated her vision and with whom she developed new missions. By working directly with this group, she was able to keep issues on the table, and political intrigue under control. Finally, she created a support structure of teams and task forces headed by divisional leaders. Because they had been hand-picked, consulted, and included in the development of the new plan, these workers were motivated, and quickly bought into the new strategy. Early on, Fiorina had created the basis of a flexible architecture that stood a fair chance of being successful.

The 1,000-Day Imperative

As executive tenure shortens, managers can no longer operate under the assumption that they have 5 years or more to successfully shift strategy or turn a business around. Major stakeholders – shareholders are an obvious example – demand faster execution. The policy of rotating managers has been tacitly operating in a few organizations for years. Global players such as Phillips the electronics giant, Tetra-Laval the Swedish packaging business, and Sun Microsystems keep their general managers constantly on the move, typically leaving them in a position for no more than 3–4 years. Only under unusual circumstances does a manager remain on the job longer. With few exceptions, this policy has served these organizations well. In a study profiling successful managers, Harvard Business School Professor John Kotter found that promotion tends to come every 1,000 days or so for most. The time-frame seems implicit in the promotional process of many organizations.[7]

So What Happened to the Time?

General managers have been rotating in and out of jobs at a faster pace over the past several years. But that is not the root cause of this new phenomena, this speed-up of time that we are currently experiencing. The real culprit is Internet time.

With the advent of the Internet, our concept of time has completely and irrevocably changed. We are in a period not unlike the one following the recognition of international time zones in 1884. International time zones developed out of the simple need to solve the timetabling problems of fast-moving trains. Because each town and city kept its own sun time, setting a timetable for departures and arrivals was proving difficult for railway companies. Officials soon solved the problem by creating time zones, an idea that moved over the globe with dispatch. Most people at that time were still moving around on foot and horseback, of course, but no matter. Before long, everyone fell in line with the new time zones. Can you imagine using the system of sun time in your office? The idea seems ridiculous today.

Yet, we humans have never found it easy to recognize and adopt a significant technological shift, not even when everything points to its efficacy.

Today's managers are often no different from their military counter-parts of the First World War – so busy in the trenches leading the troops that they fail to see the importance of the burgeoning technology around them. The main forms of communication during the First World War were runners and pigeons, though both radio and telephone had become commonplace by 1914. Military officers were unable to assimilate these new technologies because that they could not make the mental shift necessary to incorporate them into their strategies. Not until the Second World War was the power of these technologies demonstrated.

Most people, Amazon.com's CEO Jeff Bezos among them, say that the Internet is still in its infancy. Clearly though, this powerful infant has already changed our lives profoundly. Arthur Rock, legendary founding father of venture capital, put it succinctly: *'Now everything is on Internet time. Everything moves very quickly, takes a lot of money, and you have nanoseconds to make up your mind.'*[8]

Events are speeding up, a fact that almost no one can fail to notice. The surprise is not the event of it's happening, but rather the speed at which it's happening. Netscape was launched in the summer of 1994. From that point on, complex communication technology was accessible to ordinary folk. It transformed institutions like stock exchanges into readily accessible databases. In the 1980s we experienced the London Stock Exchange's 'Big Bang' which passed unnoticed to most ordinary folk. By 2000, one single broker, Charles Schwab, was measuring 76 million hits a day. The explanation for this speed-up has been neatly parcelled into Moore's Law – the prediction of Intel's Gordon Moore that the number of transistors on a single silicon chip multiplies twofold in cycles of 18–24 months. People now surmise that this law applies not only to technology but to change in general.

Internet time has forced companies to form, develop, succeed, or fail at speeds never before imagined. For instance, British low-cost airline company EasyJet – known as the Web's favourite airline – soared from £17 million in sales to £77 million in its first 2 years. Boo.com soared from a start-up to a £93 million disaster in less that 20 months. The list of hugely influential new firms that were boomed in the 1980s and 1990s is daunting: Sun Microsystems, Lastminute.com, Yahoo!, America Online, Terra Networks, Amazon.com, eBay, Excite, Qualcomm, CMGI, Dell, Nokia.

Traditional firms such as IBM, Apple, Hewlett Packard, Bvlgari and Intel managed to stay afloat during this time by drastically rethinking their organization. Internet time forces companies to experiment, invent, plan and change ideas while *simultaneously* building complex new products and technologies. Many of the key players in the new market place are technology-based companies, but they are not alone in being affected by the accelerated pace. Traditional firms once thought to be non-technological – bookstores, supermarkets and car dealers, for example – are now changing the way they do business. A business can be made overnight in this market, but can disappear just as quickly.

How does this speed translate into the life of a manager? Managers have experienced it in the form of: shortened deadlines for just about everything; constantly increasing demands from customers; intense pressure to demonstrate that they are adding value to the business; longer working hours; more extensive and frequent business trips; and, of course, the

Step 3   Guidelines to Assessing Mission Critical Leadership

(rank and proceed to end of chapter)

5. How long have you held your present job?
① 1–6 months   ② 7–10 months   ③ 11–14 months
④ 15–18 months   ⑤ 18 months+

6. Has your company's business model changed in that time?
① Not at all   ② Slightly   ③ More or less   ④ Noticeably   ⑤ Totally

erosion of their private lives as a consequence of this stress. To survive, management must be flexible enough to pause, reassess the competitive environment, and then rush on – to master 'pulsing', as MIT's Michael Cusumano has termed it.[9]

1,000 Days in the Business Model

Succeed or fail, a manager should not be on a job for more than 1,000 days. This is a fact of life in the new market place. Moreover, if they fail during this period and do not recover from their failure within 1,000 days, they are unlikely to ever regain their footing. This has had an impact on strategy implementation. Yet, organizations have tacitly accepted decreased management rotation time as a fact of life; few have taken into account how this fact has changed the speed at which their strategy moves, however. Because they have not made the 1,000-day time-frame an explicit part of their business model, they have not been able to organize in a way that helps them reap maximum benefit.

From a subjective point of view, executives and managers need to view each 1,000-day period as a *step* toward achieving mission critical leadership, not as an end in itself. Each new job is a transitional phase that challenges a manager to demonstrate mission-critical capabilities, learn new skills and then move on. Each transitional phase, in effect, opens a window of opportunity that gradually closes by the end of the 1,000 days. Being in a job for more than 1,000 days slows a manager's career and bogs down the organization's ability to change.

Simultaneous Implementation

With the advent of Internet time and the 1,000-day rule, managing processes in sequence has ceased to be a viable option. Parallel, simultaneous processing has replaced it. Now managers must develop this new skill as a crucial element of their leadership. Successful implementation of these processes is difficult at best. Imagine a small firm that is made up of twenty teams of ten people. Each person has his or her specific goals and each team has a set of specific goals. Everyone is working at the same time. Some are making progress, some are falling behind. Each and every decision has an impact on every person at the firm. The MCL is in charge of making sure that, while the clock is ticking, this elaborate, multi-dimensional chess game is being played to win. If he pauses, he will lose a turn. If he makes a bad move: checkmate.

Clearly, parallel processing can lead at unprecedented speed to great success or to total chaos. When leaders lose direction, they may be forced to fall back on expediency, resulting in poor product quality, endless technical problems at the production level, unmotivated employees and dissatisfied customers.

Short-Term Measurement

Leadership-building guides often identify the creation of a vision for the organization as a critical element to success, and focus much of their advice on how to develop one. I prefer to focus on building a new business model and, with it, the ability to measure progress in the short term. Deadlines and benchmarks certainly must be identified and measured within the phases of the 1,000-day time-frame; other elements of the leadership architecture are not as easy to quantify. Elements such as relationship capital – the network of informal relationships that employees have – often have as much value to the business model as the more easily quantifiable ones.

When a leader does not have clearly articulated and declared benchmarks against which to measure her success, failure often occurs. There are two phases during which progress measurement is crucial. The first occurs during the 180 opening days of a leader's tenure – in what I call the Window of Effectiveness. Within this window, a mission critical leader will establish the parameters of how to measure achievement in the future and, at the same time, establish credibility for being able to attain these parameters. Between day 180 and day 500 of her tenure, during what I call the Window of Efficiency, a mission critical leader will refine the overall strategy, and create measures through which early gains can be reinforced and embedded in the culture. At the end of the Window of Efficiency, around day 500, while monitoring the attainment of her goals, an effective leader will begin the process of preparing to hand over the reins to a successor.

How does this differ from what managers have always done? New general managers often begin by clearing decks and adopting 'new broom' strategies, in the process, sweeping away employees and bringing in new ones, cleaning up the books and giving a new shine to the assets. However, this house-cleaning process reaches a dead end, and can in fact be counter-productive if old business models and measurement systems are simply reinstated with fresh resources.

Waste Management Inc., the billion-dollar waste-disposal giant, provides a good example of this. In 1998, three directors of the firm, including Robert S. 'Steve' Miller, a legendary Mr Fix-It who had been involved in several turnarounds – including Chrysler's – led a new-broom strategy of acquisition, auditing-systems review and management replacement. In the old days this strategy might have worked. By February 2000, however, the company discovered it was in even more trouble. As they went back to the drawing board, Miller told the *Wall Street Journal*, 'We're all embarrassed,' and Roderick Hills, head of the audit committee admitted, 'I'm not proud of the fact that in retrospect, we didn't know what the hell was going on.'[10]

Repeating the same familiar formula is a recipe for disaster. Peter DeLisi, a consultant and former Digital Equipment Company (DEC) employee, writes about the sense of disillusionment felt by DEC employees after several waves of programmes of change failed to take root. During the layoffs, he says, 'many of us continued our attempts to influence the strategic direction of the company, but now memos were falling on deaf ears ... The system was closing down and executives would simply ignore all input.'[11]

Chester Barnard, author of the classic *Functions of the Executive*, describes effectiveness as 'when a specific desired end is attained'.[12] Fair enough, but organizations are now hugely complex. Effective leadership must be a multi-layered, almost three-dimensional capability. During the Window of Effectiveness, a new leader must sort through multi-layered changes, not least of which is a new way of doing business. As a mission-critical leader introduces a new business model, she must balance disruption with stability, uncertainty with clarity, and risk with steadiness.

Case Study: ABC Computer Company

One company with whom I have worked extensively, let's call it ABC Computing, offers a good example of the consequences of leadership that is not mission critical. John Meyer had been the head of ABC's country division for 6 months. In order to meet shifting market demands, the US-based company had been through several reorganizations in a short time. Meyer had implemented the most recent restructuring strategy, but was not confident that it had been successful.

The strategy had consisted of refocusing product units into business-orientated units – a move widely recognized in the industry as the way to go. For decades prior to the restructure, members of the ABC sales force performed the single task of selling actual computers, a task for which they were rewarded based on achievement. Now, they were being asked to provide a 'total solution package'. in which salespeople were responsible for not only selling products, but also for providing the follow-up service of coordinating consulting and service needs.

Not surprisingly, Meyer's plan was very disruptive. The company now required its sales team to provide more services to each customer. Yet, it provided no service training for the team, nor did it restructure the reward system to compensate for their added efforts. Consulting and Service no longer had direct access to their customers and were less able to help them. The customers were frustrated by the sales team's inability to help them immediately, and were further frustrated by lack of direct access to Consulting and Service, who could. Most workers had no confidence in the new system. To make matters worse, Meyer had not set up any benchmarks by which they could judge its effectiveness. Resultantly, positive results were not attributed to the restructuring. Thus substantive evidence of improvement was thin, and Meyer lost both credibility and leverage.

All the symptoms of an unsuccessful opening strategy can be seen in what Meyer faced at ABC. The company had been through serial reorganizations, led by the belief of some of its senior team that the market had shifted. Not everyone on the team was convinced of this, however, and the split within the team had diluted redesign efforts. Meyer had taken on the job of refocusing the sales team. He quickly set about retitling jobs on the sales force and explaining the new duties. But much, much more was required. To succeed in this restructuring, he needed to put into place appropriate behaviours to make the restructuring work to ensure that the sales team was able to play the role of consultants – not salespeople – and an appropriate reward system to fuel successful change. Unfortunately, Meyer did not set up such a system.

Interestingly, the old structure had actually yielded good results right along. This is not surprising because it was understood and accepted by everyone in the company. Employees had no reason to believe that it was not working. When Meyer entered the picture, and dismissed it out of hand, he sparked them to rebel against the new way. Like many other managers, Meyer failed to take advantage of the window of effectiveness. He spent the remainder of his tenure attempting unsuccessfully to correct the mistakes of his opening strategy.

Clearly Articulated Leadership Architecture

An MCL must have the imagination to envision a whole new organization and the practical skills to build it. Because of the ever-increasing velocity of activities and decision making required in today's world, MCLs need to build an integrated, achievement-focused framework wherein individuals and members of teams and task forces can work toward the same goals. While there may be multiple visions and missions within the workforce, all groups and individuals must be working toward a common, overarching goal that has been clearly outlined by their leader. This flexible construction, which I call the organizational architecture, supports the mission that the leader outlines during the effectiveness window.

As you can see in Figure 1.2, the organizational architecture is made up of two crucial components: a solid foundation and a series of flexible pillars. The foundation is made up of a firm set of personal values, vision, competencies, experience and preparation. The pillars will be based on these. The second element of the foundation is the business model that drives the focus of the 1,000-day tenure. This includes the overarching mission of the division; that is, a vision of what the business is striving for. As with any support structure, the foundation is fundamental; without a good foundation, the pillars will have nothing to stand on. Strong personal values and a clearly articulated business model are essential to good leadership.

Referring again to Figure 1.2, the pillars represent practical ways in which the firm will reach its mission. They include teams and task forces, relationship capital and performance measures that drive motivation. They also include various options that the organization can utilize in meeting its goals. Once an MCL establishes her foundation and her vision of what she will accomplish during her 1,000-day tenure, she then must focus on developing the actions and systems that will put these pillars into place to achieve her goals. Because not all pillars are likely to successfully support the firm's mission, a spread of pillars that are interchangeable is required. Thus, she

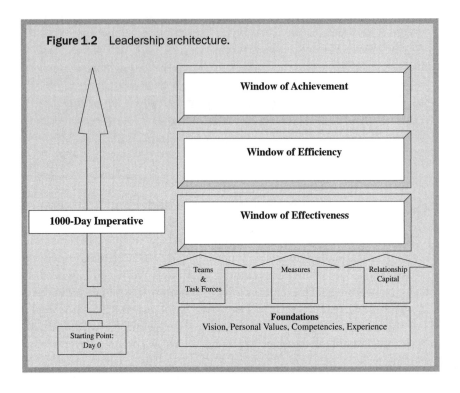

Figure 1.2 Leadership architecture.

must investigate myriad alternatives for supporting the organization. There
are three crucial elements that the pillars must provide:

- First, an effective set of strategic actions and decisions that take into
  account the compacted time-frame in which a mission-critical leader
  must act. The time-frame can be mapped out in terms of the three
  windows of opportunity afforded a new leader – effectiveness, efficiency and achievement. During the Window of Effectiveness (the
  first 180 days), the MCL must establish the major themes of what
  she intends to accomplish in the 1,000-day time-frame. This is a
  period marked by maximum disruption in which she must change
  perspectives and establish behaviours that reinforce the change
  process. During the Window of Efficiency (day 180 through 500),
  she must establish the criteria for measuring, evaluating and fine-
  tuning the results and consequences of the previous period. In order
  for the process of change to proceed at this point, the mission critical
  leader must ensure that her early moves have been accepted and understood, and that there is consensus for her plan. During the Window of
  Achievement (day 500 through 1,000), she must be able to recognize
  and accurately measure results as they become apparent. Regardless of

her success or failure, the executive should be preparing to move on at this point.

- The second function the pillars must serve is to provide relationship capital, which will derive from the human, intellectual and external resources of the business. The mission critical leader must be able to use this function to gain the support of an internal and external constituency that includes market analysts, the media, suppliers and customers. She must also be able to draw on the network of stakeholders who form the coalition of support for strategic activities.

- Finally, the pillars must provide a range of teams and task forces that form buttresses to the principal activities. Each group will have a unique mission and vision that will energize it, and allow it to participate on its own terms. Dramatic market shifts may change an organization's business model overnight, requiring that firms be able to rapidly deploy resources in order to respond to competitive tactics. Mission critical teams provide the structure for such deployment because they are market focused and reward orientated. For maximum flexibility, these teams may consist of contract mercenaries. Unlike traditional teams and task forces, each mission-critical team chooses its own leaders, develops separate and unique missions and provides strategy to energize itself. Teams are rewarded on high performance. Their existence is based on high return, though they clearly involve high risk.

I think it's important to acquaint you with the key components of leadership architecture here, at the outset. I will explore each of these aspects in greater detail in subsequent chapters. First, inherent in the MCL's architecture is the idea that no job is ever perfect. An MCL may seek perfection, but she is always in transition. Every job can always be improved on and will undoubtedly be improved by a successor. An effective leader will operate under the assumption that there is always someone out there who could close in on her market with a new business model, a new method of reaching customers, or a new way of working with suppliers. The MCL will seek out that person – that revolutionary with ideas that will change the business – as a successor.

Second, on a large scale, an MCL will create a learning organization. On a personal scale, because her leadership is always in transition, she will view each position on her career path as a prelude to the next, and each task as a building block in her own corporate education.

Finally, some portion of the leadership architecture is based in the past – for example, a system of strong values and track record – some is grounded in the present, and some in the future. These temporal aspects will integrate in the overall architectural design.

Where Do They Fail?

Unfortunately, mission critical leadership is an area in which managers are more likely to fail than any other. The lack of mission critical leadership in top management has led to unprecedented turnover rates of CEOs and general managers, even in staid organizations such as Coca-Cola, British Petroleum (BP), Xerox, Sainsbury's and BMW. Phil Pfeffer resigned as CEO of Borders Group Inc., the bookselling business, after only 5 months, commenting that it was 'time to move on'. Insiders say that the Board became impatient waiting for him to develop a strategy. In March 2000, *Chain Store Age* calculated that of the top fifty retailers in the US, twenty had new CEOs, and fully half of those appointments were 'trauma inspired'.[13] A further dozen expected to face management-succession problems in the near future. Bank One boasts $273 billion in assets, but hasn't been able to find a CEO who can develop a coherent strategy – 44-year-old Jamie Dimon is the next in line to try.

Coca-Cola provides a good example of the trend: over its 110-plus years of existence, Coke has boasted only ten CEOs. In 1997, after 16 years on the job, CEO Roberto Goizueta stepped down (because he had lung cancer), handing over the reins to a specially prepared successor. The tenure of his replacement, Douglas Ivestor, was much briefer. In late 1999, Ivestor declared that Coke needed 'fresh leadership' and announced he would leave his post after 2 years.[14] Such turnover, while completely unheard of prior to the late 1980s, is now commonplace, not only at the chief executive levels in major companies, but also in secondary management positions and smaller firms (a $1 million settlement accompanied two general managers out the door at British retailer Sainsbury). As the new CEO of British Airways Rod Eddington remarked recently: 'You live or die on your ability to compete.'[15] If so, then these events seem to signify that leaders have not got their mission-critical skills up to scratch.

Conclusion

Mission critical leadership has been evolving for several years across the various sectors of business. It can be seen in the places where you might expect to find it – high-tech conglomerates and Internet start-ups, for instance – but also in isolated pockets of traditional sectors such as financial services, insurance, construction and fashion. The search for it took me through thousands of publications and the curriculum vitae of hundreds of managers. In my interviews with general managers from firms around the world, I heard dramatic tales of success and disillusionment. I poured over dozens of longitudinal case studies about executives in organizations ranging from Hewlett Packard to Enso-Stora (the Scandinavian paper business), to Finansauto (the Spanish franchise operator of Caterpillar) and found many common themes. My research led to one conclusion: the traditional qualities of leadership are being replaced by mission critical leadership.

Mission critical leadership is not a revolutionary concept. It is merely a new roadmap that charts the dramatically altered business landscape. It is a set of guiding principles that will enable today's leader to operate effectively in today's – and tomorrow's – environment. Understanding mission critical leadership is crucial to surviving in this new world. Those who grasp these new rules – whether they are chief executives, general managers or division heads – will be able to succeed in the twenty-first century. It's that simple.

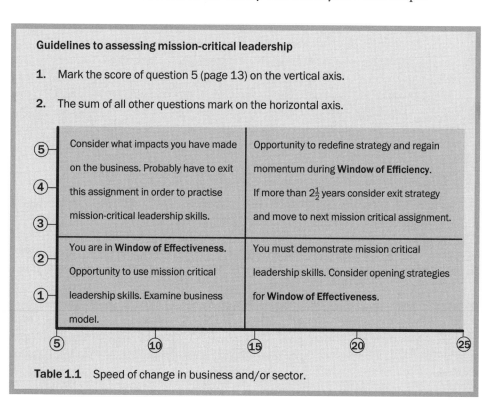

Guidelines to assessing mission-critical leadership

1. Mark the score of question 5 (page 13) on the vertical axis.

2. The sum of all other questions mark on the horizontal axis.

⑤ ④ ③	Consider what impacts you have made on the business. Probably have to exit this assignment in order to practise mission-critical leadership skills.	Opportunity to redefine strategy and regain momentum during **Window of Efficiency**. If more than $2\frac{1}{2}$ years consider exit strategy and move to next mission critical assignment.
② ①	You are in **Window of Effectiveness**. Opportunity to use mission critical leadership skills. Examine business model.	You must demonstrate mission critical leadership skills. Consider opening strategies for **Window of Effectiveness**.

⑤   ⑩   ⑮   ⑳   ㉕

Table 1.1   Speed of change in business and/or sector.

Mission Critical Leadership in Action

The pressure is on middle managers to deliver. Without the hands-on ability, knowledge and experience of middle managers, top managers cannot deliver the results promised by successive mergers, acquisitions and divestments. After years of downsizing and streamlining, companies are now running on leaner structures. This has made the middle manager's job critical, because it has incorporated a whole new set of responsibilities from over-burdened top management. The added workload forces managers to think differently about the job process and to develop strategies and structures that accommodate the added responsibility at the upper end, but continue to deliver bottom-line results. Needless to say, delivery is proving a lot more difficult than expected.

In addition, managers at all levels are spending less time in each job than their predecessors a decade ago. This is happening at the top of organizations where CEOs (chief executive officers) are being changed like coaches of English football teams, and among middle managers, who in the past could have assumed longer tenure than the three-plus years they are getting now.

These shifts have challenged managers mightily, but, at the same time, they have provided them with an opportunity to gain new perspectives on their jobs, speed up their thinking and decision making and develop their ability to deal with and create new business models – in short, the opportunity to transform old-economy management skills into mission critical leadership skills.

The Implications of a New Time-frame

In the old economy, more time in a job always meant more time for learning by trial and error. Now as each job assignment is completed and assessed within a very restricted time limit, managers have a one-off opportunity to get decisions and strategy right. Paradoxically, in the era of the learning organization, companies are, in fact, becoming less tolerant of the mistakes of their leaders. This is true at the highest level where CEOs have left British Airways, Procter & Gamble and Barclays Bank publicly, and with very little notice, as well as lower levels where middle managers regularly leave with little or no publicity.

How successful mission critical leaders address strategies and tactics for the duration of their tenure is the subject of this chapter. Clearly the opening moves of a strategy will determine subsequent behaviour. Opening moves take place during the period of the first 180 days on the job. Any decision or action taken during this time falls within the *Window of Effectiveness*.

The enduring themes of a mission critical leader's (MCL) tenure are established during the Window of Effectiveness. During a subsequent period, called the *Window of Efficiency* those themes are measured, refined and completed. The closing of a job assignment involves a period of decline and closure called the *Window of Achievement*. Successfully exiting from an assignment is as important as effectively opening one, since the assignment as a whole will be viewed as a chapter in her career. The secret of success to the Window of Effectiveness and Efficiency will always be through careful preparation and then action. Bear with me in this chapter as we discuss the ingredients of a successful 1,000-day tenure (Figure 2.1).

Opening moves have always been important in business, of course,

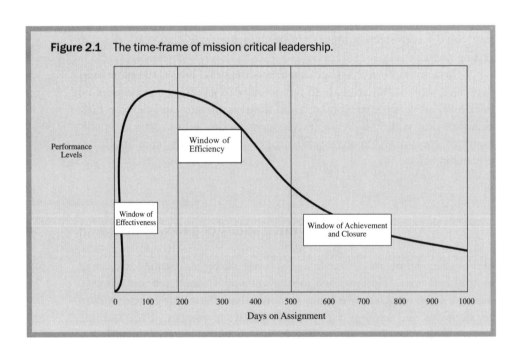

Figure 2.1   The time-frame of mission critical leadership.

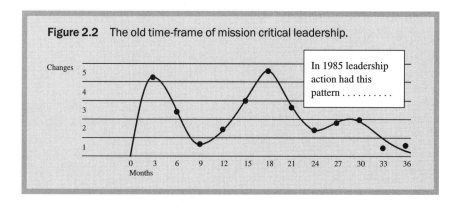

Figure 2.2 The old time-frame of mission critical leadership.

and they have also been well detailed and researched. John Gabarro[1] and Michael Watkins,[2] both Harvard professors, posited that leaders exhibited a clear pattern of behaviour as they developed opening moves. Based on the number of changes introduced by a leader over a period of time, the pattern created wavelike effects of change, the first one during the Window of Effectiveness, and the second during the Window of Efficiency. Figure 2.2 shows that the second wave is slightly larger than the first, reflecting a period of correction or reshaping as Gabarro called it. The new economy has disrupted the foundations of this process, and has undermined its predictability as well. The reasons are as follows:

Organizations Are in a Permanent State of Flux

This is because downsizing, rightsizing, merger and demerger, acquisition and disinvestments have all become a way of life. I suspect it would be impossible to find a manager today who believes that her organization will return to any sense of stability. Instability has certainly created opportunities, but, at the same time, permanent instability creates mistrust within a peer group, uncertainty about senior management and subordinates and, inevitably, insecurity about the future.

Leadership Tenure is Extremely Restricted

Consider Gabarro's view in 1985, and even Watkins' view in 1999, that after 3 years a leader would no longer be considered new, and could now be assumed to have taken full responsibility for the division or department. Today, a leader's tenure can be considered *finished* after 3 years. In effect we have *cut* the second wave from Gabarro's model as well as the tail (Figure 2.3).

Figure 2.3 The new time-frame of mission critical leadership.

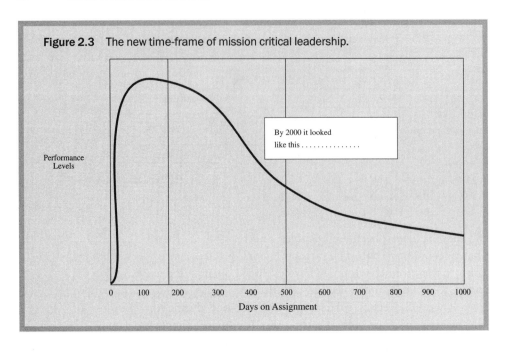

Before proceeding ask yourself these questions:

1. How long have you been in your present job? Does time appear to have speeded up while you've been in the job? Why?

2. What has been the great sources of change during this time? Downsizing, merger, demerger, acquisition, competition, markets, globalization?

3. How has your job changed as a result of (2) above?

4. What was the major impact you had on your area of responsibility while in this job? Have you added value to the business?

5. How effective has your team(s) been? With how many members do you have an electronic relationship?

Electronic Communications Dominate

The assumption of Gabarro's model, and most leadership models in fact, is that face-to-face communication is a prerequisite of success. However, electronic communication is fast becoming the dominant form of transactional relationship between organization members. Technology-driven interpersonal communication emphasizes instrumentality, utility and speed – it is passionless, brief and factual.

Globalization is Changing the Nature of Teamwork

Leadership teams in most big, international companies are comprised of members spread over all points of the compass. These teams naturally have highly diverse cultural bases, little face-to-face contact, and infrequent full-scale team meetings. Their leaders are projected to them electronically or via videoconference. They must constantly deal with the issues of weak commitment, divergent values and ambiguous power bases.

The Company Stakeholder Model Has Become Increasingly Complex

The stakeholder model has traditionally been a powerful tool for management. However, it is losing robustness in the face of increasingly complex demands from stakeholders. Shareholders themselves are increasingly diverse, and are able to trade in a company's stock virtually on a moment's notice around the clock. Traditional suppliers are clustered together in B2B trading relationships. Competitors ally with other competitors to obtain supply-chain efficiency. Customers can be multinational organizations with a presence in a hundred or more countries, or conglomerates that share a presence in the same markets. For instance, faced with global clients in direct competition with its divisions in many markets, Henkel AG spun off its chemical division in order for it to go on its own. Relationships between stakeholders were becoming too complex for the German giant to handle efficiently. Ultimately, if interpreting signals from stakeholders is difficult, responding to the signals constitutes a major undertaking.

The MCL often faces an overwhelming noise level when she takes on a new assignment. In this environment she must identify the crucial elements of her opening moves and mobilize them quickly – no task for the timid. Complicating her job is the time element; she has a window of approximately 90–180 days in which she must set the moves in motion. This window is called the Window of Effectiveness.

The Window of Effectiveness

Trevor Stone knew that the new general manager's job he'd just signed on for was going to be a tough one. The unit he was to lead, a products division of HLO Engineering in Kent, had come through 3 years without breaking even. Over that time, a succession of general managers tried, without result, to bring the division out of its slump. Each departed summarily, leaving behind an ever-more cynical group of employees.

Nevertheless, Stone was optimistic about his chances for turning things around. He had prepared a list of questions for his first meeting with the management group. They squeezed around the small boardroom table as he put several issues to them:

1. *Where are we today?*
2. *Where do we want to be tomorrow?*
3. *How are we going to get there?*
4. *What are the immediate steps needed?*

Stone was surprised how quickly the group got into the issues. After a 10-minute discussion, everyone's attention was focused on the problem. Prices were too low and margins were very tight. That put pressure on the Director of Manufacturing who had little wiggle room. 'The solution?' asked Stone. The group now turned to the Director of Sales. All agreed that if Sales could get prices up, then Manufacturing could invest in more automated equipment that would in turn bring costs down. The meeting ended inconclusively, but with everyone looking satisfied – except the Director of Sales. Stone thanked them for their insights and left.

He was waylaid by the Director of Sales, who explained to Stone that the division was only one of many suppliers to large global original-equipment manufacturers (OEMs). The OEMs kept a multiple-supplier system in place to push prices down and keep quality up. Prices would not be going up in the near future. In fact, several OEMs had formed an alliance to create even more efficiency in the supply chain, and that would push prices down even further. The alliance planned to channel all requisitions for quotations through the Internet thereby speeding up process time, reducing administrative costs and bringing prices down even further.

Now Stone felt, not just dismayed, but uneasy. Maybe his first meeting hadn't been as successful as he had hoped it would be.

Stone's unease was late in coming. The fact that there had been several unsuccessful predecessors in this job should have given him food for thought during his qualifying interviews. The position required a new manager to come in well briefed, and prepared with a clear set of tasks that could be completed in the short to medium term. Even then, he would need to solve several immediate problems before he could move forward.

Stone was neither briefed, nor well prepared. His list of questions was alright for a first-year class in strategy, but it did not fool the management group. They had seen it all before and quickly took up the game of 'strategy-strategy'. They knew the rituals of this game, both questions and answers. It was a well-rehearsed dog-and-pony show that they had run before many an earlier general manager. Stone fell back on formulaic process, and the group gave back a formulaic response.

In any assignment there are several windows of opportunity that open up, often by chance. Peter Drucker believes that such challenges as changes found in process incongruities, restructured industry and markets, new demographic trends, new knowledge generated, unexpected success or even unexpected failure, are essentially windows of opportunity.[3] An MCL cannot wait for these windows to open up, however. She must make her own windows, and the first of these is the Window of Effectiveness. It opens up as the assignment begins and extends 90 to 180 days into the time-frame.

The first task of the Window of Effectiveness is to break the frame of previous mindsets and behaviours. Until the leader gains acceptance for the need to break the old frame, she cannot begin to build the new. Initially, she must get at least an acknowledgement from the majority that frame breaking can take place. Otherwise, future strategy is likely to fail.

After 100 days in the General Manager's job at the BBC in which he made major internal announcements, Greg Dyke sent out a note that started with: 'I've no doubt some of you are thinking "OK we've got the headlines, now where's the beef?"'[4] This memo capped several early moves by Dyke that included cutting excess management, especially at the top, cutting excess expenses such as second cars for senior managers, and ensuring that the BBC got more football coverage. All of these were aimed at frame breaking – getting existing employees to think differently about what they were doing and how they were doing it.

These early moves sent out a strong frame-breaking message. It was followed shortly by a strategy statement issued by top management – the 'big idea for the future'[5] – which found an attentive audience in BBC stakeholders.

In a study spanning 10 years I examined the four general managers

> **Hewlett Packard Globalization Challenge**
>
> A former marketing manager at HP's PC Division, Bernard Merric assumed the new role of General Manager at its BCD Division. The division had been successful in the past, so Merric decided to create a sense of urgency around the time to market issue. Instead of addressing general management issues, Merric focused in on market issues in the belief that if HP didn't get there first, the competition would. His experience in PC Division had been that new product introduction should take 6 months on average. What he found at BCD was that engineering requirements stretched introduction time to 24 months. Shortening this introduction time became one of the frame-breaking themes that energized employees and enabled them to bring down that time.

heading up Hewlett Packard's BCD Division, a division that had global responsibility for large-format printers. I found that each manager addressed the issue of breaking the frame as he entered the new job. Thus, each successive manager was able to bring a new perspective to the company that forced employees to look differently both at markets and at themselves.

The division had originally specialized in manufacturing. The first general manager in the study introduced R&D. Employees were forced to change mindset and study the problems of new product introduction. The next general manager emphasized marketing and sales, forcing employees to externalize their thinking. The third general manager built teams to tackle global business problems, thus moving them from the functional perspective. The final general manager focused on the global competition and how to win at the game. Each general manager in my study could rightly claim to have broken away from previous perspectives when he took on the job. Each achieved a successful frame break during the early days of the Window of Effectiveness.

Frame breaking can only be accomplished by a leader with knowledge of the sector, the company and its employees. Stone seems to have missed this point. He starts his strategic process in a knowledge vacuum, thus setting himself up for failure. Little wonder he failed to do any frame breaking at his first meeting.

Every leader needs to work through a series of challenges that faces her in the opening phase of a job. The challenges are the hurdles that the MCL must clear and the tasks are a series of actions that will best help the leader clear them (Figure 2.4).

The Challenges

Knowledge Entering a new job invariably means acquiring new knowledge quickly. No new leader-in-the-making can expect from the onset to know everything she needs to be fully effective. Stone was an engineer, but that background was not sufficient for his new position. He needed to develop his knowledge of technology as soon as possible. A new leader must have not only managerial knowledge, but technical knowledge as well. Leaders who fail to fully understand the complex ramifications of the business model are doomed to failure.

For many years management believed that technical and managerial knowledge were separable, that leadership effectiveness could be achieved without an in-depth knowledge of relevant technology. That idea no longer holds because, in order to stay in touch in a competitive environment where most new business models are based on technical competence, leaders constantly need to update their technical knowledge.

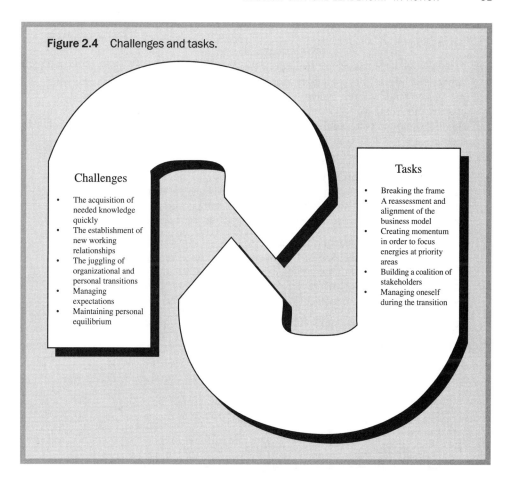

Figure 2.4   Challenges and tasks.

Challenges

- The acquisition of needed knowledge quickly
- The establishment of new working relationships
- The juggling of organizational and personal transitions
- Managing expectations
- Maintaining personal equilibrium

Tasks

- Breaking the frame
- A reassessment and alignment of the business model
- Creating momentum in order to focus energies at priority areas
- Building a coalition of stakeholders
- Managing oneself during the transition

Establishing New Working Relationships   The quality of being able to build relationships quickly and effectively seldom finds its way on to leadership competency lists. Yet it represents a critical success factor for new leaders. Stone's first meeting was not successful in this regard. He had come in cold, having neglected to establish for himself where power lay in the management team. He had not identified the aspirants to his job. These people will prove very troublesome in the future as they block his every move.

The inimitable nature of the 1,000-day imperative means that the MCL does not have time to make mistakes about relationships in the workplace. In order to succeed, she must establish them, though some relations may involve high-risk initiatives for her. As earlier noted, Carly Fiorina at HP established relations almost immediately with senior managers who had earnestly aspired to her job and probably continued to do so.

J. C. Penney

Compare that with the entry of Vanessa Castagna into J. C. Penney in August 1999. For almost 100 years store managers at the company had taken responsibility for what got packed on their store shelves. They had great latitude both in selecting and purchasing products. With the arrival of Ms Castagna as COO all of that was due to change. Castagna believed the real job of managers was to welcome customers, sell products and make sure inventory levels were kept to a minimum.

Castagna's opening gambit was to announce that she had formed teams to deliver an eccommerce solution for coordinating suppliers with the purchasing process. With such rapid developments in ecommerce J. C. Penney could not afford to get this wrong. At the same time, taking on such an established culture was not easy. Ecommerce was a sensitive issue that her successors had not wanted to address.

But succeed or fail, Castagna set herself the task of examining the business model at the beginning of her Window of Effectiveness. Once she redefined that model she moved on to implement changes quickly. Results are still not in, but Ms Castagna cannot be accused of dawdling. Her opening moves had ensured her a place on the short list of candidates to replace the retiring CEO James Oesterreicher.

Stock Performance: July 1999–July 2000

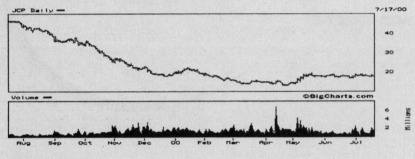

1999 Sales: $3.7 billion

Website Address: http://www.jcpenney.com

The new leader will find herself confronted with a range of electronic relationships. The dominance of electronic communication means that she will seldom meet face to face the people with whom she interacts, from direct reports to customers to suppliers. The electronic medium is a valuable tool for getting things done; its power to command loyalty and nurture emotional involvement is severely limited. It is as ubiquitous as plumbing and usually just as inspiring.

Juggling Organizational and Personal Transitions   The incoming MCL is herself undergoing transition from a previous assignment and may be struggling to find an effective way to transmit a new message. Her appointment will have had a tremendous impact on the perceptions of organization members. Some perceptions will be positive, some negative, but all will have to be dealt with eventually. With the advent of a new leader, the organization itself is in transition. That will translate into a latent sense of uncertainty and even urgency – qualities of which the MCL may take advantage.

Managing Expectations In order to positively exploit the uncertainty and urgency of the situation, the MCL must understand both her own and her employee's expectations. She may have to deal with unduly high expectations of herself, raised by her appointment to the position. She will likely have to deal with unduly high employee expectations especially if the team is highly talented. Expectations have risen generally, mostly as a result of the changed perception of self-worth engendered by the 'instant Internet and computer billionaire' tales that abound in the new economy.

Despite that, an MCL can always return to the time-tested formula of attention to employees, participation and caring to draw top performance from her employees. Companies still find this formula effective, particularly during troubled times. As the Calico Commerce share price plummeted by 80 per cent from a November 1999 peak, many of its employees shifted seamlessly from being paper millionaires to ordinary well-rewarded employees again.[6]

Earlier, the company had begun a programme to increase company loyalty, a rare value in Silicon Valley where job-hopping is a way of life. First, management met with employees candidly, keeping them generally informed of new developments. Then management acknowledged that employees do have lives beyond the company gates by making adjustments for personal problems and events. Finally, by sharing ownership broadly across the organization Calico gave employees a strong sense of belonging that they felt was unique to their company. Small wonder that when the chips were down employees rallied behind Calico.

Managing Personal Equilibrium Sit in a business-class airport lounge and listen to people trying to stay in touch with their networks. If not banging out messages on their laptops, they're having themselves plugged into a mobile phone. Often they're using both laptop and mobile phone. The new technologies, telecommunication in particular, are enablers of fast, immediate communication. Never before have organizations focused so intensely on information flow through personal networks. For new leaders, this presents a problem, in that communications technology is almost relentless in its consumption of every available moment. Life has become increasingly more difficult trying to maintain balance. In the case of global operations, the possibility of maintaining equilibrium with a 24-hour work shift is well nigh impossible.

Being able to handle the stress of the initial period calls for emotional balance. During this period, it is almost impossible not to find pressure influencing every aspect of one's life. Keeping family in focus becomes increasingly difficult and important.

The Tasks of the Window of Effectiveness

As the MCL works herself into the job, and provided that she has defined tasks well, the challenges will evolve. She may face challenges that are contradictory or paradoxical. Realistically, however, the objective is to achieve tangible results targeted by the MCL and team as being profitable and significant. Clearly, results that are neither profitable nor significant don't count. For example, management can show quick profits through the sale of fixed assets. However, these are not usually significantly sustainable. Achieving tangible results will involve several core tasks, including:

- Reassessing and aligning the business model.

- Creating momentum to focus energies on priority areas.

- Building a coalition of stakeholders.

- Managing oneself during the transition.

A Reassessment and Alignment of the Business Model   The real challenge for the MCL is to identify the existing business model and then start the process of challenging that model. Internet technology has driven a re-evaluation of business models though it has not changed the basic economic principles on which they are based. The economic principles you learnt in your first year at university are pretty durable. A matchless new business model can lead a company to market domination. Of course, this is meaningful only if it is sustainable. Sustainability is achieved through time-tested criteria: cost leadership and/or differentiation. In early 2000, many dotcoms learned the hard way that a lack of these two elements in their business models can lead to collapse of the company. The UK e-tailer Boo.com failed because, even though it could generate a turnover of £650,000 a month with an investment of £90 million, profitability had receded into the distant future. Even with first-mover market domination, Amazon has difficulty justifying its model. Because it seeks to dominate through cost leadership *and* differentiation it requires huge turnover to

Hewlett Packard's BCD Globalization Challenge

When Rich Raimundi took over running HP's BCD division in Barcelona, he wanted employees to refocus their energies on running a global business. Under the previous model they had exercised regional responsibility but that model was changing, and he wasn't sure that everyone understood the full implications of the change. Therefore, during a 200-day Window of Effectiveness, Raimundi set aside 22 hours a week for coaching and mentoring his direct reports. The first 8 hours of each week was spent in meeting with his team of seven direct subordinates. At this meeting new-product development and strategy was discussed, using a fairly rigid process format. After that Raimundi would spend 2 hours with every direct report individually making sure that the mindset was changing and that appropriate behaviours were appearing in the workplace. Micro-management? Perhaps, but after his 1,000 days on the job, Raimundi left a business which had almost doubled in sales, and a workforce that was greatly empowered to deal with globalization.

show a minimal profit. Business models are discussed in more detail in the next chapter.

Creating Momentum in Order to Focus Energies on Priority Areas Change in the business model is always going to create problems with employees. Employees have become used to the old model. They will not necessarily jump up and shout – 'Yippee, new boss, new model, new ways of doing things around here!' On the contrary, they will have difficulty understanding why the model should change, especially if the old one has been successful in the past. They may have difficulty in understanding the new business model.

This juncture requires the hands-on involvement of the MCL. She must emphasize very specific areas for employee focus. When motivation is low and people are distracted, they need to be refocused – sometimes on a daily basis – on what needs to be done. Hershey and Blanchard's situational leadership model would term this as an S1 situation – low morale, low commitment and high insecurity. Hands-on involvement will be time consuming, critics will belittle it as micro-management, but, in the end, it will keep everyone's energy focused.

Building a Coalition of Stakeholders

New-economy business models go much further than the old ones in extending stakeholder coalitions. For example, take the extent of the buy-in that the Dell model requires of both suppliers and customers. The business model cannot work without the total commitment of suppliers. It will take a lot more than just in-house commitment from employees given the extent of outsourcing by Dell – it will take internal and external commit-ment to the model. The MCL must commit for the long term to make the business model work. Relationship-capital management plays an important role here, something to which we will dedicate attention in Chapter 5.

Managing Oneself During Transition

The networks that the MCL brings to the job, as well as those created during each assignment, are, in effect, support systems that link past and future. They provide community, continuity and security for the MCL, which becomes stronger as she progresses through each 1,000-day phase of her career.

Her own strong sense of values will also provide continuity. An MCL carries these values from assignment to assignment, expecting that they will be regularly tested, and confident that they will withstand.

Juha Korppi-Tommola is a veteran of divisional turnarounds. A native of Helsinki, he has completed mission critical assignments in companies such as Polarcup the packaging business, and Stora-Enso the global paper company. He has worked in the US, Brazil and Spain and has headed up six major divisional turnarounds. Assignments often required survival strategies that involve dramatic cost cutting, disposal of assets and refocusing of strategies into completely different markets. Moving every 1,000 days or so, Korppi-Tommola feels that his value system has to be well thought out and articulated, 'You act like a surgeon in an emergency ward, you often have to cut without being able to gather all of the facts. And after down-sizing a business you have to energize those people who remain – the survivors. After every assignment, regardless of how tough it has been, people must remember you for your integrity under all circumstances. What else do you really bring to the business?' he says.

Window of Efficiency

So far in this chapter I have emphasized the fact that the MCL may have only a one-off opportunity for success in her 1,000-day tenure. If she has moved quickly, she will have opened her Window of Effectiveness with varying input – intellectual in the case of the new business model, and practical in terms of actions directed at various stakeholders. We now turn to the period immediately after the Window of Effectiveness, when results start to come in – the results that will measure her impact. Her management efforts will undoubtedly reap varied results. She may even have made a lasting impact on the organization but not on the bottom line. To view her effectiveness, we need to analyse the Window of Efficiency.

As CEO of British Airways, Robert Ayling was at a management level above most MCLs. However, his tenure at BA presents an interesting blueprint with which to track the Windows of Effectiveness and Efficiency.

A British Airways gold-card frequent flyer was turned away at the gate one Friday night. He had a boarding card and an assigned seat, but a BA staff member shouted out that he had been denied boarding, an action ordinarily used for football hooligans or drunks likely to cause trouble during the flight. The passenger was not drunk or troublesome – he had been accidentally thrown off the flight because of an administrative hitch.

Upset, he wrote to Robert Ayling, CEO of the airline. Weeks passed. He wrote a second time. Finally, months after the incident, Ayling replied. In March 2000, when Ayling resigned as CEO, most of BA's 60,000 employees celebrated his departure. I would not have been surprised to find this passenger – and hundreds more – joining them. By the end of Ayling's tenure, he had brought morale among both staff and passengers to an all time low.

After privatization, British Airways had changed its business model. It invested heavily in its people and the service they could provide. BA reasoned that its product – aircraft, seat configuration and food – could not be differentiated in the medium to long term from competitive products. So BA threw its weight behind service, investing heavily in the training and development of a crack service crew, and eventually achieving enviable levels of service.

BA's costs were extremely high as a consequence. When Ayling came on board, he immediately set about reducing overall costs as well as cutting back on staff levels. A lawyer by training, Ayling appeared to have made a sound opening move. He immediately moved into turbulent airspace. He displayed what some people saw as arrogance, and a notable lack of charisma, and soon found himself short of support among stakeholders. Staff turned against him, and the media picked up on the trouble fairly quickly. Passengers felt the turndown in enthusiasm from the staff, or heard about it from the media. Eventually the Board of Directors turned against him.

The competition was embodied in Ayling's nemesis – Richard Branson. In contrast to the abrasive Ayling, Branson enjoyed popular support from both the media and the public. While stories of passengers roughly handled by BA staff were increasing, Branson's staff at Virgin seemed to be having an Indian summer in which nothing could go wrong.

Ayling had taken up the new role of CEO on October 1996. In one of his first attempts to change the business model, he set about to forge an alliance with American Airlines. Ayling believed that the resulting new alliance would quickly dominate the lucrative trans-Atlantic route. Ayling worked hard at getting approval for this alliance from stakeholders, who ranged from employees and customers to the British Government and the European Union. But Ayling quickly entered into disputes with Washington and Brussels about the alliance, and BA's image took a pounding as a result. From the start the alliance strategy showed signs of strain and by day 300 of his tenure was in serious trouble, though Ayling himself felt confident that the deal would go through. Eventually Ayling failed to deliver.

HP's Carly Fiorina and the Window of Efficiency

Compare this to Fiorina at HP. By June 2000, HP's share price had plateaued at $134. This was up 100 per cent from when Fiorina had taken over the reigns of the business, but HP had been sorely affected by a falling stock market which had seen many Internet companies fail entirely or lose most of their value. Not that HP was an Internet company but its stock had moved in line with the earlier euphoria of the markets.

Fiorina had now been in the job for 210 days and the results were starting to come in that suggested that her shaking up of HP was working. She had refocused managers on HP's innovative history and wanted more new-product introductions. She had appointed key people to important new roles ranging from e-service to retail relations in an effort to speed HP up into the Internet age. Some people like Antonio Pérez had been vital to her during the initial Window of Effectiveness. As Fiorina entered the Window of Efficiency, however, she discovered that she was going to have to appoint someone to Pérez's position. He had been Head of the Imagining Business, a major portion of HP's overall business and a stable cash cow but they had decided that they would part company. He had supported her during the initial stages but now wanted to move on himself.

Stock Performance: July 1999–July 2000

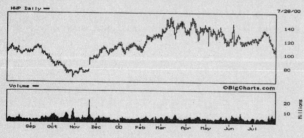

1999 Sales: $42.4 billion

Website Address: http://www.hp.com

The other element of Ayling's opening strategy was to cut costs in order to boost profits. Here again, Ayling ran into trouble. Employees had generally rallied together around the previous charismatic CEO Colin Marshall (now Lord Marshall). Ayling not only lacked the charisma of Marshall, he was positively abrasive. Employees refused to go over the top. As his Window of Efficiency opened, day 180, Ayling had a strike on his hands. He had no relationship capital to cash in on during this rough space, and, from then on, relations with employees were strained.

Insiders later said that it wasn't Ayling's vision for BA, nor his drive to cut costs that ultimately caused him to fail. It was his confrontational style that destroyed him. 'He could have tried encouraging staff just now and again,' a BA pilot said. 'Let's hope that Bob's replacement is someone who knows how to get along with people.'[7]

Ayling exacerbated his problems further by issuing a brusque admonishment to frequent flyers, cautioning them to limit hand luggage because extra handling was causing late plane departures. This coincided with a precipitous drop in business-class passengers, a group Ayling very much wanted to court.

Although well into the Window of Efficiency, day 280, Ayling created another stir, ironically, mostly with first- and business-class passengers, when he initiated a drive to change BA service colours to fit with a new 'cool Britannia' image.

Well over the 1,000-day period in 1999, Ayling was preparing the markets for a precipitous drop in earnings and a BA first: losses. By this time, Ayling realized that the results were not what he had expected. He began a re-examination of strategy.

'Three years ago, we realized then that the assumptions we had been working on previously were probably invalid ... I think that was not a bad bit of futurology,' he said cryptically as he set about changing strategy.[8] In terms of the principles of mission critical leadership Ayling should have left at this stage. However, he continued in the job. The share price had plummeted from 760 pence in 1997 to 299 pence at the time Ayling announced a £250 million loss. Still, Ayling appeared not to have read the signs. He clung on tenaciously from November 1999 to March 2000 before withdrawing from BA. Amazingly, in his final week, even as the Press was reporting Ayling's removal, he was resisting the decision, still seeking to find support among board members. Several days passed before he realized that his time was up, that the Window of Efficiency had long closed, and that he had mismanaged even his own exit, leaving no successor and a

> *share price which could only be improved by his departure. Like one of his disgruntled passengers he was denied boarding the flight the second time round.*

The Window of Efficiency opens approximately 180 days in the job, and stays open until day 500, sometimes further. During this period, the measures put into place by the MCL start to register. Its opening marks a period in which the MCL can take stock of the major changes started earlier.

This period is not necessarily quieter for the business, but action within the company now moves from the decisive, shock-filled implementation pace of the Window of Effectiveness to a more incremental, steady flow. Having swung the boat around by 180 degrees, the skipper now keeps it on course by making small adjustments to the wheel, perhaps 5 degrees to starboard or port. The changes introduced during the Window of Effectiveness now need to be maintained or redefined. This reshaping process benefits from the leader's increased understanding of the business and its impact on people.

Not surprisingly, many MCLs run into trouble at this juncture. During this period in his tenure, Ayling definitely seems to have lost the plot. The resistance he was experiencing from stakeholders should have suggested that he was going to encounter significant problems in dealing with people. Problems of ineffectiveness in the MCL usually surface during the Window of Efficiency. At the opening of Ayling's tenure, abrasiveness had seemed a minor problem – just another quality of character – in the face of the crisp opening moves that promised so much benefit for the business. Though strategy stuttered along, because of implementation problems, it might cumulatively have moved the company forward, providing Ayling with a respectable track record. It did not, however. Ayling's troublesome management style seemed to create too many roadblocks. The reasons for his downfall:

1   *He could not maintain momentum* During implementation, the major challenges for an MCL lie with people and relationships. Ayling would have few problems dealing with the technical aspects of the airline such as online booking or new aircraft. In fact, all his problems seemed to revolve around his inability to get on with people – though he seems never to have picked up on that fact.

2   *His results didn't support his strategy* The reason most leaders are removed 12 to 24 months into a tenure is because results are coming in and strategy simply isn't measuring up. Ayling was prepared to

adjust and reshape his strategy but never got a second chance at getting it right.

3   *His reassessment of the business model fell short*   Ayling had departed from his predecessor's service-focused business model in order to make BA more competitive. His decision to invest heavily in business-class travellers seemed to contradict his original decision to undermine the service function. The business model he was reshaping was widely criticised as being high risk for the high-volume, low-margin transatlantic route. In view of BA's poor track record with business-class travellers, airline-industry leadership publicly questioned Ayling's ability to channel huge numbers of new business passengers on to his flights. Their seemingly expert negative opinions of the strategy made it difficult for stakeholders to see how it would work.

4   *He had made no investment in relationship capital*   Near the end, Ayling had alienated almost everybody in his network, from employees right up to Board members. Relationship capital is nurtured during the tenure of an MCL and cashed in times of trouble. From the outside, it seemed that Ayling remained ignorant of that principle throughout his tenure at BA.

5   *He groomed no successor*   Ayling left the airline with no one to take his place. He seems to have assumed that his tenure would proceed for some time, that no contingency plan was needed even should he be run over by the No. 9 bus, and that grooming a successor was superfluous to running a company.

6   *He mismanaged his exit*   The 1,000-day imperative assumes that the leader is responsible for handing over the reins in an efficacious way and moving on. Ayling clung to his dwindling power until forced out. His track record indicates that he might well have made a messy exit under any circumstances.

Within the time-frame of the Window of Efficiency, and from a psychological point of view, two things have happened for the MCL. The first is that she has lost the fresh perception that was possible at the beginning of the assignment. In other words, as the newness and unfamiliarity has rubbed off, it has become increasingly difficult for her to maintain her unique vision. She has herself become assimilated in the culture, thus frame breaking has become increasingly difficult, if not impossible.

The second change in the MCL is that with the increase in her comfort level, her credibility and power are becoming firmly established. This development is, of itself, empowering. Provided the Window of Effectiveness has been successful, the leader's chances of success have probably increased.

Step 1   Guideline to assessing Window of Efficiency:

1. How effective are you communicating with your team? What contact – electronic, face to face, group or one-to-one – do you employ, and how often?

2. Does your team understand the mission and the vision? Have they communicated it to their people?

Now she can turn some attention to areas on which she has not previously focused. Like the saucer spinner in the circus, however, she must balance time for new issues with attention to her original strategy.

Maintaining Momentum

Maintaining momentum consists primarily of keeping people going. When her teams are halfway through the race, the MCL needs to think about rewarding them for the distance covered thus far. She must also decide what each individual needs to spur motivation and creativity. Arrival at the halfway point is an accomplishment that should be celebrated. It reaffirms the vision and reinforces enthusiasm for reaching the ultimate goal.

Technology and process can cause problems at this stage as well. They are usually more easily solved than people problems. On the other hand, people issues can be readily identified in the early stages of development, and addressed before they grow too big. Though they are sometimes complex and messy, involving pride, envy and ambition in various quantities, they are better resolved promptly and quickly on discovery. Lingering people problems can have a devastating effect on morale. The patience of Job as well as the wisdom of Solomon are useful qualities in trying to resolve them.

Measures Assessing the Consequences of the Window of Effectiveness

The real proof of successful change is the results that start emerging at this time. Many MCLs will have actually changed the company's measuring systems, and will feel the consequences of this as well. If measured too soon, some of these results will only be signals. More time will need to pass before final results are in. If changes were introduced very late in the Window of Effectiveness, or if implementation of a measuring system stretches across both *windows*, results may arrive too late to allow the MCL to reshape action.

Redefining the Business Model

Would that competitors could be put to sleep as a company introduces a new business model! The competition watches the situation like hawks and if the model is good, they copy, refine and try to do it better themselves. For that reason redefinition of the business model is an ongoing process, and cannot be left unattended for any length of time. At Intel, Andy Grove

Bibby's Acquisition of Finanzauto S.A.

Some mission critical leaders stake their entire tenure on implementing new measures. During his Window of Effectiveness, Tony Phillips focused on new controls in Finanzauto S. A. in Madrid. The firm had been acquired by Bibby's, a subsidiary of the large South African conglomerate Barlows, in a hostile takeover. Phillips felt that although company results were poor, the business model was a robust one. Provided he could change the control system, he would be able to turn the business around. Changing the accounting system would allow him to focus the energies of employees on areas of importance, such as the *after sales* service area. A key person for the implementation of the new control system was a financial director Phillips had brought in from outside the Spanish organization. Phillips delegated the detail of the control system to his new FD while he worked on motivating people to buy-in to the new system. By day 500 the results had turned positive, cash flow had improved, bad debts had been reduced, inventory had been slashed and unproductive assets sold. Shortly after the acquisition, the Financial Press had questioned the wisdom of Barlows's decision to acquire Finanzauto. Its scepticism vanished as Phillips's systems started to deliver results.

Stock Performance: July 1997–July 2000

1999 Sales: $3.5 billion

Website Address: http://www.barlows.com

closed the DRAM (dynamic random-access memory) business on the basis of his own revolving-door technique. In it, management asked itself 'What would a new leader who came in from the outside do about this existing business model?' 'Close it,' was the consensus. Once that action had been defined, the team had only to walk out, come back in again and do it! Grove wrote at some length about the difficulty of actually getting the team to articulate the problem and the solution. He took months to even get himself to be able to see the problem differently.[9]

Still, every organization needs enough stability to enable it to bed people and systems down for a time, to pilot test them and to release

Step 2   Guideline to assessing Window of Efficiency:

3. Does everybody understand and perform to established agreed up measures? Identify low or no performance and reasons.

4. Is the business model still valid? How is it evolving? How have competitors responded? How to react?

them. Consensus building requires a model that is intellectually robust and emotionally appealing. But to believe that the model is unique and unbreachable is naïve. Quite simply, if the MCL does not revisit and refine the business model, the competition will.

Adventures in the new dot.coms seem to have produced an even stronger message. Once the results have come in, a revisit to the business model may not save the business, but it could produce a hybrid of the business for leadership. As Boo.com collapsed, it took with it £90 million of investors funds – more than any other dot.com company had ever lost. e-Boo had seemed to be a symbol of the dot.com phenomenon. It had high-energy level, young, soon-to-be-wealthy people and scads of brainpower and creativity. Nonetheless, it couldn't survive on £650,000 per month revenues. Within weeks of Boo's demise, its key employees stepped up to the plate to develop a new business model that would use the company's innovative technology to help sports retailers. They moved to negotiate new deals and funding quickly, and in practically nanoseconds a new business was born.

Relationship Capital

Of all the intangible assets, relationship capital is the most difficult to measure. Nonetheless, it is a critical element of the business model. Because it doesn't appear in the profit-and-loss statement, it can drop below the MCL's radar. During the Window of Efficiency, a leader should be able to tap into every level of stakeholder in order to gauge reaction, acquire different opinions and motivate people. This applies to suppliers and customers as much as it does to employees. In this way, the MCL can measure relationship capital and factor it into his measurement.

Reassess Key People
The MCL is incapable of making change happen if she doesn't have the right people in place. Elsewhere in this book I talk about selecting team leaders, mavericks and teams to create a change environment. These opening moves

cannot and will not take place if key roles are occupied by inappropriate people. Key roles can be staffed inappropriately if current occupants are in place as a result of incumbency, best-available placement policy or simply bad-judgement calls on the leader's part.

When people in key roles have been identified as being unable to handle the job because of lack of skills, vision or commitment, the MCL has to move fast. The early opening of the Window of Efficiency provides the opportunity to make changes and to shift people into areas where they will have maximum impact. These activities are actually part of the process of maintaining momentum.

Paul M. Tanner took over the UK-based division of his company, IBB, a large West Coast-based hi-tech company. Tanner's brief was to make the division more marketing focused, while at the same time ensuring that sales would be substantially improved and a British successor to his job would be identified by the end of his tenure.

By day 30, Tanner had identified marketing function as a major problem area. More specifically, he identified the fact that the Marketing Manager was weak in international marketing. Tanner replaced him. By day 100, he felt that he had put the right person in place and was now concentrating on refocusing the business model.

Things went well for a while. The team worked on getting the international focus right. This involved constant travelling for the team, who were making contacts with customers across Europe and the Americas. There was very little time to meet face to face; emails were the main means of communication for almost 6 months. On day 400, Tanner was called in by the now-not-so-new Marketing Manager, who said: 'Sorry to do this to you, Paul, but I've accepted a better offer. It involves less travelling, and I need to be nearer my family.'

Tanner was devastated. His strategy depended on having this person in place. But Tanner had neglected to stay personally in touch with this key staffer, preferring to assume that his silence signalled happiness. With the loss of this person, his entire change programme had been undermined.

Conclusion

This chapter examined the Windows of Effectiveness and Efficiency using examples such as Robert Ayling's tenure at British Airways and Carly

Step 3   Guideline to assessing Window of Efficiency:

5. Have you and the business's relationship capital increased or decreased? Where are there holes? What strategies are being developed to plug the gaps?

6. Who are the people and roles key to successful implementation? Do they know that they are key? Are they empowered to perform? Are all the roles covered for the period of the Window of Efficiency?

Fiorina's at Hewlett Packard. With careful preparation of tasks the MCL can be well set to establish herself from day 1 as the Window of Effectiveness opens. The Window of Efficiency measures the returns of those earlier decisions and actions confirm if the MCL is going to make it.

Reassessment and Alignment of the Business Models

HEADLINE:
COMSTELLAR LAUNCHES WITH INNOVATIVE BUSINESS
MODEL AND PREMIER MANAGEMENT TEAM; ARCHITECTS
OF TOMORROW'S COMMUNICATION TECHNOLOGIES

On 11 July 2000, this headline announced the formation of a new telecommunications start-up, Comstellar Technologies Inc. The new company would focus on 'disruptive' technologies that would provide dramatic improvements in communication networks. The company had assembled an interim management team experienced in telecommunications for its start-up and would appoint a permanent team as the business matured. Comstellar aimed to be one of the world's leading technology companies and its new CEO (chief executive officer), Sanjiv Ahuja, explained why: 'Comstellar is built on a unique business model. It is based on the belief that if you combine the agility of a start-up with the resources of a large organization, you can launch and build new companies at an accelerated pace and with a higher success rate.'[1]

Comstellar had raised more than $140 million in investment capital, from investors that include Clarity Partners, First Analysis Venture Capital, Goldman, Sachs & Co., J. P. Morgan Ventures, Lehman Brothers.

This company has raised a lot of money around the claim that it has a unique business model. Like many companies in the new economy, it uses the term to signify idea or concept rather than an entire model shift. Comstellar understands that its business model is 'based on the belief ...' that a strong start-up management team combined with the resources of a large organization can be used to build new companies. In the old economy, business models were based on harder data, usually something like the 5-year plan, but the new economy has introduced some very soft business models, some of which have been successful. As Michael Lewis has commented, '"Business models" is one of these terms of art that were central to the Internet boom: it glorified all manner of half-baked plans.'[2]

Many of these models are based on vision and faith. They do not particularly move managers exposed to 15 years of the budgetary system of a large corporation. The challenge for business in the new market place is to move its business models to the middle ground – a little less faith and a little more substance.

In the past, business models reached various levels of sophistication, some were far more than just 5-year plans, but, for the most part, they faced a common challenge, which was to try to predict the impact of decisions on future behaviours. In the 5-year plan this was a fairly simple financial exercise. It involved forecasting expenditures against future buying behaviour of customers. Michael Porter's five-forces competitive strategy (see Note 5) model sets forth a more in-depth, analytical approach. Still, many old-economy companies fell back on a relatively faith-based model; they made their projections intuitively rather than scientifically. Only recently has a format started to emerge, even for old-style models. A lot of interest in shifting business models was generated by companies such as Dell, Amazon and Yahoo! In common parlance these companies had new business models, but few people understood them fully or knew how to apply them to their businesses. What this discussion will provide is a framework for understanding the existing business model, a test bed for assuring its robustness and a means of comparing it with competitors' models. My aim is to help reduce the surprise that most companies experience when confronted by the innovations of the competitors' business models.

The stages of this process are:

- outline and develop the business model;

- identify how your company's business model has changed;

- determine how the business model should change;

- develop a comparative analysis of your company model and that of competitors.

How big is the shift to new business models? The word revolution is used often these days. If the staid and conservative chemical industry is going through a business-model revolution, will any company remain untouched? No, if we are to believe survey after survey. *Chemical Market Reporter*[3] showed that more than 60 per cent of all chemical companies expect ecommerce to be central to their activities by 2002 – $100 billion worth of projected revenues. Giants such as Dow Chemical are developing a business model that would emphasize customer interface, extend value to supply partners, make leading-edge use of electronic channels and create several new e-businesses. Dow's introduction of myaccount@Dow, a customer-specific-extranet that provided customers with online access to transactional ecommerce functions, was only one of several innovations.

The problem with almost every survey conducted during the period 1996 to 1999 was that they consistently underestimated the impact of ecommerce on the global economy. In that period actual results were from two to seven times larger than analysts' estimates, some of which had been made only 12 months previously! In early 2000 BCG was predicting growth from $92 billion in 1999 to $2 trillion in 2003. It is easy to see where that growth was coming from when sectors such as the chemical sector were estimating $100 billion growth in 2 years.

When a new manager seeks to understand the business model of a company, he will look first at its value chain. When we left Trevor Stone, our erstwhile hero from Chapter 2, he had just exited his first management meeting as new General Manager, stymied by both a cynical management team and his own lack of knowledge about the company he had been hired to run. Logically, Trevor's next move will be to study the value chain. The value chain not only identifies each of the activities of the business and sets them up in an orderly manner, it also allows managers to search for activities that create and capture value. These latter terms – value creation and capturing – are strong conceptually but rather difficult to put into practice. Let's take a look at some of the original theory on value chain.

The hypothesis of the value chain makes certain basic assumptions about processes and technologies of the business. A generic business model will outline five primary business activities together with the four functional processes of integration. The primary activities cover 'inbound logistics', 'operations', 'marketing and sales', 'distribution logistics', and 'customer interface'. The primary business activities of the company should be driven by the common goal of creating value for customers. A company's related functional integrative processes should be driven by the common goal of making the primary business activities more efficient and effective. These processes cover 'firm infrastructure', 'human resources', 'technology development', and 'procurement'. A manager will analyse the value chain to discern how each of these nine activities interrelates within the company and what value is being created from the various interrelationships. This information will help him determine the relative strength of the company.[4] As Michael Porter, Harvard professor of value-chain-theory fame, noted:

Each of these activities can contribute to a firm's relative cost position and create a basis for differentiation. The value chain disaggregates a firm into its

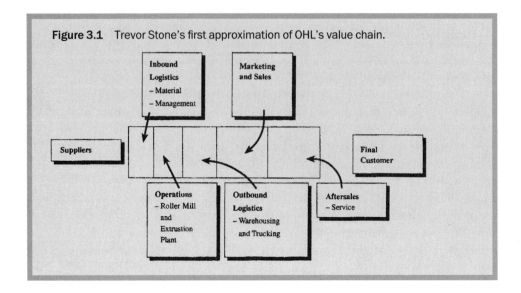

Figure 3.1 Trevor Stone's first approximation of OHL's value chain.

strategically relevant activities in order to understand the behaviour of costs and the existing and potential sources of differentiation.[5]

So, for example, in an alloy-products division of OHL Engineering, we look in on Trevor Stone studying the value chain shown in Figure 3.1.

OHL locates its primary activities in different parts of the country, so Stone must look for elements they have in common, such as management, human resources, IT and possibly the brand structure of its products. He needs to ascertain where value was being created. This quickly becomes obvious – the only activity that adds value is operations. The final customers, global original-equipment manufacturers (OEMs) are actually demanding that OHL process and transform the raw material at the lowest cost possible and provide free delivery for the finished product. Stone cannot identify any value creation in outbound logistics, marketing, sales or after-sales service. These activities seem to exist because they have always existed in this business, and for no other reason. Stone quickly begins to understand some of the problems the company faces, not least that their current business model is obsolete.

Let us withdraw from Stone's rather grim situation for a moment, and compare OHL's value chain with a company such as Dell Computer Corporation. Dell is famous for its 'be direct' business model and hence the value chain looks something like that shown in Figure 3.2. A quick look tells us that Dell creates and captures value in a number of areas:

- Creates competitive advantage by using leading-edge Internet technology to create customer and supplier links.

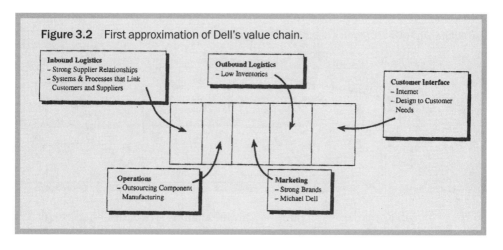

Figure 3.2   First approximation of Dell's value chain.

- Develops strong supplier relationships in order to have high-quality outsourced operational response.

- As a result of strong supplier relationship, is able to keep inventory down to 6 days.

- Patents many of its processes and systems so that it can take the strategy of differentiation beyond product.

Looking at the value chain in Porter's old-economy way has some limitations. Examining physical assets and activities alone will yield an abridged view. If a new-economy manager develops a business model focused on tangible assets, products and services alone, she is likely to make wrong assumptions. Think back to the example that opened this chapter. That business model was based on 'a belief' – something highly intangible.

New business models are concerned with value creation and capture a combination of both tangible and intangible assets. The most important intangible asset, the one capable of creating immense value, is information. Information runs through an entire organization and keeps it functioning. Yet it has no place in the accounting system. Interestingly, shareholders have realized this, which might explain why stock prices far exceed book value. Book value measures the

Step 1   Guideline to articulating your company's business model:

1. List, in sequence, the major activities of the business. What tangible and intangible assets support these activities?

2. In which activities does your business create value? Where is value captured? How has this model changed in the past 5 years? How should it change in the next 3 years?

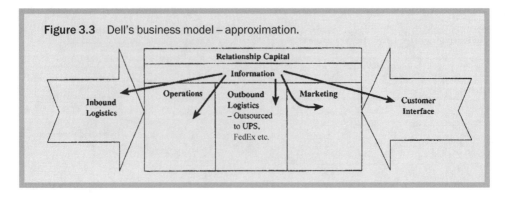

Figure 3.3   Dell's business model – approximation.

tangible; market capitalization, the intangible. The stock market takes a much broader view.

The second most important intangible asset is relationship capital. Relationship capital is the combination of human, intellectual and external capital. Human capital is the experience, expertise, knowledge and skills that employees bring to work with them each day. Intellectual capital is the sum of knowledge and experience as seen in process, systems and innovations accrued by the company. External capital is the value of external relationships that link the company to its external environment. There are links with customers, suppliers, alliance partners, the community, government and so on. We will look more fully at relationship capital in the next chapter.

In effect if Dell's model were to include information systems and processes and relationship capital, it would give a better reflection of the business (Figure 3.3):

- suppliers and customers back up into the business: Through managing the resulting relationship capital, Dell captures value created;

- suppliers have been integrated into operations: Dell captures value created;

- customers have been integrated into operations and marketing: Dell captures value created;

- Marketing and customer-interface management allows customer personalization and customization of the product – creating market differentiation: Dell captures value created.

Within Dell, there are levels of information gathering, organizing, selecting, packaging and distribution. The intangible forces of information and relationship capital permeate that physical world of resources. With that understanding, we build a differentiated business model.

Suppliers are as important as customers in the new business model. Provided the information process is robust, a manager can outsource the activities of inbound logistics, creating value in the supply chain. This reshapes the business model again. Most large companies, including the OEMs to which Trevor Stone had to respond, are attempting to transfer responsibility to suppliers by getting those suppliers to back up into the

> **Step 2   Guideline to articulating your company's business model:**
>
> 3. How well are intangible assets being managed? In particular, information and relationship capital?
>
> 4. Where do your core competencies lie in your business model? Are you capturing value in these activities?

business. Stone must therefore factor this customer's business model into his own value-chain analysis.

In the new market place, suppliers are taking on activities that were traditional company activities. Automobile manufacturers have been aggressive in backing suppliers into the business with a two-stage process. First, they have grouped suppliers to take on research, design, manufacturing and assembly of major subassemblies of cars and trucks. The company outsources full responsibility for each unit up to the point where it is fitted to the main platform. Second, they have formed an alliance across several automobile manufacturers. Thus, OEMs reach for greater cost efficiency from suppliers as well as from the industry as a whole.

FedEx and UPS must realign their business models to the external environment on a priority basis. On the face of it, FedEx and UPS have physical value chains that are similar to that of the Post Office. The Post Office has moved letters and packages from one locale to another for centuries. However, when one factors information into the value chain, the new entrants have a great advantage. They integrate information on every item they move into their distribution logistics. This information is easily transferred to both sender and receiver at almost no cost. The ability of each customer (in this case sender and/or receiver) to back up into the business and keep track of what interests him most (i.e. the physical movement of a particular item) transforms the business model. Customer interface, the value-creating activity that encompasses the old *sales* and *after-sales* services, becomes a process that allows the customer to take on certain aspects of the service chain. It combines low physical presence with high investment in IT. Instead of calling in to ascertain where an item is, the customer merely searches for it through a computer link-up.

Customer interface is where most of the Internet start-ups claim advantage. Through sophisticated management of databases these

Inbound Logistics means nothing more than the receipt, storage and distribution of the inputs an organization uses in the creation of its services and products. Traditionally this was a closely guarded cluster of functions. Those functions are now shared or outsourced through alliances and partnerships. The development of many of these partnerships and alliances may be based on the relationship capital of other groups in the company so that, in addition to cultivating partnership and building trust with customers and suppliers, the MCL and her team need to examine all initiatives that create ripple effects across multiple tiers of the value chain. That means looking at things like:

1. inventory strategies – everything from JIT (just in time) delivery to CPFAR (collaborative planning, forecasting and replenishment);

2. information sharing – attempts to provide access to real-time information on production, sales and inventories;

3. collaborative initiatives with customers and suppliers – aimed at improving product development;

4. adoption of web technologies – including attempts at e-business, logistics management and cash-to-cash cycles.

For example, Dell Computer's business model asks a fundamental question – does a computer company have to carry inventory? Dell came up with an answer of 'As little as possible' and got its inventory down to 6 days. Jeff Bezos at Amazon.com asked a similar question but added distribution to the question – does a book supplier have to distribute its products? And Yahoo asked – does a company need inventory, does it need production or distribution? There is no secret to the questions that are asked about these business models nor where value in the model is going to be captured. The secret is developing a team and organization around capturing that value.

companies are able to identify personally each customer and thereby customize their products and services.

Transparency of process is fundamental to reconfiguring the business model in this way. Transparency allows the customer to understand the process and thereby assume certain responsibility for the successful delivery of the product or service. Business models will vary depending on the degree of responsibility transferred by the company.

This is nowhere better demonstrated than in Swedish retailer IKEA's business model. The world's largest home-furniture supplier, IKEA has outlets in sixty countries. In this most diverse of markets, IKEA has managed to provide low-cost quality goods to customers provided they take on some of the traditional activities themselves. Amazingly, IKEA customers readily agree to take on the task of managing their own distribution logistics, and at-home assembly. Why would anyone agree to rope an unassembled cupboard to their car roof and take home what are nothing

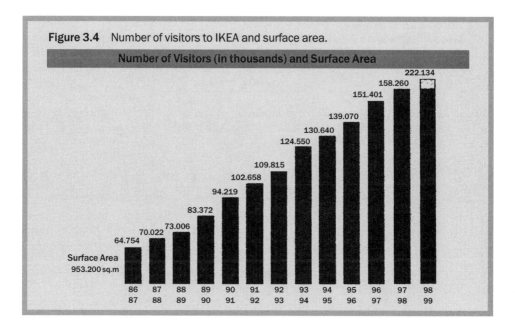

Figure 3.4   Number of visitors to IKEA and surface area.

more than reshaped bits of wood? The answer lies in the power of IKEA's marketing presentation. Using both its catalogue and a visual Internet link that allows customers to walk through a virtual store display, IKEA offers customers more than bits of furniture. It offers them a certain lifestyle – represented by the IKEA image. This creates value in the mind of the customer. Moreover, this lifestyle is affordable if the customer is willing to take on certain activities. IKEA facilitates these for the customer by providing easy store access, clear assembly instructions and a guaranteed return policy.

IKEA's business model emphasizes information control flow that is generated in operations, and progresses to customers via catalogue and website, and to suppliers, who can ascertain exactly how their product is doing in the market place (Figure 3.5).

The Virtual Corporation

It is possible to adapt the business model to create a virtual corporation through extensive outsourcing. The idea of leveraging efficiency through value-chain partners is appealing, provided the company is prepared for high levels of collaboration and information sharing. If the company

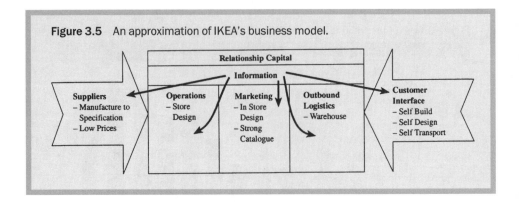

Figure 3.5   An approximation of IKEA's business model.

decides to set about improving performance, for instance, it must include value-chain partners in its programme.

Outsourcing like this has a clear implication – the company doesn't believe that it has a proprietary knowledge or expertise in these certain activities. Also implied is: that value creation is more likely to occur in another activity of the business; that the final product or service will be improved; that greater value is created for the customer and that more value is captured within the firm by outsourcing inbound logistics.

The logic of outsourcing can probably be applied to all activities of the firm. There is no reason not to question every activity. New business models show that some very successful firms leave nearly all the traditional activities to outsiders. For example, when Rome-based Bvlgari International wanted to extend its exclusive brand name to perfumes, its natural inclination was to do everything in-house. This had been the tradition for decades. Bvlgari had always chosen its raw materials carefully, designed and made its own jewelry pieces and sold them directly to a clientele that included movie stars, Arabs sheikhs and captains of industry. However, CEO Francesco Trapani and Perfume Division Head Gianluca Brozzetti saw that new thinking was required. The recently appointed Brozzetti argued that the company would need many years to build up the competence to compete with established fragrance houses. The strength of Bvlgari lay in image and market creation. Provided that suppliers of quality products could be contracted, the main focus should be on building

> **Step 3   Guideline to articulating your company's business model:**
>
> 5. In the new-economy model what activities will you discard, out-source or share?
>
> 6. How does your model stand up to that of your competitors? Where do they capture value? Where is your competitive advantage?

the brand. Brozzetti set about finding the finest fragrance manufacturers, and the finest package designer and manufacturers. Within a year Bvlgari had introduced a major brand (Bvlgari Pour Femme) on the global market – record time for market introduction in the industry. To prove that this was no fluke, Brozzetti launched a second product, Black, some 18 months later to even greater success.

Bvlgari S.p.A

- Website address: http://www.bulgari.it

- 1999 Net Income: $59.3 million
  1-Year Net Income Growth: 14.7%

- 1999 Sales: $487.3 million
  1-Year Sales Growth: 13.7%

In this case the business model outsourced all activities other than concept design and marketing where Bvlgari believed it had strength.

The decision to outsource operations should not be taken lightly. Most leaders prefer to take the route of the ex-CEO of Compaq. In 1991 Eckhard Pfeiffer was plunged into the role of CEO of Compaq Computer Corporation after the firing of its founder, Rod Canion. The market had shifted, and computers had become a commodity. Customers were moving to competitors in droves. The company was in a state of shock at the firing of its founder. The first thing the Pfeiffer did was to go home and work through all of the problems. 'I spent two full days just going through specifics. I worked on it very intensely. Prior to that it was just fragments. Why aren't we doing this, or why did we keep resisting such and such, or why are we not dealing with the market demand or that customer complaint.' Pfeiffer decided to stay in operations but, unlike Trapani of Bvlgari, basically reconfigured Compaq's business model to make the company a low-cost designer and manufacturer striving for market share in every market segment of the computer business.[6] This proved highly successful for several years until Compaq was laid low by Dell's business model. Pfeiffer left Compaq in 1999.

Core Competency

In the model used by Bvlgari Parfums, activities such as outbound logistics – all the activities required to distribute these products or services, and marketing and sales were outsourced. Though simply formulated, the model allows the mission critical leader (MCL) to pose questions about where the core competencies of the business lie and whether the business could prosper without undertaking some of these functions internally. Trevor Stone's model has revealed that OHL's core competencies lie solely in operations. The company could start to benefit from a redesigned model that would outsource some or all of the activities that currently generate 'no value added' to its value chain. However, Stone needs to balance this with the problems that arise out of the outsourcing itself.

First Movers versus Slow Movers

Markets generally punish those who are not 'first mover' into a market space. This fact of life generally accounts for business models having taken centre stage. 'The reward for joining the first-movers club is market valuation that is five times larger than your second player', says Bruce Richardson of the Boston-based AMR research consultancy. In recent times, the lesson has been clear; first movers not only define the parameters of market space, they often become the benchmark against which all subsequent entrants are judged. One of the advantages of having a revolutionary business model is that it endows the company with a dominant mindset – one that can be shared with prospective clients and partners. Customers are more likely to remain with first movers, because dealing with second players presents a small but tangible risk of underperformance.

First-mover arguments are very persuasive. However, firms that are not first mover, but well established in solid markets, have not necessarily fallen to the status of runners-up. Many old-economy firms have demonstrated that being a big, albeit slow, mover may still very well win the day.

Merrill Lynch was once best known for the claim of one of its executives that online trading threatened customers' financial well-being. It had been written off as an Internet also-ran as recently as late 1998. But by the end of 1999, Merrill Lynch was able to roll out its unlimited-advantage accounts, wherein high rollers could trade online. By choosing to delay the launch of its online trading site the company had run the risk of being left behind. At the same time, the very length of its development stage assured customers that the programme would meet all of their expectations. Rather than frustrate customers Merrill Lynch made sure of the quality of its site and got an overwhelmingly positive response.

Business Models and the Internet

The Internet is not benign. It has created the most aggressive market space ever seen. While many of its proponents preach that the Internet is an open non-competitive forum, the reality is that it breeds the most aggressive kind of competition. Businesses must learn quickly how to develop and defend their business models, and, equally, how to attack and counterattack those who would put them out of business.

A case in point is Thawte Consulting, a small South African firm that had developed encryption software which would ultimately corner most of the US market. CEO Mark Shuttleworth negotiated with three possible partners in the US and eventually struck a deal with VeriSign for $575 million. However, the losers in the negotiations did not skulk back to their corners hoping for better luck next time. They immediately counterattacked through the US courts, hoping to destroy the deal using anti-trust legislation. In the old economy this would have been considered negotiating in bad faith. In the Internet Age, losing the first round translated into making aggressive attempts to close the business entirely in the short term.

This aggression has led to all-out war between companies. Operational strategies are now aimed at disrupting, denying, destroying or otherwise doing serious damage to the competition and their allies. The difference between the old and the new economy is that in the old the warfront was out in the market place – on the supermarket shelf, the showroom floor. The

But old-economy sectors – like the automobile industry – follow companies such as Price Online, Amazon and Webvan into focusing on the customer interface. Driven by Internet technology and the challenge of new entrants with diverse models in the market space the automobile industry has individual firms trying to develop models that had several elements in common:

- intense customer relationships as a result of improved communication, emphasis on customer service and innovations in after-market services;

- enhanced branding and customization in order to emphasize differentiation;

- real-time communications with suppliers that will reduce transaction costs, improve design planning, scheduling and logistics as well as improve inventory management and cash flow;

- the creation of 'super suppliers' that are taking over many of the aspects of designing, engineering and manufacturing functions.

In early moves in the industry in the US, Ford announced an alliance with Yahoo! Inc. while General Motors linked up with America Online – both Internet firms offering personalized services for customers. In the UK, GM in the form of Vauxhall did something similar with Delphi Automotive. Even traditional rivals such as Ford, GM and Daimler Chrysler were joining forces to rationalize the purchasing of $240 billion worth of parts from thousands of suppliers. This alliance shadowed a similar one in the retail industry backed by Sears Roebuck & Carrefour to procure $80 billion worth of products online. In comparison, Amazon's $1 billion sales pales into insignificance.

goal was to persuade customers to shift their allegiance. Now the battlefront has moved into the organization. The struggle for scarce resources – human and financial capital, information and product technology – has been escalated to include a push to dominate the opposition's business model with one's own. Whether you want to hire private detectives (as did the senior executives of Oracle in their battle with Microsoft) is a moot point. It has become critically important to understand the competitor's business model and attack its weakest links.

For instance, by acquiring one of its major book suppliers, Barnes and Noble knew that it could deal a serious blow to Amazon's business model. As Barnes and Nobel developed a strategy to acquire Ingram, its own distributor, Amazon mounted a counterattack through the Federal Trade Commission to close off this acquisition avenue. On this occasion Amazon was successful but Barnes and Noble would be back.

The creation of a new business model is not a static process, it is a dynamic one that requires constant reiteration throughout its development. At Cisco Systems the goal was to establish the company as a leading player in every market it touched. Within this framework, the company aimed to become the single source for heavy-duty computer-networking equipment. If anything, Cisco's overall success is based on having a dynamic business model that is obsessive about technology. Its core philosophy is to aim at the future, though the future is a moving target. Cisco acquired Cerent – a fibre-optic-technology developer which, at the time, generated $15 million a year and employed a mere 275 people – for $6.9 billion. Cisco saw the acquisition as an investment in the future.

Traditional travel agencies like the Thomas Cook Group Ltd and Preussag AG have long realized that value could be captured in management of outsourced facilities and in customer interface. What they have been unable to do is create new value at the customer interface at a time when companies like Yahoo! and Amazon are maximizing that process. On the face of it, the traditional travel agency has been abysmal at managing the customer-interface issues of identification and individualization to meet customer needs with special products. Their mass-marketing models are doomed to fail unless they can turn that model on its head.

Conclusion

Starting with the soft intangible 'belief' model that was introduced by Comstellar we have progressed to providing much more substance, more beef, to the model. When we look at measurement systems in Chapter 7, we'll find that the most leading-edge business model is still based on hard financial measures that test its robustness. The lesson of the Internet gold rush was that investors were often not as demanding of business models as they might have been. They now have the opportunity to be more analytical.

Relationship Capital

Relationship capital is the hidden treasure of any organization. It can be found sequestered in that all-embracing network of relationships that form the nervous system of business. It is embedded in an organization through the networks of formal and informal relationships that people have with people inside and outside the firm. Though information systems often give relationship capital the appearance of tangibility, they are difficult to measure. Thus, relationship capital is often a hidden force in business, though it can often spell the difference between a successful company and an unsuccessful one.

Relationship capital permeates every aspect of the business model; yet, few companies have learned to identify it as a force, and to recognize its importance to their business models. For most businesses, relationship capital remains invisible and private. However, leaders who do not understand the value of relationship capital are doomed to ignore it, and ignorance in this area can sabotage even the most promising of alliances. The recent spate of partnerships and mergers in Europe has spawned some stark examples of this. After the initial excitement of the merger has worn off, many a manager has found his division isolated, not because of a lack of motivation or technology, but because its network system has become severed and obsolete.

With the merger of two of Denmark's largest companies – Danisco and Cultor – a DKK 19.219 billion business was created. Putting the deal together for CEO (chief executive officer) Alf Duch-Pedersen was relatively simple compared with meshing the operations of two companies. Several divisions in the new company overlapped and needed cutting back. Leadership set to the task. A former manager later told of the disorientation he felt as the new business systems were being created: 'There were too many new faces around – people who had come from the other side. They were [seemingly] good people but I didn't know whom to trust. To whom could I take a problem? I felt that both my job and my ego were under attack.'

What happened to Danisco Cultor is common to many mergers. On the face of it, Danisco Cultor leadership set about adapting the formal structure to the requirements of the new situation. People were moved into roles that apparently fit their personal capabilities, as well as the organization's needs. However, the existing relationship capital in the informal structure was ignored, and eventually discarded. As connections were broken, nodes moved or removed, so the basis of relationship capital was destroyed and the capital lost. Of course, the new structure can foster a different and perhaps equal network over time – but in the new economy, will it be allowed the time required to accomplish this?

A good instinctive grasp of the importance of relationship capital can be a powerful leadership skill. Emphasizing its importance merely confirms what we always knew, that 'it's not what you know, it's who you know and who they know that counts'. Virgin's Richard Branson has an uncanny ability to draw on relationship capital, often in the nick of time, as he proved when he seemingly pulled an alliance with Singapore Airlines out of his hat. Branson took the Business Press by surprise. The Press had Branson figured for a goner, and was highly sceptical of his chances of pulling out of the tailspin *they* said his airline was in. What the media didn't factor into its analysis is that Branson is a long-term investor in relationship capital. He used it to ensure the alliance with Singapore as he has used it skilfully throughout his career. Even his personal popularity in the market place is based on a carefully nurtured media image that portrays him as an affable, approachable and thoroughly normal guy. In deciding to end hostilities with British Airways when Robert Ayling left he formed another potentially powerful alliance – one which ultimately allows the two former adversaries to present a unified front against heavy regulatory interference. Branson inherently understands that good business is based on a robust and all-encompassing human network and he plays that network with artistry. Don't be misled, relationship capital is not only the domain of the CEO. As can be seen in Figure 4.1, it permeates and influences every aspect of the business model.

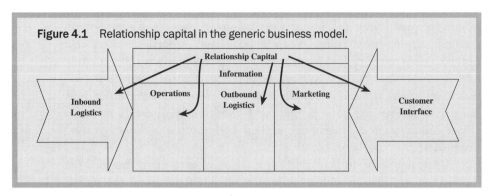

Figure 4.1   Relationship capital in the generic business model.

Figure 4.2   The dynamics of relationship capital.

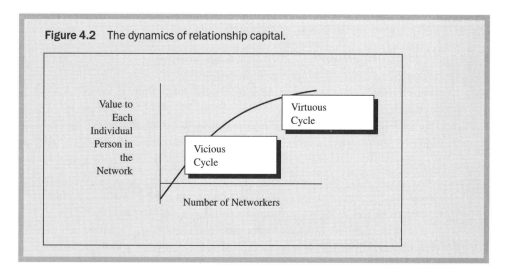

Informal relationship networks have been around since humankind started getting organized. They work for several reasons. Networking is a natural social phenomenon that most people enjoy; repeated interaction between individuals and groups develops trust and improves cooperation; networks based on advice and information transfer can be powerful assets. As the old saying goes 'knowledge is power'. Networks which occur within and between organizations can transcend boundary barriers. These same informal networks are inherent in every business today.

In business, the network of relationship capital shares a basic characteristic with traditional networks as well as other virtual networks; as the number of people in the network grows, so the value to each individual increases. This creates a pattern of vicious versus virtuous cycles (Figure 4.2) in which membership limited to a few creates dearth, and ultimately death for the network, while membership expanded to the many creates plenty and ultimately success for the network.[1]

Take, for example, a relatively informal social network such as Rotary International or Round Table. In a community where one of these organizations has many members the cycle is virtuous. Individual members gain perceived value in terms of numbers of friends and contacts. At the same time, stakeholders – the community at large in this case – gain benefit from the group. Where group membership is limited to a few people and new members are not forthcoming, the life of the group will be fairly short and will add little or no value to the community.

Three Components of Relationship Capital

Relationship capital in business is much more than a series of private networked relationships, however. Even in small networks, it can be broken down into a series of components: human capital, intellectual capital and external capital (Figure 4.3). Human capital manifests itself as the experience, expertise, knowledge and skills that people bring to the network with them each day. Through improved hiring techniques in business, better training and development, and attractive incentive schemes in the workplace, human capital can be increased.

Working in tandem with human capital is intellectual capital. Intellectual capital is defined as the sum of a company's knowledge, experience, processes, systems and innovations. Many companies have begun to focus on knowledge management. However, the knowledge area of relationship capital remains an issue that is neither well measured nor managed. Most knowledge-management systems attempt to capture tangible explicit knowledge and information rather than the tacit implicit knowledge inherent in relationship capital. As Jeffrey Pfeffer has noted: *'Knowledge-management systems rarely reflect the fact that essential knowledge, including technical knowledge, is often transferred between people by stories, gossip and by watching one another work.'*[2] Most knowledge-management efforts emphasize technology, focusing on the storage and transfer of codified information such as facts, statistics and written reports and presentations.

External capital defines external links with outside stakeholders with whom relationships may be found or established. They include customers, suppliers, alliances, community, competitors and even other departments or divisions within the greater company.

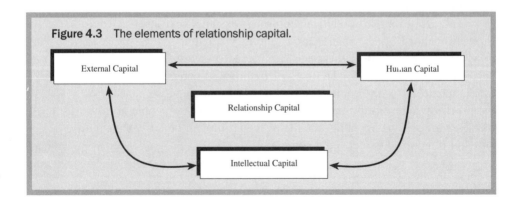

Figure 4.3   The elements of relationship capital.

Motor Rallying and Knowledge Management

Behind the recent headline news of the battles on the racing circuit between Colin McRae, Tommi Makinen and Carlos Sainz lies another tale of knowledge management in the world of sport.

Motor rallying is a tough sport that requires teams of drivers and technicians to endure extreme climatic conditions for days on end in different parts of the world. Running a rally team requires a combination of physical stamina, technical competence and the ability to learn fast. In fact the World Rally Series is really a succession of opportunities for teams to test and improve their cars through the process of trial and error. The challenge of maintaining a world-class standing is so great that the majority of automobile companies outsource their rally teams to a diverse group of specialist companies.

Seat, three-time rally-kart winning team, is the exception. Under José Aguilera, the Seat team has worked its way up from service provider to independent rally team and also to full-fledged world-class team – the Formula 1 of rally motoring.

The secret to this success is not the hard codified explicit knowledge that is recorded in motor manuals – but knowledge management, the soft, tacit, embedded knowledge that is created in a team and cannot be written down – maybe not even articulated clearly.

A rally car is a sophisticated machine that is constantly monitored by computers. The hard information gleaned is combined with the knowledge that drivers acquire when they have crossed the circuit a few times. Much of this knowledge is intuitive. Drivers and technicians work in close-knit teams, putting 'feel' and hard data together to give them faster times and more durability. Aguilera says 'It is a combination of selecting the right people for the team and then focusing total and immediate concentration on the challenge at hand.'

Human and intellectual capital, when linked to external capital, give rise to relationship capital. Although the three are closely related, and can be firmly linked, companies often have difficulty organizing and measuring them. Other than their more tangible aspects (i.e. payroll and training, which can be measured in the financial statement) they remain largely invisible. Ironically, even when those aspects are measured, they usually appear in profit and loss as expenses, and not in the balance sheet as assets.

A Rogue's Gallery?

Harold Geenen and Lord Hanson were probably the last of the 'balance sheet' leaders – staunch believers that business models revolved exclusively around the financial statements. Each of them believed in strong, financially driven control systems managed by 'kick-ass' accountants. Each of them

Relationship Capital Cautionary Tales

Let's look at Robert Horton during his term at BP, or Al Dunlap at Sunbeam. Horton was known as 'Hatchet Horton' and Dunlap as 'Chainsaw Al'. Neither of them wasted much time on developing relationship capital, either before or after they took over their respective jobs. When Dunlap took the helm at Sunbeam – and fired 70 per cent of the management – the share price soared by 43 per cent. The survivors of that massacre were subjected to Dunlap's confrontational management style, including public humiliation at meetings. He made few friends among the people he came into contact with, prompting Tom Peters to say 'Al Dunlap is a first-class jerk and I wish you would quote me on that and throw in a few four-letter words!'

Fired by the Sunbeam Board, Dunlap left behind a legacy of questionable financial practices, stock price that had plummeted 80 per cent, and a slew of shareholder lawsuits. It had taken Sunbeam 2 years to wise up to Dunlap.

Ironically a *Fortune Magazine* article marked the beginning of the end for Bob Horton, ousted from BP. In the article, Horton claimed to be much brighter than his peer group in the company – surely not a wise investment in relationship capital. Shortly afterwards, it became clear that he had lost the support not only of his peer group, but of the company board as well. Exit Horton, also after 2 years.

was highly successful while he remained on the bridge. The moment each stepped down, however, problems arose – successors were unable to perform at the same level. The unacknowledged problem was that both Geenen and Hanson had built huge funds of relationship capital, which they neglected, or refused to pass on. For example, Hanson had a legendary 30-year partnership with Gordon White who complemented his skills in every way. What Hansen lacked White had – particularly in managing human relationships. Since none of this collective wisdom and cooperative effort ever found its way into the very hands-on control system that was the business, it was lost when they left the building.

Virtual Networks

Networks in the new economy present a dichotomy: they can deliver tangible results if well managed, yet are the most intangible element of the value chain. One of the real differences between the new economy and the old is that, in the old economy, networks were very real and tangible. They were the physical connectors of nodes essential to the business model. The airline industry's zeal for hub operations or the energy industry's emphasis on the grid network are examples of how networking was perceived in the old economy. In the new economy, businesses are just beginning to identify relationship networks, to recognize their value and to develop the ability to integrate them into their economic systems.

What has truly changed the dynamics of the new economy, however, is the 'virtual' network. The virtual network can provide the element of network externality, which can be defined as invisible linkages between individuals or groups. The arrival of that element has reconfigured how companies think about business models. In brief, network externality is the value that is attributed to the business model by virtue of the number of people in the network.

For instance, let's take a look at Apple MacIntosh, generally considered to produce a quality computer. Yet, in spite of quality, Apple is not a leader in computer sales. One reason for this is that Apple represents a small, somewhat disconnected network within the computer industry, and consumers have been made very aware of this through media and advertising. Potential customers hesitate to invest in Apple computers because they recognize the fact that joining a network of few users might not be a good idea – the vicious-cycle effect, as described above, is working here. In spite of the fact that Apple MacIntosh *users* believe mightily in their product choice, and are known to be quite verbal in their praise, their small number does not prevail. The power of perception works to the advantage of Apple's competitor, Wintel, which is seen to have the larger, more comprehensive network and, therefore, to be the better investment. In this case, perception and expectation create positive feedback in the form of customers for Wintel. Carl Shapiro and Hal Varian[3] say that 'positive feedback makes the strong get stronger and the weak get weaker, leading to extreme outcomes'. Witness the battle between Apple and Wintel.

Positive feedback is, in itself, important to relationship capital because together with the effects of the virtuous cycle they make a potent force. As the network of informal and formal contacts grows it effectively feeds on itself swelling exponentially the perceptions and expectations of the strength of its centre.

An excellent example of this is the case of South Life Ltd. The company appointed John Slater to head up its claims division which was experiencing considerable difficulty. The division was fielding ongoing complaints from its branches and customers that claims took too long. In addition, field staff found employees in claims to be unhelpful and unfriendly.

Slater soon got to work on the problem. First, he set up an interchange of employees at lower levels. Field staff were asked to spend a few days in the division learning how the operations were run. Divisional staff were required to go out into the field to view operations there. Employees were not happy about this; each group believed that they knew what was

Slater used a simple checklist to start this process:

1. What information is important to us?

2. Where are we in the information flow?

3. Who do we know that has the information we need? What is the basis of our relationship with each of these: friendship, business and social group?

4. Who do we *need* to know in that network, and how are we going to establish contact and build relationships?

5. With contacts we've lost, when was the last contact and what is the basis and strategy for renewal?

6. Do we have time to build the network?

7. What resources are available for building this network?

8. Can we alter the reward systems to fuel behaviour changing?

9. How are we going to coordinate the renewal strategy across the division?

happening in the other's operations. Slater persisted – this was only part of his objective. What he was really trying to do was to establish a criss-crossing network that would allow both field and divisional staff to enter each other's domain informally, and without recourse to supervisors and managers. Eventually these relationships started to develop. Now Slater focused even more on the network, eventually encouraging senior staff to set about developing similar networks. Keeping the networking process going over time was no easy task, however. To keep the process dynamic and functional, he developed a programme to reward people for using and developing it further.

The bottom-line goal of the programme was speedy claim processing. Provided this was accomplished, and staff could show that they were using networks to accomplish it, they would earn points that would accumulate and ultimately reward them with a half-day off.

Soon operations staff was calling field staff to alert them that a claim was being processed. Often they would call customers to tell them that a payment would be in the mail within 3 days. The flow of information from the division to its major stakeholders increased substantially – and claim-processing time came down. Just as important was the realization outside of the division that real change had been accomplished, and that attitudes had shifted. Claims were no longer a millstone around everyone's neck. It had become a value-adding division of the company.

Network Management

Despite all of the attention that is given to knowledge management very little is said about network management. Yet, as already stated, *network development and management is crucial to recognizing and developing relationship capital.* We know that organizations could hardly operate without the informal networks; what we currently do not know is how to systemize ways in which an organization can derive its competitive advantage from networks.

We know that informal networks are established primarily by individuals and then by groups. Networks exist either inside the firm or external to it. Some businesses like to keep their networks inside the organization, developing what we used to call cliques. Others avoid these. Some companies and people are excellent at building external relations; others, not so good. All of this is extremely difficult to measure, since most networks are invisible and private. To add to the complexity, individuals develop their own networks over time, but are simply unaware of the true power of the informational network they've built. Others are intuitively aware that they nurture relational capital, but feel they should protect their investment.

On Internal Networks

Bruce McIlveray was a general manager at what is now Reckitt Benkiser, the large pan-European fast-moving consumer goods (FMCG) company. McIlveray, an Australian, was famous company-wide for turning difficult businesses around. He had headed up divisions in Asia, Africa and Europe, and his success was based on the informal networks that he had developed within each of those divisions. He was extremely systematic, working on the network virtually everyday. On taking an assignment, he would identify the thirty most influential people within that business. He had developed

Internal networks, and the way McIlveray approached them, looked something like this:

- Basic assumptions: people enjoy and are motivated by being in the General Manager's network. Problem solving is best achieved when it is done close to the individual's place of work.

- Database management each day is essential. Updating of data is also important.

- Relationship capital is built on both social and business contact, combining those in one call is acceptable.

- Relationship capital is increased through giving; going out to people, meeting at their places of work, putting them together with others for their benefit, pays off.

A fast build-up of personal knowledge is possible through focusing on relationship capital.

a simple database that included everything he knew about each person – hobbies, family names and vacation information etc. Pretty simple stuff. He would make sure that by the end of each week he had spoken to every person on that list. Complemented by McIlveray's walk-around-the-plant management style and his refusal to meet anyone, other than a stranger, in his office, he built a network of employees who judged him a great communicator and motivator for whom they would go the extra mile.

On External Networks

The ability to bind two different company cultures and make an alliance work often falls to a limited number of individuals within the company, a fact that the recent proliferation of alliances across Europe has obscured. Carlos Garcia-Pont, Professor at IESE, has posited that in industries such as the automobile industry, there exist strategic blocks of business, firms that derive strength from interconnected networks. Firms in the strategic block are privy to information such as the introduction of new products, the movement of key people and other opportunistic events. These strategic blocks often expand the network using the concept of a two-step leverage – 'I know someone, who knows someone … etc.'. The strength of each block depends on every individual's ability to use such leverage when necessary.

Slome's system of external networks is based on the following premises:

- Basic assumption: people enjoy being on someone else's network. Everybody has the potential of being an important member of a network.

- Maintaining a database is essential. Data may include the person's business position, name of partner and favourite food.

- The network must be constantly maintained, though this can be a fun process because it involved socializing with people.

- Reciprocity is essential – if you want people to help you, you may have to help them first.

Benny Slome, a highly successful entrepreneur, built Tedelex, the South African domestic-appliances conglomerate, and for which I happened to work at one time. Slome was of the old school, and had little time for contracts, lawyers and litigation. Apart from being somewhat eccentric Slome believed that a handshake on a deal was more potent than a contract, and that alliances were built on honest and open relationships with people he could trust. He had developed international alliances with many firms, notably, Sony in Japan and Blaupunkt in Germany.

The basis of Slome's relationship capital was a vast network system that he had developed over many years and continued to develop throughout his career. It was a simple and effective system. After meeting someone and exchanging business cards, he would write basic information about the person on the back of the card. On returning to the office he would enter it into a database. Of course, this was not revolutionary. However, Slome went a step further. The next time he was in the vicinity of that person's office, Slome would call them. The call would be nothing more than a social call – but it represented a renewal of the relationship capital. Each day that Slome travelled, he would call at least ten to twenty people, apologizing for not being able to see them, enquiring after family and business and inviting them to call when next they were in Slome's hometown, Johannesburg.

Slome made contact with people from many walks of life, some chairpersons and CEOs of businesses, others entry-level employees, but everyone went into the database. Slome believed that CEOs weren't the only people who could make things happen. For some of the contacts, being called to help with a problem by Slome, the CEO of a big corporation was as big a motivator as being called by their own CEOs. In fact, their own CEOs had probably never called many of these people. Slome used the network to solve many an internal issue.

Building the Network

Relationship capital is built on three types of networks: the advice network made up of those persons from whom you would seek advice or, alternatively, to whom you would give advice; the trust network, made up of people in whom you trust and who trust you; and the communication network, the most obvious one, made up of all the people to whom you speak.

Analysing these three networks will give the mission critical leader (MCL) some insight into how fast her team can manoeuvre. Provided she is systematic about unearthing some of these embedded networks, she, and the team, can identify strengths as well as gaps in the network structure. Each network has a structure that reflects the nature of the flow of information from one person to another. Mapping information flow means that gatekeepers, bottlenecks and fountains can be identified.

The analysis can be made in a straightforward way, using a questionnaire that focuses on the following areas:

1   the communication network – to whom do you speak inside and outside the organization?

2   the advice network – as an individual to whom do you give and from whom do you seek it?

3   the trust network – whom do you trust outside the organization and who do you think trusts you?

Communication Networks

This is by far the most obvious of the three networks because it maps all the contacts of all the individuals on the team, both internal and external. Internal communication networks are good for binding and cohesion as well as interdependency within the team and external links are important for orientating the team to what others are doing in similar or related areas. Each area of information should be considered separately, then as part of the whole.

Advice Networks

Advice networks facilitate fast learning. When a team member is faced with a problem, she can tap the network for a variety of outside information and experience. Networking prevents members from having to reinvent solutions that may be common knowledge outside the team.

Advice networks cross the boundaries between internal and external networks. They are not constrained by location, and can cut across different companies as well as across different industries. Companies like HP (Hewlett Packard) seem to be particularly skilled at getting advice to flow across different divisions as well as from outside the company. For example, HP managers combine openness and a willingness to stake almost everything except closely guarded technology secrets in order to develop and nurture advice networks with suppliers, customers and colleagues.

The following checklist can be used to analyse the advice network:

1   Create a database of your critical advice relationships. Advice relationships are those in which you seek advice as well as give it. As you noted in the case studies above, a simple index-card system will serve you well as the readily available software on most computers.

2   Categorize advice relationships *by type* – internal, external, vertical, lateral – and *by importance* – Which of these is critical to my/our success? On which are you dependent? Which consume most of your time?

3   Note the difficulty level of each relationship? Which ones are easy? Which cause you trouble? Which are in bad shape?

4   Develop an investment strategy for those relationships critical to you and your organization. Can these be turned to a trust relationship?

Rover and BMW

The acquisition of Rover by BMW was little short of a disaster. Many jobs were lost and the management team was rationalized in order to make sense of a new formal structure. But if the formal structure is the skeleton then the networks are the nervous system. Managers in this case found themselves with trust networks that were reduced to those people with whom they had previously worked. Newcomers (i.e. from the *other* company) were clearly not to be trusted. Within a short time the company was in trouble because managers were guarding their information, not delegating and definitely not sharing their problems with colleagues although many of them felt they were in the same boat.

Some would put this down to xenophobia. But the BMW experience was a dramatic contrast to long-term trust that managers within Rover had build up with their Japanese counterparts in Honda. During the Honda years Rover managers had spent a lot of their time focusing on trust specifically.

5   Use a hold strategy for those that are in good condition and need little attention. (In fact, consider a hold strategy even for contacts that seem unimportant. Circumstances may change, bringing to prominence a relationship that may have been considered dead.)

Trust Networks

Like advice networks, trust networks can move both horizontally and vertically, but because they tend to be limited to people with whom the leader and team have had close personal contact, they are usually smaller. A leader's analysis of trust networks will not differ all that much from advice networks, but it will hinge on the problem that trust is difficult to define in practical terms.

Peter Drucker believes that organizations of the future will be formed around their trust networks, 'Organizations are no longer built on force, but on trust. Trust between people means that they understand one another.'[4] But even his attempt at a practical definition of trust does not translate into a readily applied tool because trust is usually the result of dynamic process. It is most often established through consistent and predictable integrity and concern for others, but everyone does not possess the skills to engender it. People who are self-serving have difficulty with trust networks and might find themselves with only one or two individuals in their network. Improving such a situation means direct and personal intervention, probably over some time. As leaders come to depend more and more on trust networks, however, the pay-offs may be worth the investment in time and effort.

The checklist for analysing the advice networks above can be applied to an initial analysis of the trust network. For a long-term view or for a leader and group with trust-network problems, use the following:

Step 1   Guidelines to assessing relationship capital:

1. How does relationship capital fit into our business model? What value can you attribute to relationship capital?

2. Is your group in the know or the last to know? Can you readily map your three networks? Are you strong in internal or external networks? Who are the individuals and groups who have access to or control the network?

1   Does a trust relationship exist? If not, why not?

2   Why is the trust relationship a problem? In what ways has it broken down? What are the causes of the breakdown – member experiences that predate the group; reputation of one or more of the players; or politicised organization?

3   What resources are needed to successfully improve and amplify trust in the network?

4   Can the advice-network members be converted to create a new trust network? What resources would be required?

5   Would the 360-degree appraisal system, a system for giving all-round feedback, help this team to sort out its trust issues?

Mapping the Communications Networks

Create a density chart for each of the three networks, listing all contacts, and then labelling them as you go. Because networks are private, this method attempts to bring some of the hidden treasure to the surface.

Next, have all team members gather around the map. Identify where gaps exist and what needs to be done to fill the gaps.

Now map the three different networks searching for overlaps, holes and potential synergies.

Structure, Roles and Membership

When an executive decided to take up his next assignment in a packaging company after 10 years in the computer industry he discovered some unsettling facts in the process. He found that his old computer-industry network was of little use to him in his new job. Undaunted, he began to build a new network on the job. Then he discovered that the packaging industry did not use the informal, interfirm, cross-functional network typical of the computer industry. Instead, he found himself faced with a completely new and foreign network. In the new network he was forced to focus almost exclusively on the internal network, primarily to establish credibility for himself; he had little or no time for the external networks which he believed would ultimately be most important for the business.

There is a valuable lesson to be learned from our executive's experience. Networks often institutionalize certain behaviours that are completely unique to the industry. The network also develops rules or etiquette primarily to protect the network itself. Often an industry will itself determine the structure of networks. All networks, whether individual, intrafirm or interfirm, have rules about acceptable behaviour. For example, breaking a rule like supplying the name of a network member without permission is usually unacceptable in networks. In some cases, these behaviours may lock in or lock out certain members. For instance, forming a network with someone in a similar position to oneself in another organization may prevent one from developing a relationship with a third party in that, or even another, organization.

Membership in a network gives you access to 'who's in and who's out'. Being a member gives you access to the rumours, of course, but it also plugs you in to resources. Everyone knows that if you need to get something done you need a network to pinpoint the person who can do it. So, as with our executive, you take the best qualities with the worst in networks.

Step 2   Guidelines to assessing relationship capital:

3. Have we mapped three networks – communication, advice and trust? From this analysis which team member forms a natural bridge to a client or supplier?

4. Do we maintain a network database? What resources are available to establish one?

Density and Holes

If value is to be created and captured through relationship capital, a leader will need to determine the density of the network and then to consider structural holes. Among professional groups such as lawyers and doctors the density of the network is an important factor. A new entrant to a profession soon discovers that many of his colleagues operate in dense networks where referral, advice and trust is developed. She quickly realizes that building a successful practice will depend more on the density of the network she can form than on the number of successful surgeries she can perform.

In mapping networks, leaders must make a focused analysis of structural holes. Often the analysis will uncover surprisingly blatant holes in the network. These may need to be filled quickly in order to protect oneself or the group. On the other hand, they can give rise to opportunities and should be given longer consideration. If a leader finds herself or her team on the periphery of a network, then she should develop strategy to improve the position, and assign qualified members to fill the gaps.

The following relatively simple actions will increase the density of any network:

1   Joining sector, social and community associations where counterparts may be found;

2   Attending conferences, seminars and courses, especially those targeting the sector;

3   Cultivating stronger ties with suppliers and customers – perhaps socializing with them.

4   Setting up informal gatherings for employees and customers to find out what's really going on.

International Relationship Capital

The business model is increasingly built on the strength of international relationship capital for a lot of organizations. This is an area with which expatriate managers in global business often struggle.

Research supports the idea that having local networks is crucial to innovation and to success. The success of Silicon Valley, Cambridge and Modena as industry Meccas bears out Porter's idea that the clustering of companies in a region enhances performance. The networking effect seems to have impact no matter what types of companies are clustered. Little wonder that regional governments offer attractive inducements to get companies into industrial or high-tech parks in their regions. The spin-off to individual communities is often large.

On the international level, however, local networks can be problematical. Often large organizations have difficulty locking into those local networks in faraway places. One proven way to successfully establish remote networks, as well as to build relationship capital, is to hire local nationals to run the business. Because of their familiarity with the area, they are more able than expatriate managers to develop both internal and external networks with alacrity. The reasons for this are worth exploring:

•   Language – Networking is a social phenomenon which, naturally, takes place in the local language. This provides special challenges for expatriates that few of them are able to overcome. Being able to order dinner in Italian in Rome is certainly an advantage, but does not require the fluency necessary to master the complexities of networking amongst Romans. What one tends to forget is that the language of networking is steeped in history and meaning. Nuances that come in the form of nods and a raised eyebrow or special in-jokes are impossible to learn without spending years in a country. If you consider the complexity of your own network in your own home community you realize how difficult that would be to master with rudimentary – or even mid-level language skills.

- **Culture or social norms** – Salutations are quite different from one society to the next, as most of us have discovered at one time or another. When we meet an acquaintance, the greeting may vary from a casual 'Hi' in one society to vigorous handshaking and back-slapping in another. Almost every public gesture and behaviour is influenced by the social norms of a society and unwittingly expatriates often run afoul of those norms. Fortunately, most cultures are welcoming and overlook the gaffes of foreign visitors; some even find them charming. Social intercourse is one thing, however; breaking into a local network is quite another.

- When Clive Callahan, a British expat with many years' experience in Mediterranean countries, opened up Dunlop Slazenger's new offices in Sant Cugat in Spain, the company needed essential telephone services installed by Telefónica, the Spanish telecommunications company. The telephone company sprang into action and a technician was sent around to make the necessary installations and connections. Alas, declared the technician, installation was complete, but connection was not possible. Telephone lines were still overground in this a new industrial area; that is, strung from pole to pole. Unfortunately for Dunlop Slazenger, the nearest pole was some way down the street, too far to string a line into the building. The telephone company did have a department that dealt with poles; it couldn't provide a pole without a requisition, and that took several weeks. The technician would continue with installation inside the building but connecting to the outside world was beyond his domain. Here Callahan's local experience swung into action. After a few well-placed calls from his mobile phone, he uncovered Telefónica's supplier of poles. The following morning when the technician turned up for work he found a pole erected outside the building.

- **Local knowledge** – Understanding how things 'work' can take forever in communities where everything is taken for granted and nothing is recorded or in places that offer little to local citizens other than tax

Step 3   Guidelines to assessing relationship capital:

5. Do we fully understand the (local) structure, rules and membership of our networks?

6. Do we have GDTs? If so, how well are members of the GDTs networked? How are we leveraging relationship capital through our GDTs?

collection. Finding contacts in local industry can sometimes be achieved by doing something as simple as driving around the streets. Because expatriates tend to cluster together in groups, they may not venture out to reconnoitre in the community. When a general manager of a global British firm visited his office in Beijing, he was appalled to find that while people were comfortable travelling to Shanghai, no one had actually left the office to survey markets outside the city precincts. By mixing with a largely expatriate community this group had actually overlooked some basic requirements of working in an international setting.

A business is able to grow exponentially when it can access knowledge with ease at all levels internally and externally. Training, development and promotion of local talent can be a more practical investment for a company than trying to maintain expensive, often insulated expatriates in senior roles. In a systematic approach to the development of international relationship capital, a business would consider sending an expatriate only when there is a lack of local talent and know-how.

The Power of Globally Distributed Teams

Globally distributed teams (GDTs) may have shortcomings in the face-to-face business of running things locally, but they have a great strength in their ability to *plug into* local networks. For this reason, GDTs can be valuable in leveraging relationship capital. Videoconferencing, conference calling and electronic-chat discussion are globally so accessible and efficient that it is possible to leverage the relatively weak international network of the GDT into the strong local network within minutes. Thus companies have only to learn how to articulate and evaluate international relationship capital in order to draw on it with élan.

The power of GDTs is demonstrated in Figure 4.4. The leader is at the centre of the net and has contact with each member. Members have contact with the leader, and with each other. However, the real power lies in the fact that each member has her own network on which the leader or other members may draw. This leveraging of relationship capital means that the GDT has a web spreading over many regions and countries. Nurture of the network is crucial and can be accomplished using the suggestions that follow.

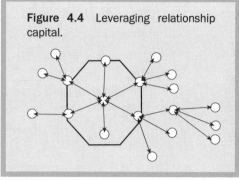

Figure 4.4 Leveraging relationship capital.

- Have each member of the GDT draw up a list of their communication, trust and advice networks. If team members are doing this remotely, they'll need 24 hours or so to complete the task.

- Ask members to share the numbers of their respective lists as well as to name the most important member of each list. This may prove difficult since some people may feel that these names potentially represent their power within the organization.

- Challenge members to increase their lists during the next fortnight. This might be done by exploring holes in their density maps. This way they attempt to develop new relationships.

Conclusion

As we have seen in this chapter, a network is not an accidental, irregularly occurring phenomenon. The cases we've looked at illustrate common themes. Networks have to be worked on consciously all the time. They need to be maintained and renewed. They are not only about seeking advice, they are also about giving advice, socializing with people, making contact, noticing and being noticed.

Networks '*provide individuals with the benefits of access, timing and referrals that allow them to make the most of their stock of physical and human capital*', say Nitin Nohria and Sumantra Ghoshal.[5] Because networks are so deeply embedded in the organization, focus ultimately and inevitably narrows down to each individual. In building outward, the firm is an organic system of networks of which the structure is comprised. The more dense and robust the networks, the stronger the organization.

Once we begin thinking about the organization in this way, we realize that the alignment problems we perceive between different sectors of the

Before proceeding, take a moment to reflect on these issues. To see relationship capital as a whole, ask yourself the following questions:

1. How can we rethink our existing relationship capital?

2. Can we estimate the value of relationship capital? Can we add value through developing innovative networks? What is the cost of a whole network, or a part?

3. How can we redesign performance appraisal and reward criteria to incorporate the recognition and harvesting of relationship capital?

business are often created by thinking of the business as a mechanical system. The very term 'alignment' is itself a mechanical term suggesting mechanical solutions that resemble calibration of an instrument rather than organic resolutions in human terms.

Networking has no such terminology and therefore doesn't suffer from alignment problems. Networks have strong and weak ties, holes in structure and commitment to the process or lack thereof. Alignment problems are often nothing more than weak ties within a network system.

Winning Teams

In December 1998, *Time Magazine* announced that for the first time since 1852 a human tower of ten levels had been successfully completed. This achievement formed the background to the boom of *castells* in Spain, quite literally the building of castles in the air. The centre of the boom is Catalonia where 10,000 active members belong to 58 *collas* or clubs. A ten-level tower requires as many as 700 people to support it at the base while at the top, an *anxaneta* – a small girl or boy – raises a hand to indicate successful completion. Towers often collapse because of weaknesses at various levels. But on 23 November 1998, Los Minyons of Vilafranca successfully completed the highest tower in almost 150 years. We come round to discussing these on Page 88.

The Castell

In Chapter 3 we saw Rich Raimundi at HP (Hewlett Packard) dedicate more than 20 hours a week to building a team during his *Window of Effectiveness*. Raimundi wanted his division to be able to take on global responsibility. He set up a programme of close coaching and mentoring to ensure that each individual understood his role and what was expected of him. Members of the team came to see Raimundi as their trainer, and themselves as fledglings learning to fly. Week after week, in a series of team and individual meetings, Raimundi laid down a standard of high performance, reinforcing it until it became second nature to the team. When he exited from the division, he left behind a team that was capable of running a global business.

Now this story would not be so remarkable were it not for the fact that the vast majority of managers spend less than 3 or 4 hours a week in contact with their direct reports. After speaking to hundreds of managers at Raimundi's level in companies all over the world, I have discovered that managers who spend more than 10 hours in direct contact are an exceptional minority. In fact, only 20 per cent of managers spend 5 hours or more a week with their teams. It has led me to believe that there is more lip-service paid to the concept of teamwork than any other idea in management. It has led Margot Cairnes, author of *Approaching the Corporate Heart*, to be thoroughly sceptical of the whole team business,[1] 'I am often approached by corporate leaders wanting me to engage in team-building exercises with their people. I find this whole notion laughable and quaintly old fashioned … Over the years, I found it increasingly difficult to get the whole team in one place, at one time … Moreover, the life cycle of teams seemed to be speeding up. I gave up completely when working with the top team of one organization which, by the end of my valiant team-building effort 1 year later, had none of its original members!'

The fantasy of the intrepid manager surrounded by his faithful team of people is so appealing that managers will declare they lead a team, that they take decisions as a team, and on and on. Those around them recognize this company-speak and usually ignore it. They know that bosses go through this charade when either they dedicate no time to teamwork or they are simply not team players. In fact they may often be closet dictators. However, even dictators know that no business can rely on intelligence and wisdom residing exclusively in the heads of those at the top of the organization. That's why so much lip-service is paid to the concept of teamwork.

The TMT is Not a Team!

Unlike Cairnes, I am not cynical about teams. I believe that confusion has arisen because we compare the top-management teams (TMT) with mission critical teams. They are not the same. The TMT is made up of the most senior managers of the business. It includes the CEO (chief executive officer) and his direct reports. Having a strongly cohesive team at TMT level is desirable and even possible, but not essential. Moreover, though CEOs pay a lot of lip-service to the idea of the TMT being a real team, they seldom are. As Cairnes implies, all the evidence suggests that most TMTs operate successfully without being real teams at all. Jon K. Katzenbach, of *Teams at the Top* fame, says[2]: 'The best performing companies are run by strong CEOs operating in single-leader configurations rather than in teams.' As Dave Pottruck, co-CEO of Charles Schwab, would put it: 'Sure, I'm a team player. As long as I'm the captain.'[3] Admittedly, he said this before being miraculously converted to a teamworker. Miraculous conversions, however, most often signify the afterglow of arrival at the top for someone who may well have been a rotter on the way up.

Self-proclaimed 'teams at the top' tend to underachieve. Before rising to CEO of HP, Lew Platt had been a successful leader of a strong mission critical team that had turned around HP's Medical Equipment Division. After he rose to the top job in HP, he continued to lead in the HP way with a strong emphasis on team. His TMT couldn't get HP results to lift above the horizon, however. During the final stage of Platt's tenure, profits fell into a slide, declining by a few percentage points each year.

TMTs seldom display real team characteristics. We seldom observe cohesion, team spirit or shared intent. Based on my own observations, TMTs can be riddled with politics and intrigue. When combined with inflated egos, group chemistry can be cursed with conspiracy and double-dealing that would make a Borgia blush.

If intrigue is tantamount at TMT level, quite the opposite applies to mission critical teams below TMT level. Mission critical leaders (MCLs) cannot afford intrigue. A functional team is critical to an MCL's success. Going it alone can and invariably does prove disastrous. We all recognize the manager who tries to cover all of the bases by himself. He usually takes a lot of work home at night. He believes that if you want something done you should do it yourself. He is always self-seeking and seldom pats anyone on the back for a job well done. He usually burns out along the way.

MCLs know that they need high-performance teams. They also appreciate that no new business model can succeed without massive commitment to team performance. They are conscious of the fact that a good team will exceed the potential of any individual member, that a great team will beat records and give a towering performance. At the same time, the new economy has brought with it a new perspective on the way teams function. Leadership now faces team issues that didn't exist before. In the old economy teams could get away with being internally focused (i.e. essentially introverted and naval gazing). Now, as companies become more and more market driven through increased customization and individualization of products and services, they require teams that are externally focused. Externalization has brought with it a new set of challenges:

Rewards – For the first time in corporate history, company compensation plans linking individual performance to stock options have been widely adopted. As a result, rewards are being fixed by stock-market performance, and individuals are looking out for themselves. Within these new parameters, working in teams presents special problems for the compensation plan. Companies must now look to indicators such as revenue and stock price as criteria for feedback on team performance. In spite of the problems involved, Diageo decided to keep responsibility for change focused in teams. CEO John McGrath believed that it was simply too difficult for any single individual to fight the system. The reward structure had to be adapted accordingly, sometimes grouping as many as thirty people together for bonuses based on bottom-line results.

Risk – Because new products and services derive from new thinking within mission critical teams (MCTs), they can easily become high-risk propositions. If not well managed, MCTs can easily upset the status quo by challenging the organization itself. Or, if *they* are challenged by the organization, they can bolt, starting up their own companies or hawking their ideas to competitors.

Companies can lose profitable properties when they fail to recognize the value of the work of MCTs or the MCTs themselves. The MCT itself is not slow on the uptake, however, and will often leave as a group, to start up on its own. For example, MusicMatch, producer of what the *Wall Street Journal* (WSJ) rates as the best music-download software on the Internet, is a company born within Hewlett Packard. Denis Mud, currently CEO of MusicMatch, and his team of HP employees developed the basic concepts of MusicMatch over a bottle of wine in Mud's kitchen. Once they had refined the concept they left HP and started up their own business. Remarkably, they departed with the blessing of HP.

Outsiders – Business has seen an exponential growth in outsourcing, joint venture and alliance. Within a company, strategically critical activities are often performed by outsiders such as suppliers, consultancies and other service providers – even competitors! MCTs that include outsiders often run into internal problems that prevent them from delivering. External or temporary members of the MCT will naturally bring their own, usually hidden agendas with them, and can put tremendous strain on the team. Even the most well-intentioned relationships with outsiders require special management, as we discussed in the previous chapter.

A New Culture?

These days, employees are only too aware that companies will compensate performance with stock options, profit sharing and other incentive bonuses. They are also aware that no company in the new market place can guarantee them job security and longevity. So, in lieu of the prudent paths of their parents – a steady job, good pay with long-term prospects – bright ambitious people sign up for the big pay-out in the short term. Their dreams of 'castles in the air' are almost exclusively established on one simple motivational model – the money model. This phenomena guarantees that company culture will be as important as ever. But it spells trouble when either the company or the team get into difficulties and the big pay-off starts to recede in the distance.

Even before interconnectedness became a buzzword, most managers in the West were sharing common experience. The enlightenment brought to us by our Japanese managerial counterparts showed that teamwork made a difference. Never mind that the intellectual groundwork had been done in the West or that European companies such as Volvo had long been experimenting with teams. These were little more than theories. Japanese management made it work and show up on the bottom line – business was booming in Japan. What we were doing as we trotted around the Toyota plant was observing how the knowing–doing gap had been closed. From that point, teamwork became a pervasive theme in management circles. It has been repackaged several times since the 1960s – usually to great effect. The basic concepts of team building are widely known and applied. However, the results can vary; depending on the organization and environment, they can range from disastrous to magnificent.

3M, Motorola and HP are notable Western examples of team building. They are also notable exceptions to the rule. Despite common experience, the majority of companies, especially European ones, do not have strong team-player cultures. They are unlikely to ever have team cultures. For that matter they are unlikely to have even a single culture permeating the entire organization. They are large and growing larger, too diverse and global at this stage to undergo such a cultural flip.

MCLs find themselves bound to operate within this constraint. They have to breathe life into existing pockets of culture that may be moribund. Here is where the mission critical approach begins to differentiate itself from traditional leadership. Forming and building a team is not that difficult. Most people have been on team-building retreats and understand how the process works. The challenge comes when one gets back to the office. That's when the MCL takes steps to sustain the intensity of the experience for her team.

The second issue is to avoid falling into a *castell*-effect trap. The Catalan *castell* creates an illusion. Observing it, you tend to focus on the people in the tower, and to think that the winning team is made up of that group alone. Your focus ignores the supporting masses, several hundred people with varying levels of commitment and understanding who form the foundation of the *castell*. So with an organization, a functional pyramid made more complex by having foundation members stretched across the globe. Figure 5.1 provides a simple hierarchical representation of teams in companies. It ignores the fact that teams, groups and MCTs form and operate vertically and horizontally across functions. Only the TMT remains static and isolated in its position. It seldom even draws membership from below its own level. Your focus must take into account all of the people in the network, as well as all of the dynamics it engenders.

The inherent national characteristics of various countries do not of themselves inhibit team cultures. People often believe that they do, but this is more often a response to stereotype than to reality. David Pottruck, previously mentioned teamworker at Schwab, says that 'the presumption that people are naturally going to work together as a team is in fact a disguise. My experience suggests that the natural state of affairs in American business is entropy. Chaos is more likely than teamwork'.[4] This rather sweeping indictment seems to reflect dramatic overstatement, rather than sound judgement.

What is evident is that Italians form teams that are different than Swedish teams. Latin teams seem to be more individualistic than Scandinavian teams. Italians seem to communicate in an animated way and often interrupt each other as they try to get airspace. Scandinavians are more subdued and reticent. But they have

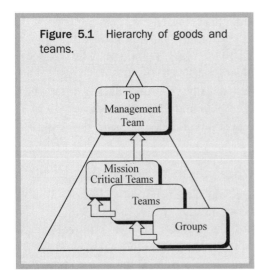

Figure 5.1 Hierarchy of goods and teams.

been this way since they set out on hunting parties from the caves. Despite these differences Latins and Scandinavians are both unquestionably capable of forming formidable teams that will take some fierce beating. To both nationalities, team activities are simply natural.

Take, for example, Bvlgari International. At the movies whenever you see James Bond or The Saint checking the time, he is invariably wearing a Bvlgari watch. How a small Roman business became a global player is a story in itself. As you would expect, because Bvlgari is a traditional Italian family business, its culture is somewhat paternalistic. Many people are second- or third-generation employees and had grown up in the shadow of the company. In developing an expansion strategy that would open stores around the world and market on a global scale, CEO Francesco Trapani had to adapt the company's overarching paternalistic culture to conditions in other parts of the world like the US and Asia.

He also needed to give MCLs the freedom to create a strong sense of team within divisions. Trapani recruited leaders who had demonstrated knowledge of global operations and the ability to develop and market a high level of Italian sophistication. These MCLs came from organizations like Procter & Gamble, American Express and McKinsey and all had inter-national-operations experience. The idea of actually marketing and distri-buting globally was a strange concept, a daunting task that required dramatic cultural change. The company also needed to recast its production and distribution processes to global-scale efficiency. The majority of its employees were Italian, and Roman to boot – people who might have been hugely resistant to change that challenged deeply rooted cultural mores.

The situation had all the chemistry for failure. But it succeeded bril-liantly. In the expediently short period of 18 months, Bvlgari moved from being a very famous Roman business to being a global player. Within this same time-frame, MCLs in the organization were able to build strong com-mitment to particular aspects of the overall mission. In the watch division, for example, the company needed to break with its tradition of being so elitist that you could only buy a watch in a Bvlgari store – teams accom-plished this. Now it was taking on competitors such as Cartier and LMVH.

Contrast glamorous Italian design with Scandinavian engineering. ABB's hard engineering business has changed the way we think about global business. ABB was created in a merger between ASEA AB of Sweden and BBC Brown Boveri of Switzerland. Under its first leader, Percy Barnavic, it developed a decentralized structure with tight financial controls. Basically, what Barnavic wanted his MCLs to do was take on the 200 disparate businesses of ABB and report on how they were doing. Each MCL had to develop her own team at a local level, and motivate and reward them accordingly. Each leader's goal was to create a strong, customer-focused culture at a regional level that corresponded to the overall mission of making 'economic growth and improved living standards a reality for all nations throughout the world'. By 2000 it was becoming apparent that, as a global player, ABB was not thinking of itself as a Scandinavian or even a Swiss business though it had just moved its HQ there. The company moved major operations to the Far East where something like 40,000 jobs were created. ABB has moved from being a business with strong Scandinavian MCTs to a global business with a heavy mix of international MCTs – and the move has not cost it any of its agility and profitability.

The issues that concern an MCL in a large corporation are: What constitutes a MCT? How do MCTs differ from other teams? What are the skills required to move from being a team leader to being an MCL?

What Makes a Mission Critical Team?

To build a Catalan *castell* takes a huge organization of people, not just for the highly visible tower, but for the enormous less visible foundation. As seen in Figure 5.1, there is a difference between group, team and MCT. In fact, in most organizations, there are usually fewer real teams than there are groups. Groups such as committees, councils and sometimes even task forces, meet to share information, perspectives and insights that help individuals in their own areas. There is no group accountability for results, however. What differentiates a team from a group is that the team members deal with a wider scope of the goals and accept greater accountability for their completion. Where there is no shared responsibility, then there can be no team.

An MCT is an enthusiastic set of competent individuals who have chosen to work cohesively in trusting relationships with a commitment to common mission, accountability and performance. What ratchets up teams into MCT is the level of mission set for the team, the performance levels required of the team, and ultimately, the rewards and recognition they are given for achievement. The main characteristics of an MCT are as follows:

- an MCL who is upwardly mobile and has influence in the TMT (top-management team);

- a mission that is directly correlated with the organization's mission;

- clear demonstrable measures that will be reflected in the bottom line;

Working groups	Teams	Mission critical teams
Strong, clearly focused leader	Shared leadership roles	Team leader with upward influence
Individual accountability	Individual and mutual accountability	Individual and mutual accountability
Group's purpose equals broader organizational goals	Specific purpose that the team itself delivers	Mission strongly correlated with organization mission
Individual work products	Collective work products	Collective work products to be shared with other MCTs
Runs efficient meetings	Encourages open-ended discussion and active problem-solving meetings	Demanding, often conflictive, passionate about changing things.
Measures effectiveness indirectly by its influence on others	Measures performance directly by assessing collective work products	Bottom-line measures
Discusses, decides and delegates	Discusses, decides and does real work together	Discuss, create, formulate and obsessive about implementation

Table 5.1 Groups, teams and MCTs. How to tell the difference between (adapted from *The Work of Teams* by Jon Katzenbach, 1998b, p. 37).

- rewards that are tied to the measures;
- a feedback loop that passes through the MCL;
- a life is no longer than that of the tenure of the MCL.

The differences between working groups, teams and MCTs are outlined in Table 5.1.

Table 5.1 outlines the difference between teams and MCTs but operationally it might be quite hard to differentiate them. Quite honestly, they are often very similar. The strong determinants are outlined below.

Upward Influence
In order to acquire vital resources – financing and talent – MCTs need leaders who have influence with superiors and peers. The MCL must

build relationship capital inside the organization. With each new assignment, the leader should be concerned about broadening her networks.
Because the leader and the team are going to need influence in various
part of the organization, these are not only communication networks but
trust and advice networks as well.

If the team has no access to power and influence, a vacuum is created
that can set it up for failure. We often encounter teams that are extremely
loyal to the leader and who sympathetically share in his frustration when
he is having trouble upstairs. 'If only the bosses understood what we're
about' ... or 'What we need is someone from upstairs to try and do
this ...' A succession of moans and complaints about lack of progress can
mark the team with the kiss of death – particularly with important stakeholders. The problem usually lies in a leader who doesn't understand how to
get power or how to use it. The team leader must have (and be perceived to
have) influence in a direct line into the top-management team. Though this
seems an obvious statement, many team leaders start off at war with the rest
of the TMT – a bad start to any change process. A team leader must be seen
to have the political clout to successfully open a dialogue with the majority
of the TMT.

Mission
MCLs differ from teams because the focus of the MCT's mission and the
impact of the team's output are directly connected to the overriding mission
and results of the business. That doesn't mean that an MCT has a mission
that exactly echoes that of the overall organization. In complex businesses
many teams are globally distributed. To expect them to have the same
mission would be madness. Working that closely in tandem would
introduce a level of rigidity that would stop effective action from ever
occurring in the company.

To what lengths should a leader go to get commitment to a mission?
Without commitment, the MCT will undoubtedly underachieve. So the
question that arises is when does the MCL draw the line and accept lower
than expected performance? Some would say that the owner and founder of
the famous restaurant chain, Hard Rock Café, might have gone beyond the
call of duty. The business had been under considerable competitive pressure,
results were down and employees were drifting. CEO Isaac Tigrett,
consulted a noted Indian guru. He took a retreat at his headquarters in
India.

Having spent several weeks in meditation, Tigrett was finally granted
an audience with the Master. They looked at each for a few minutes and
then the Master spoke – 'Love All, Serve All' he told him. Enlightenment!
Tigrett rushed back to the business. He quickly spread the new message

amongst his team. They too must have been enlightened, because the end of this story is a happy one. With its new mission the company started doing well and turned its results around. The owner was able to sell the business to a large multinational.

The mission of the MCT has to be well focused in order to succeed. Some general guidelines for most MCTs are:

- Is the mission focused on a customer issue? Most restructuring in a traditional business is driven by getting the business to be more responsive to market. That has meant rooting out complexity and simplifying systems so that the company can become customer obsessive.

- Is there a high risk tolerance among members? This is the team that will have to rethink the business model for the future. You don't want a mob of bureaucrats working on this, they'll tell you why it can't be done.

- Is the team characterized by flexibility? Markets are changing so fast that an MCT that is locked into a rigid process will not survive, nor will the company.

- Is there enthusiasm and zest in the team? Are team members excited about the work they are doing? Do they believe that they are going to make a difference?

Measures and Rewards

MCTs operate at the cutting edge of the firm and therefore must have measures and rewards tied directly to bottom-line performance. Measures of performance that are ambiguous or non-quantifiable will substantially lower achievement levels, a subject we will discuss further in Chapter 8. As someone once said 'If you can't quantify it, you probably haven't understood the problem.' Using a scorecard method, together with some hard measures like EVA (economic value added), brings focus to actions.

The Internet is restructuring businesses fast, chiefly by putting customers at the forefront of the business model. Because of its speed capability, the Internet has become a meritocracy. It rewards and punishes immediately. Rewards have to be based on performance. Stock options are always attractive because they are inexpensive and lock a successful MCT into the future performance of the firm.

Companies often find establishing cash rewards very difficult because they destabilize the rest of the organization. Establishing individual rather than team rewards can also cause problems because they cause division within the team itself. Many companies now reward MCTs with non-financial rewards, such as personal time and sabbaticals. However, when MCTs are formed with outsiders, non-financial rewards are not viable. In cases where the business model encompasses a supply chain of large-scale outsourcing, the MCT relies on the supplier to achieve its mission as well as to support the mission of the overall organization. For example, in outsourcing Internet websites, major organizations often find that their marketing strategy is directed by an MCT that consists primarily of outsiders, with a few company insiders scattered throughout. Companies will then reward outside members of the MCT in cash while rewarding insiders in kind. This disparity can create problems of demotivation on the part of insiders. To avoid this, MCLs are going to have to face implementing financial rewards across the board.

From Team Leader to Mission Critical Leadership

The shift from team leader to MCL is an important one. Successful team leaders often have very focused internal skills for building and leading teams. The MCL needs to have these, but, more importantly, she needs to have focused external skills as well. By the time she takes over the team, she needs to have developed the upward influence necessary to remove barriers to success. In addition, she needs to have learned how to align herself and her team with her immediate external environment as well as with other areas of the business. The MCL also differs from a team leader in that she must know when and how to divide and subdivide the team into subteams. When this occurs, she becomes a leader of team leaders. The structure and approach become decidedly more sophisticated. An MCL needs to enter the field with a clear understanding of how teams work, since she will need to take a long view on all of her teams, factoring in the probability that, inevitably, some teams will fail. She can reduce the failure rate of teams considerably, however, by selecting her membership carefully. The criteria for selecting an able MCT are:

- Select people who have the potential for being outstanding team leaders, then let them loose on the job.

- Acknowledge the limitations of the top-management team. Though it is made up of team leaders, they don't expect it to be a real team, and you shouldn't either.

- Spread the risk of team failure across several teams and be prepared to discard dysfunctional and destructive teams; as with ideas, it's not only finding the new one, but knowing when the old one has passed its time and should be scrapped.

- Reinforce a team-orientated culture; getting the culture right for teamwork is almost as important as determining mission critical teams because hostile cultures destroy teams and their output.

- Recognize individuals who are potential winners – they understand how teams operate and they facilitate successful team development by removing impediments.

- Protect mavericks; a smart MCL needs to pay close attention to what the rebellious new thinkers in her industry are doing in the way of new products, new marketing and new services. She has to make a place on her teams for these unusual, sometimes difficult, people who can find the right way through rapidly changing global markets.

Selecting Potentially Outstanding Team Leaders

When the MCL gets the team selection process right she achieves two things. First, she ensures continuity within the assignment by building a foundation of excellent people. Second, she ensures that the assignment as a whole is successful. The speed with which business is now moving means that, more often than not, potential team leaders are being drawn from outside the organization. Studies show that 93 per cent of companies now seek their leadership from the outside because the company lacks in-house talent, time and an in-house development process.[5] When looking for an effective team leader try to identify these special skills:

- **Emotional intelligence** – The attributes of self-awareness, regulation, motivation, empathy and social skills that Daniel Goleman calls the sine qua non of leadership.[6]

- **Ability to deliver** – A track record of team rather than individual delivery.

- **Learning capability** – Demonstrating insight into learning points having failed previously.

- **Experience of teams** – Having led a team that had real behaviours and results.

- **Understanding** – Of how to manage collective knowledge and expertise.

When Corning Inc. identified a need to become more market driven they chose Suzanne Welch to do the job. An outsider, she left her job as General Manager of Kodak's Internet marketing and quickly set about forming a team that would get a difficult job done. The team's assignment was to develop a centre of excellence for marketing within Corning. This centre would be the touchstone for all of the company's marketing intelligence and knowledge. The team would increase the overall marketing competence within the company and drive the culture to being more market orientated.

Senior managers realized that they needed a strong team leader to get things changed within the group. Welch didn't rely on doing this all herself, however. She needed her own team leaders to help her achieve the mission. She decided that the centre for excellence required its own separate leader and champion. She chose a second team leader to develop a marketing strategy.

Recognizing Potential Winners

Over the centuries kings and princes would hire knights and their entourages as protection. For a fee, these knights would go out to do battle for the king. This has its counterpart in modern corporate life where team leaders now bring their own teams to resolve important issues. Sometimes these are merely consultants, other times they join the organization with a view to a longer relationship and greater rewards. The case of the mercenary knights was never more clearly demonstrated than Volkswagen's hiring of Ignacio López.

Before joining Volkswagen, López had developed a high-performance team that delivered in the critical area of purchasing. López had been a charismatic leader developing an almost cultlike following among subordinates. Working his way through General Motor's Germany subsidiary Opel to the senior ranks of GM in Detroit, López and his team had delivered demonstrable bottom-line results. They were the scourge of industry suppliers as a result. Then López moved to Volkswagen, taking his team with him. That is when GM decided to bring in the heavy machinery. GM effectively paralysed López in a long legal battle, thus effectively paralysing as well Piech's strategy to gain competitive advantage in purchasing. By May 2000, Volkswagen CEO Ferdinand Piech had to accept that he had lost the battle to retain Ignacio Lopez and his team as part of his global strategy. In a civil case in the German High Court, López – or Super López as he was known in the auto industry – had been found guilty on six counts for having stolen secret documents from GM and bringing them to Volkswagen. In a conciliatory package to General Motors, one of its main rivals, Volkswagen agreed to suspend several other members of the Super López team. Thus ended one of the most bizarre chapters in business history. This was an MCT that wielded real power, and its demise hurt business. Was Piech damaged in this battle? Yes. Was it fatal? No. As with most MCLs Piech had spread his risk. The failure of the Super López strategy was not the end of his strategy.

One of the biggest problems that traditional organizations have today is attracting and keeping talented people. Piech tried to solve this by contracting a knight and his team. Today, really smart people ask why they should work for large organizations when they can work in smaller operations where they not only get their ideas implemented speedily, but share involvement in the project from beginning to end. The MCL recognizes talented people in the organization and draws them on to MCTs where they can make a difference. Then she identifies whether their talent has been well applied within the team. Finally, she ensures that the processes are in place to best derive maximum potential from them.

Teams do not always create a happy picture. Commitment levels are broadly spread among most organization members. Some employees are entranced by the concept of teamwork and have enthusiastically bought into the vision of their respective team leaders. Others are just bothered or bewildered by the whole team thing. Members of the 'bothered' contingent sense that they are being manipulated or betrayed. Those who are bewildered can't make sense of what's happening and what they do understand, they reject.[7] Both can spell trouble for mission critical leadership; understanding both constructive and destructive processes is important.

Spread the Risk

Large organizations have learnt an important lesson as they make their transition into the new economy. They recognize that they will probably have to acquire or form alliances with several partners before hitting on the right business model. So, too, with teams. The MCL may have several MCTs working on the same or similar themes in order to improve chances of success. One of the strongest learning points to come out of Intel is that buying options in different technologies has given the company the inside edge. As venture capitalist Arthur Rock says, 'In the process Intel has become one of the biggest venture-capital companies on the West Coast.'

Since not all teams are equal to start with, the MCL must spread her options over several. Some teams are bound to fail, others will perform below expectations. Some will start off well, then lose creativity and drive. Some will never become real teams at all, they will merely go through the motions. There are rules for developing and sustaining teams. They are not rules in a mathematical sense, but, rather, in an artistic sense. They stem from an interpretation of complex behaviours. Thus, learning to lead such teams requires practising the process, learning from experience and improving performance. There is probably no short cut to acquiring the secrets of this art.

Reinforcing the Team Culture

MCTs must find a cultural context in which to operate successfully. Because the concept of team is often quite vague and ambiguous, a team approach may seem easily applicable, yet fail.

All organizations have a culture. Some may be conducive to teamwork, and others will be closed to it. Cultures are value laden; they are imbued with attitudes, beliefs and sentiments. Companies often overlook this when deciding to farm work out to consultants and contractors. A look at the prevailing 'team' metaphor reveals much about whether teams could successfully operate within the culture:

- If a business is a start-up or is still quite small, the organization itself is seen as a team. Teamwork is widely accepted and applied, though this may taper off as the organization grows. The problem for many dotcoms is that they fail to maintain a sense of team after the start-up of the company. As the firm grows, its very size dilutes the team ethos. Much is lost in the process.

- If a business is larger, teams may exist in 'off-line' functions, usually operating within informal structures to solve problems. To all intents and purposes the organization continues, while these teams spin off to tackle specific issues. They often create tensions, particularly when trying to implement their solutions. This distancing of the team from the reality of the organization has its own organization. Working in the automobile industry in South Africa, Ken Dovey found that the application of teams was largely superficial and had no serious impact on the long-term future of a company, unless management was willing to engage workers in a broader context; for instance, in their settings outside of the workplace.

• Teams may exist in a formal structure as a basic unit. Extreme examples of these exist in companies such as Opticon where the entire value chain revolves around teams.

Protect the Mavericks

Though Nick Earle didn't quite match the stereotype of the maverick who would overturn a whole business, his 18 years with Hewlett Packard had prepared him to take on the role of team leader of one of HP's most revolutionary concepts. The team was a new e.solutions.services group. It would cluster small firms that made the hardware and software that supported HP's solutions to approaching ecommerce. HP's culture had always supported maverick behaviour and strong team values. This had allowed CEO Carly Fiorina to earmark him for the job. His target was clear – to add a new business to the ecosystem every week. With sufficient resources (a budget of $150 million was a good start), and the protection of Fiorina, he hoped to build an organization of 120 people, 25 per cent of them from outside HP. He and Fiorina expected that, in the process, HP would undergo a sea change.

The Problem of Globally Distributed Teams

Henkel's Alois Linder found himself with a team that stretched from Spain all the way over to China. Getting this team together for an eyeballing meeting was a major undertaking. Even getting his team together occasionally was difficult, inefficient and costly in financial terms. What he needed was for each of his managers to be an effective team leader, who could deal directly with her people *in situ*. The regular meetings that Linder had with his team were by conference calls, videoconferencing and chat mails. Linder himself needed to make a major shift: to move from being a team leader to being a leader of team leaders. This was probably the largest and the most personal change he had made in business. Some of the skills he required to do this might be innate, but he learned others from scratch.

Imagine it's your first day at work. The company has an orientation programme to establish a minimum level of knowledge and skills. The first day is spent teaching you how to read and write. No, not financial statements, nothing as complicated as that. They are teaching you to read simple things like names and addresses with joined-up letters! The second day you learn how to use a telephone, 'using the index finger, point at a number, then press firmly'. On the third day, you learn how to tell the time, aided by the free issue of digital watches, because all that big-hand-on-the-twelve-and-small-hand-on the-two stuff is a bit confusing.

Hard to imagine, isn't it? That's because we take it for granted that most people come to work with basic skills and knowledge already established. To all intents, these technologies have become invisible; we hardly notice them unless they're missing. They are what we used to call satisfiers. They don't motivate us any longer, though they have the capacity to demotivate us if they are missing. Consider how many technologies are fast becoming invisible in the present. Computers (some time ago), mobile phones (going fast), email (hi, has anyone had a handwritten letter recently?), voicemail, spreadsheets, power point presentations ... soon someone will offer seminars on how to give a presentation *without* PowerPoint.

Videoconferencing is going the same way. Working on this book, I had occasion to speak to senior managers of 3i via videoconference. 3i is Europe's largest venture-capital company, and the UK's third largest company by market capitalization. I was struck by how polished they were at the whole process of running a videoconference meeting. Admittedly, the technology is outstanding compared to a few years ago, and it is improving all the time. Nevertheless, the whole concept of videoconference is going the way of the telephone – fast. A spin-off has been the proliferations of globally distributed teams (GDTs) all over the place. GDTs are teams that have certain peculiarities:

- **Limited contact** – They seldom meet face to face because of the high costs involved. Yet, in most discussions on high-performance teams, the sports metaphor predominates. Whether basketball team or football team, the analogy of the playing field (whether level or not) becomes the model and the basis of team discussion. Now this metaphor is as inappropriate as it is stale. Can you imagine your players taking a field that exists in twenty different countries, playing for 24 hours each day and never being able to make physical contact when they disappear into the locker room? A richer metaphor is to be found in hospitals or ships because they have teams with different members on duty 24 hours a day. How these teams maintain cohesion and standards would provide better insight into GDT behaviour.

- **Superfluous membership** – GDTs often include members for the sake of 'keeping someone in the loop'. These people become passengers not because they are relevant to the team, but because someone thought it was a 'good idea' to include them in the conversation. As Debra Freitag of Sun Microsystems says, 'You eventually belong to so many groups the problem becomes how to structure them meaningfully in your life.'

- **Inability to assume responsibility** – Because most technologies are fast becoming invisible, GDTs have become reliant on them and suffer from indecision when they break down. Think about how lost you are when you lose your watch or your mobile phone, and spend a day in limbo. GDTs stumble when the technology breaks down. One way to look at this is to pass it off as a short-term issue – the technology will soon be up again. Another way is to realize that GDTs often have an accountability vacuum. Technology is not good at teaching self-reliance, independent thought or action. Like sailors who become 100 per cent dependent on GPS (Global Positioning System) technology for navigation, they forget that it can't nurture skills on how to get home when the technology collapses.

- **Lack of Trust** – In a virtual-reality simulation within air-conditioning giant Carrier Corporation, academics ran a scenario of globally distributed teams working together in the US, the UK and Spain. Teams were connected daily by videoconference, telephone, email and so on. Several teams had to produce different sections of an important market survey that was to be submitted to senior management. Most of these failed miserably. Although members of the GDTs (all students at various top business schools) were interconnected on a daily basis, they had established only one level of relationship capital, communication. There was no trust in the team and no one had thought to establish a process for delivering trust. Trust is a requirement of GDTs which is most conspicuous by its absence. In close-contact team seminars, there are exercises that actually build up trust. For instance, 'the trustful walk' challenges you to allow yourself to be led blindfold through a country field. There is no equivalent training available to GDTs. They will have to leave trust to be built up over time relying only on occasional meetings and consistent behaviour patterns established during the initial stages of the GDT's life. In the Carrier simulation, the GDTs suffered from mission drift and failed to deliver. Ultimately, the entire assignment was completed by a subgroup situated at one location.

- **Power** – What we learned in the Carrier simulation was that teamwork could only succeed if power was entrusted locally, if responsibility was accepted at a local level, and if, at the end of the day, the local team had a mission with which it could identify, and which had been developed by the team itself. This whole experience indicates that the task of the MCL is doubly difficult. She needs to build up trust within the GDT to give direction and guidance, while at the same time devolving power into the region to get on with the job. If managers were forced to choose between the MCL's situation and the situation of Rich Raimundi with his twenty hours of face-to-face meetings, most folks would opt for Raimundi's job.

Conclusion

In this chapter we have discussed why TMTs are seldom a good example of how teams should work. The MCL must move direct reports from groups into MCTs. Without such teams the MCL is unlikely to succeed. Thus, the processes of MCT building must become second nature to each MCL. Two perspectives are important. In one the MCL must meet all the primary requirements of facilitating MCT formation; in the other she must actually understand the processes that drive team formation. Those processes are the subject of the next chapter.

Teams, Task Forces and Tantrums: Getting Mission Critical Teams Working*

'There are no sacred cows'. John Parson remembered the line well. His boss had delivered it when giving him the mandate for his present job. The brief had been vague, 'as open as you need it to be'. His boss had said, 'See what you can make of the new Technoltrip technology – tell me what we should be doing with it.'

During that first briefing Parson's boss had given him his full support and had assigned three people to his Internal Board of Directors: Bernard Hill, Head of Special Projects; Jack Cashmore, Head of Marketing; and Douglas Weekes, a senior manager from production. They, together with 'as many people as necessary', would comprise Parson's 'committee'. Parsons had misgivings about the Internal Board from the outset. At the first meeting they all came racing in. Weekes had a face like a weasel and a matching character. Hill was known to be a brilliant scientist but had an ego so large that Parsons wondered how he got it all in under the same umbrella on a rainy day. Cashmore was a tall elegant man with greying sideburns. A good marketer, he was known behind his back as 'Lord Flashheart', a snipe at his general smoothness around the office amongst other things. Parsons had seen this group in action and could almost predict what people were going to say.

Nevertheless, the initial meetings passed uneventfully and the weeks went by. The committee co-opted several individuals into the group full time. At first, the co-opted members had behaved like carbon copies of their bosses; Parsons began to suspect that they had been briefed to toe their respective departmental lines. But as he continued working intensively with them individually and as a team, he noticed that they slowly started to get personally involved in the project.

* I would like to thank Professor Pablo Cardona for his contribution to this chapter. On a long train ride between Barcelona and Madrid, we created the model now known as the Carmill model (Cardona and Miller 2000). Apart from the Carmill model, his insights to the presentation of the ideas in this chapter have been very important and are greatly appreciated.

Parsons felt that the close involvement, and the fact that they were full time was making a difference. He constantly emphasized to them the importance of the project to the business and the interest the CEO (chief executive officer) had in its success.

The new technology raised a plethora of issues because it overlapped with activities in virtually every part of the company. In terms of existing products, the technology would upset marketing, production, distribution, customers and suppliers. Parsons knew that any proposal his team made would step on somebody's toes. So after several weeks of research and preparation, the project team went for broke. They proposed the following strategy:

1. launch a Technoltrip product that combined the new technology with existing technology, some of it purchased from competitors;
2. manufacture and assemble it in a special plant set aside specifically for this product.

To ensure success, spin off the entire operation to create a new business that would take on its own distribution and marketing.

The proposal immediately ran into trouble with the Internal Board of Directors. 'I believe that there's very little new in here that we haven't discussed before – in fact, years ago,' was Hill's comment. 'My dear boy,' Cashmore said to Parsons irritatingly, 'we have some very special customers in that end of the market and the margins are good. I would be very reluctant to go messing around with them – we could lose out in the long run.' At least the weasel Weekes hadn't been that predictable – or had he? 'I'm not sure that I agree with either of them ... but we can't give the go-ahead for a new production unit without their approval for this.' (Weekes had confided to Parsons that he was actually on his side and would support him. This wasn't evident at the meeting. So Weekes had covered all the bases.)

What chance do you think this project has of seeing the light of day? Has the CEO set it up for failure? Does this situation seem familiar? Do you have colleagues who play Jekyll and Hyde in and out of meetings?

The history of successful firms that fail is riddled with tales like this.[1] Intuitively, we all know why mission critical teams (MCTs) fail on assignments like this – they get snarled up with bureaucracy. Large companies have difficulty kindling innovation, even when they have mandated change. They often put impediments in the way of the very leaders who are attempting to accelerate it. Instead of allowing them to use their full talent to lead, the organization throws bureaucratic rules and archaic structure into their paths. On occasion, large, tired old-economy companies are offered the rejuvenating chance to lead out with a disruptive technology such as Technoltrip. This allows the company to leap from one technologically innovative period to another. Companies can squander these opportunities if they do not appreciate how to develop and exploit teams. The design, composition and process of a team profoundly influences the outcome. Enlightened management of these factors is key to the project's success. Notwithstanding, many companies spend valuable time managing the mis-management of team processes.

Technology-driven companies are not the only businesses to fail the litmus test of accelerated change. Companies in construction (such as the ill-fated German monolith Philipp Holzmann), airline services (such as the ever loss-making Olympic Airlines), and automobile manufacture (such as Fiat and Rover) have all struggled unsuccessfully to stay in step with the competitive forces in their sectors.

Parson's boss is on the right track. He knows that the company needs to develop its new technology. He mandates a research team, then gives Parsons the go-ahead to develop it. Parson's team eventually comes up with a typical solution for disruptive technologies – spin off this new business and let it go on its own. The problem is that the CEO has set up a reporting structure that has 'no' written all over it. From the outset, Parsons' proposal is bound to fail.

Design of the Support Structure

Companies like General Electric (GE) and Boeing have learnt that the starting point for creating the agility required to respond to the new economy is to get the report structure right. Parson's boss has set up a committee that comes between himself and the proposal. We know what this committee will do – it will block or adapt the proposal to such an extent that it will be 'committed' out of existence. We've all been on committees like this. Like actors playing themselves as characters, individuals take on behaviours in such a coded predictable way that the chance for spontaneity is remote. There is more chance of Boris Yeltsin making a comeback than this type of committee coming up with something new.

External reporting has to break free of embedded roles and structure in order to give a good proposal a fair chance. There should be very few people external to the team who are involved in the final decision. MCTs need a reporting structure which contains certain key members:

1   *The champion* Usually a member of the top-management team (TMT). The champion must have responsibilities in the area of the

proposed changes. In Parsons' case, since the proposal is to have impact on every aspect of the business, the CEO is the best champion for this MCT. The champion has to make sure that barriers are removed and resources made available. He should certainly be involved with Parsons and the MCT during the development stage.

2   *The sponsor*   The frontrunner for the assignment. He is not a member of the MCT but is able to respond to recommendations, supply some resources, and follow up on MCT initiatives and problems. In essence the project must have a home during its inception, and the sponsor provides that. As champion, the CEO needs to solicit someone who can take Parsons and the MCT under their auspices. The sponsor will anticipate problems and smooth egos that get ruffled in the process of the assignment.

3   *The facilitator*   Usually an experienced facilitation professional, possibly an outsider, who gets involved in the planning and design of meetings and presentations. This person is good at moderating meetings with various stakeholders, and at briefing the champion, sponsor and decision panel.

4   *The final-decision maker*   In this case the CEO and an appropriate panel. Ultimately, we can probably ascribe this failure to Parsons' inexperience and the committee's interference. The outcome might have been very different, however, had the team been provided with this reporting structure.

Companies like Intel and Royal Dutch/Shell have broken from their traditional structure to form flexible informal structures. These structures ensure that projects of the Parsons' type get a fair hearing. Moreover, these companies provide quick decisions and plenty of resources to make the projects happen. At Shell, the *GameChanger* process is an innovation laboratory where teams work on venture plans. These they submit to a panel made up of senior managers and members of Shell's Technology Unit for final approval.[2]

Getting a fair hearing for your project is important; getting a fast decision is equally so. Parsons' project will wend its way through a committee process that resembles a federal bureaucracy. Eventually, instead of an innovative venture supported by a team of enthusiastic entrepreneurs, Parsons will end up with an exhausted compromise that will in no way resemble the original. Whatever support he had marshalled in the early stages will disappear quickly.

Unilever, Boeing and GE are trying to get one thing right about decision making: keep it simple, rational and straight. A proposal has to be presented to a decision maker, that's rule number one. And rule number two is that the decision has to be taken right there. If the proposal looks viable, if the figures add up, if the resources are available, if the team has the capability to implement – let them run! The rationale behind this is so simple, so lacking in political intrigue, so obvious, that it is hard to believe that large organizations would choose any other way.

How could Parsons have shown mission critical leadership in this case? He could have diplomatically rejected the CEO's proposal for a committee approach and counter-proposed an MCT structure. He could have clarified the terms for the assignment before setting out. For example, if the proposal was approved who was going to head up the project? If Parsons was to be the nominee, did he want the job? If so he needed to make that clear from the outset. This would clarify leadership issues with heads of other departments. He could have ascertained that his team would have the appropriate champion and sponsor, and that it would have direct access to the final decision maker.

Best practice with MCTs has the following features:

- a **process** in which those closest to and impacted by an important change in the business model are brought together;

- a **solution** and a short-term action plan for the issue or opportunity is explored, created and presented by the MCT to a decision panel for active support within 90 days of the opening of the *Window of Effectiveness*;

- **responsibility** for implementation is retained by the MCT. Follow-up will be supported and monitored by the champion and sponsor.

Of course, the reporting structure can go wrong in many different ways, as Table 6.1 suggests.

The Design of Mission Critical Teams

Figure 6.1 outlines some of the issues of which Parsons should have been aware. The external roles of champion and sponsor are requisite. However, there are several other forces that can influence the success of the project if managed with care. External and internal influences to carefully watch might be a rapidly shifting market place; existing customers and their loyalty; marketing department and its lock-in to existing products; and the Hills Special Projects Unit and its resistance to anything not invented

The champion	Brief too vague, unclear issue selection
	Lack of communication and agreement
	Shifting priorities
	Implementation responsibilities not clarified.
The sponsor	No commitment
	Not coached to understand role
	Too many issues to implement
	Lacks follow-up on problems generated
	Politics too fierce to handle.
The facilitator	Lack of clear boundaries to areas open to change and areas that are closed
	Insider with too much baggage
	Wrong people in the room.
Decision panel	Can't take decision – wrong people on panel
	No support or clarity on implementation
	Action items assigned to non-MCT persons.

Table 6.1   Where report structures go wrong.

here. Parsons will have little direct control over these, but he needs to bring influence to bear in these areas – either through his own or that of the sponsor.

Team Composition

Winning teams are made up of winning people. The art of creating such teams is not self-evident, however. The recipe for a winning team must take into account not only the role of each potential member, but her particular mix of skills and flexibility. Beyond that, it must factor in how each member contributes to group dynamics, and, ultimately, what those dynamics will be. This is a complex issue for any leader to tackle. Even a single component – diversity within the group, for instance – can be complex. Experts suggest that *too little* diversity leads to inbreeding whereas *too much* produces lack of common understanding and shared interests.

Figure 6.1   Linking design/process and results.

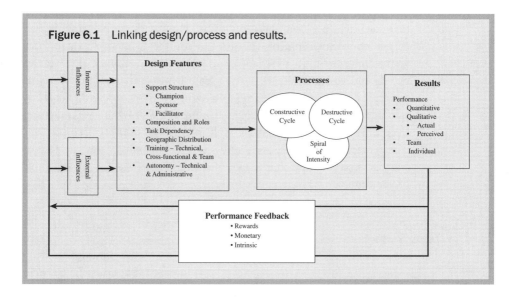

Ultimately, however, team composition must be determined by the nature of the assignment. The following gives a cross-section of teams:

- **Teams that solve a specific problem** – Usually this requires a multi-skilled membership with specific problem-solving experience. For example, teams that introduce change interventions in quality, safety or cost-cutting fall into this category. Such teams are usually semi-autonomous and function in a very directed way. The leadership role is directive, and focused on achieving limited objectives. In cross-functional, new-product-development teams, the degree of involvement for marketing, engineering and manufacturing members may vary through different phases of the project. At Honeywell, for example, a team exists *ipso facto* from beginning to end of a project. Marketing people assume predominant responsibility and workload in the initial phase of concept development and product requirement. Engineering people are more devoted during the design phase. Manufacturing people take charge in the manufacturing phase.[3] These efficiently run teams can have a positive impact on the bottom line.

- **Teams that have a broad brief** – While all assignments are by nature problem solving, some assignments are less specific than others. Parsons' team has a broad brief with no defined constraints to address an issue. These teams run better when self-managed, and can be very successful, provided they build sufficient momentum. Parsons correctly spent the initial phase in close contact with his team to nurture vision and motivation. He was then able to withdraw to get on with preparing the ground for the team's proposal. Such teams have their greatest impact on established culture (i.e. values, beliefs and vested interest). Their greatest problem arises in the implementation process. If the team has a highly abstract brief and is mainly self-led, it will form and dissolve around different members and issues over time. Such teams operate well in research and creative settings. Their major impact is on innovation. Leadership in these circumstances is so low-key that it may not even be physically present most of the time.

Team Roles

The mission critical leader (MCL) must have a solid grounding in team composition and the dynamics of team development. She must be particularly clear in the area of role development. There is sufficient research to support the idea that high-performance teams require intensive development of essential roles. For example, Meredith Belbin found that high-performance teams did not achieve noteworthy results without the inclusion of a 'plant' – a bright loner who constantly questions the status quo and comes up with ideas that are out of the box. Though teams without 'plants' are often more harmonious, they are less creative and less willing to raise the level of the debate. They are most often searching for uniformity where creativity is required.[4]

Regardless of the nature of the team, certain roles are essential to the survival and achievement of the team. These include:

- team coordinator;
- analyst;
- team builder;
- implementer;
- broker;
- plant.

Team coordinator – If this is not the MCL, it should be someone who is a mover and shaker. This person acts as a catalyst. She gives direction, inspiration and strong support for the mission of the team. On many occasions the coordinator is required to be no more than an effective administrator of the team, organizing schedules, structuring tasks and maintaining order. This person could be an emergent leader.

The analyst – This is someone who systematically evaluates and develops a case for the strategy chosen. This person is by nature analytical, and will ask quantitative rather than qualitative questions. He may also play the role of reviewer, auditing and evaluating outcomes. He asks questions of the strategy such as: 'Is this logical?' and 'What do the numbers tell us?'

The team builder – This is a person who is good at building coalitions and nurturing allies. She tends to be a highly political individual who builds support for the change process. She is process-orientated by nature and is constantly aware of the team's development and progress. She will often be heard to ask: 'Do we have everyone's ideas?' and 'What about you Bill? – you've been quiet for a while.'

The implementer – This is an action-driven person who delivers the targeted results. He is the member who actually ensures the implementation of the vision. An important contributor to the team, he usually does a lot of tidying up around the periphery. He will be heard to say: 'I'll follow up on the details of that' and 'Are we going to make the deadline, or is there something that we've missed?'

The broker – This is the power broker who facilitates the change process while making sure that alignment is taking place. He has a big investment in relationship capital, and uses it to the best advantage of the team, especially in tight spots. He will say things like: 'I know someone who can help us with that problem' and 'Don't worry about production, I'll take care of those guys.'

The plant – This is the loner, the outsider, the bright person who questions most things and brings a different perspective to what the team does. She could become the maverick of the team and company. She can often make outstanding contributions, provided the leader nurtures her. She gets bored very easily. She can be expected to say the unexpected.

Training

Working in teams might come naturally, but it is greatly improved by training. Sometimes the simplest techniques help MCTs to get focused and gain momentum. For example, Bev Davis of the Greenwich Group in Toronto suggests using the toolkit in Table 6.2 for commonly encountered problems found in MCTs.

There are also gains to be made by moving away from 'talk 'n chalk' training formats. Most company employees have been on so many change training courses by now that they could almost run them better than the trainers. For them, the issue is not learning the concepts of the training course, but getting the learning points implemented. Many companies are

Tools	Application
In/out frame	Scoping a project
Fifteen words	Developing common project definitions
Threat/opportunity analysis	Determining driving rationale
3D's (data, demonstrate, demand)	Proving the need for change
More of/less of	Describing future behaviours
Elevator speech	Communicating vision
Stakeholder analysis	Identifying resistance
Communication charting	Developing communication plans
Calendar test	Determining the support of leaders

Table 6.2 Toolkit for MCTs.[5]

changing to an action-learning training methodology. Companies such as Motorola, Unilever, BHP in Australia and Boeing have applied action learning with great success.

Action learning tackles learning by doing first. It moves the burden of learning from the trainer to the participant. The trainer enables the student so that learning can be applied to real business problems. Motorola University has Action-Learning Teams (ALTs) that focus on real problems in the company. Members of ALTs devote only 25 per cent of their time to the team. The concept of ALTs doesn't differ much from MCTs. They are comprised of:

- a champion – who is a member of the Board;

- members capable of influencing decision, resources and implementation;

- a broad mix of expertise, experience and responsibilities;

- ability to draw from both line and staff functions;

- up to twenty-five members;

- candidate nomination by business units.

Through providing process support and resources Motorola University assists participants to become better leaders and team members.

The pressure to get employees up to speed through intensive learning such as this cuts across all organizations. Unilever's Executive Committee's 'Foresight' project was set in motion in 1998 to challenge twenty high potential, unconventional middle managers to identify 'megatrends' that would influence their business in the next 20 years. An intense action-learning, total-immersion process was used to create a paradigm shift for participants. As a result of its success, the 'Foresight' experience continues to spawn several offshoots.

Teams are not just about getting the right leader and roles into place. There are three specific steps that make teams work (Figure 6.1). Design is only one of the elements. The remaining two are the team-development process and the monitoring of results.

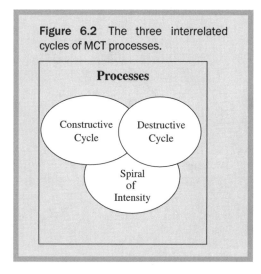

Figure 6.2 The three interrelated cycles of MCT processes.

Team-Development Process

From an action-learning experience, MCTs must learn the three interrelated cycles of MCT processes (Figure 6.2).

The Constructive Cycle

The constructive cycle is one through which all groups pass on their way to becoming teams. As the intimacy increases and the newly formed team passes through the constructive cycle, on a number of occasions the spiral of intensity notches up. Soon the team is capable of high levels of performance (i.e. it is becoming an MCT). When things go wrong in terms of internal dynamics the team is in danger of passing to a destructive cycle. Once the team passes through the destructive cycle, it is unlikely to make a comeback.

The development process for a winning team is mapped out in terms of forming, storming, norming and performing (FSNP).[6] This is a classic four-stage-development process model. In the *forming* stage, individuals get to know each other and try to establish membership criteria within the team. They overcome insecurity and anxiety until they feel accepted by other team members, and reach a basic level of mutual expectations. In the *storming*

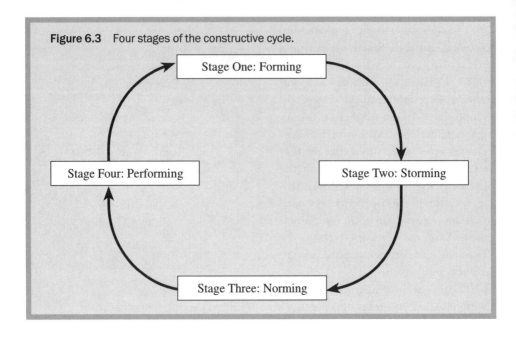

Figure 6.3   Four stages of the constructive cycle.

stage, individuals with different perspectives start responding to the group's challenges. There may be bids for power and influence, and emotional arguments. Until these are resolved, the group struggles to proceed. In the *norming* stage, members decide rules and procedures for accomplishing tasks. Also, tacit norms of acceptable behaviour develop that help the team work as a coordinated unit. Finally, in the *performing* stage people work together in a collaborative way. People cooperate with each other in order to accomplish the team's objective.

The four stages of the constructive cycle (Figure 6.3) form a cycle that is repeated. The experience of successful accomplishment that results from the performing stage further unifies the team, its identity as a team is reinforced. Each time the team re-enters the forming stage, individuals acknowledge and value other members' efforts and capabilities. Knowledge of the other team members increases, as does the level of mutual respect and trust. The team is now ready to take on more challenging tasks. Now they face a new storming stage that will lead to an improved norming stage, and so on. The team develops and matures through this cycle, until the tasks require a different type of team, or the members change abruptly enough to vary the identity of the team.

The iterative development process is itself a spiralling process. The team constantly passes the same point but in more depth. The first cycle of this spiral can be seen as a kick-off cycle, the second cycle around as an operational cycle, the third as a review cycle. A team can pass through a

Stage	Forming	Storming	Norming	Performing
PROCESS	Trust development	Communication	Organization	Collaboration
OUTPUT	Cohesiveness	Decision	Action plan	Results

Table 6.3   Stages, processes and outputs of the constructive cycle.

Figure 6.4   Spiral of intensity – kick-off operational and review cycles.

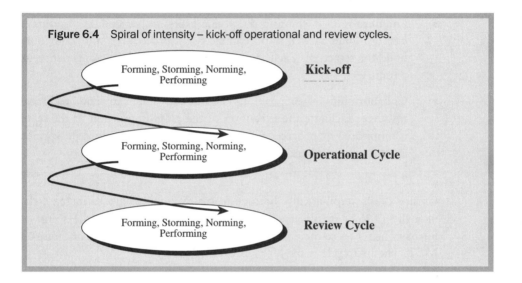

single cycle many times before moving on. For example, when a team meets only occasionally, and has several new members at each meeting, it passes through the kick-off cycle repeatedly.

The processes of the constructive cycle and the spiral of intensity have to be seen working in conjunction. Winning teams have to master these processes. At each stage, the constructive cycle has a process and output. The first stage – forming – is a process of trust development. The output is team cohesiveness. The second stage – storming – moves through communication to action decision. The third – norming – moves through organization to action plans. The fourth – performing – to collaboration of eventual output (Table 6.3 and Figure 6.4). The action-learning programmes mentioned earlier can be powerful tools in focusing teams on learning from experience. The team's objective evolves into creating knowledge and transferring it first among team members, then throughout the organisation. This is a challenge that action learning meets by looping learning back into the organization. Though initially focused on the individual, and then on the team, the process eventually permeates the whole organization. The process can be broken down in more detail:

- **Trust development** – Mutual respect, acceptance of interdependence and emotional stability within the team create cohesion.

- **Communication** – Exchanging information, defining problems, developing alternatives, meeting challenges and articulating mission eventually lead to making informed decisions on issues.

- **Organization** – Definition of specific tasks, responsibilities, resources and deadlines as well as acceptable rules, procedures and behaviours build the structure. Tacit and explicit rewards and sanctions define its parameters.

- **Collaboration** – Acquisition of human, financial and technical resources facilitate the execution of the plan. Interaction of the team is monitored by progress reviews. Key points of measure mark specific results, recognize and celebrate accomplishments.

Groups don't automatically become teams. Members have to increase the intensity of their involvement in order to create a team. As the spiral of intensity increases so the group is transformed until eventually it becomes an MCT. The first cycle is the kick-off cycle (Figure 6.4).

The Kick-off Cycle

This cycle initiates basic team formation. The embryonic team moves through the four stages (FSNP) at a superficial level – trying to establish the basics of trust, communication, organization and collaboration. More importantly, they explore the potential for shared objectives or common purpose. The mission for this team soon becomes the early identification of shared objectives. A minimum level of physical and psychological security has to be ensured to get the team through this cycle. Team members have to feel safe – they need to feel secure in the fact that they can express their opinions, expose their feelings and ideas without being held to ridicule. They search for a fit with others in the team. They look for a fit between personal mission and the potential team mission.

During this kick-off cycle individuals learn about each other, gain mutual respect and start to commit themselves to cohesion and eventual interdependency. If members of the team are unaware of the stages and cycles, the MCL can be of limited use. She is working alone. She must have a team which understands the process and is capable of initiating moves. As we will see later, the kick-off cycle can be reapplied to teams that have become stale or destructive.

The Operational Cycle and the Destructive Cycle

Teams that achieve early success in identifying common goals and missions usually celebrate in some way. There is anticipation of further cohesion and success, the team now start going through the cycle again. Here the intention is to move through each stage (FSNP) but in much greater depth. Team members can now share problems, and general apprehensiveness, as well as move to integrate efforts to achieve the mission.

If the kick-off cycle is about intense cohesion, the operational cycle is about achieving the mission. The team is able to focus all of its efforts on producing output. Provided that the team is able to solve internal issues that occur along the way, it will succeed in achieving its goals. During this cycle, the team is highly likely to divert energy into a destructive cycle. The tasks become more complex, and many require simultaneous completion. Team members often question the mission, the contribution of others and even the usefulness of the team leader. Team leaders often risk losing the team as it struggles to resolve issues internally.

A team need not self-destruct because it performs below expectations. A winning team is basically a learning team, and thus should be able to isolate the causes of the problems it encounters. Ultimately it should be able to find solutions to improve its performance. Low performance may be due to internal or external causes. The team leader may need to propose changes in the composition of the team or in some of its roles or rules.

However, we have all observed and been members of teams that have entered a destructive cycle. Whether initiated by excessive competition, lack of direction from an MCL, or an inability of the team to resolve its problems, a destructive cycle can start at any stage of the operational cycle. At the storming stage, when the team should be creating a sense of urgency and commitment, it can derail into anxiety, lack of commitment and distrust. At the norming stage, instead of creating an action plan with specific milestones, the team can become distracted by a perceived impasse and become powerless to proceed. At the performing stage, instead of having a systematic format for performance measurement, it faces chaos and lack of performance. Internal fighting destroys cohesion in the team, and it disintegrates.

All successful groups and teams go through this series of stages and cycles, improving gradually over time. However, the MCL can be in for a surprise if she takes over an existing team. The team may have experienced crisis and negative behaviours that have weakened its capacity to perform. When Robert Horton took over BP's worldwide operations, he immediately set about putting new teams of young ambitious employees into place. These teams in essence had the brief to rethink the business – an exciting challenge for any bright newcomer. Unfortunately, Horton's actions seemed to bypass old-established groups and teams in the organization, possibly signalling that they had little future in the newly restructured business. From the outside, he seemed to misread both the intensity and destructive capacity of these teams as they set about resisting him at almost every turn. Horton lost the battle with them and was soon seeking challenges elsewhere.

Such destructive potency in teams is not unusual, though it may not be focused on the leader so much as on individual members of the team. When teams have to choose between team mission and their own individual objectives, and they opt for the latter, the team has already begun the process of self-destruction. This is a moment of truth for the MCL, because withdrawal of support and resources will only reinforce the destructive process, confirming everyone's suspicion that it's now every person for herself.

Some authors believe that organizations most often set MCTs up to fail because they do not understand team processes. They do this primarily by maintaining focus on the individual and squelching movement toward interdependence. Pfeffer[7] questions the very concept of internal competition, saying that in more cases than not it has negative consequences of demotivation, information hoarding and extreme political behaviour.

The destructive cycle can give rise to chaos and eventual collapse of the team. Defining its stages are difficult, given its complex sources. However, Table 6.4 shows probably the most distinctive aspects.

A destructive cycle can start in a number of ways. It can begin with the formation of coalitions that obstruct team consensus and commitment to team decisions. The team takes a route that leads to violation of team norms and rules. This produces disorganization and misunderstandings. Disorganization and misunderstandings result in low performance and flagging commitment to team objectives. Finally, the team members are reduced to frustration and blame, which produces distrust, and destroys team cohesiveness.

Stage	Storming	Violating	Failing	Dismantling
PROCESS	Division	Disorganization	Disinterest	Distrust
OUTPUT	Lack of decision	No action plan	No results	Break-up

Table 6.4 Stages, processes and outputs of the deconstructive cycle.

- Hire, reward and retain people, in part based on their ability and willingness to work cooperatively with others for the company's welfare.

- Fire, demote and punish people who act only in their individual short-term interest.

- Focus people's attention and energy on defeating external competitive threats, not on fighting each other.

- Avoid compensation and performance-measurement systems that create internal competition.

- Have measures that assess cooperation.

- Build a culture that defines individual success partly by the success of the person's peers.

- Model the right behaviour via leaders acting collaboratively, sharing information and helping others.

- Promote people to top-management positions who have a history of building groups where members cooperate, share information and provide each other mutual assistance.

- Use power and authority to get people and units to share information, to learn from each other and to work collaboratively to enhance overall performance.

Table 6.5   Methods for dealing with destructive competition.

When detected early, the team leader can move the team back to the storming strategy and redirect it towards a more constructive route (back-pedal strategy). When the team is in a dismantling stage, the team leader can take advantage of a new challenge (and even create a special one) in order to change the cycle (forward-pedal strategy).

If winning teams can learn how to detect when they are entering into a destructive cycle, they have a better chance of survival. The symptoms are obvious to observers, though often not to insiders. Incoherent mission, strong emphasis on individual objectives, the emergence of coalitions that reject the constructive processes, failure to commit to or complete parts of the action plan, and a sense of distrust pervading the whole unit are individual or collective signs of self-destructing teams. Pfeffer proposed the list of ways of overcoming destructive forces as shown in Table 6.5.[8]

The Review Cycle

Problem identification and resolution is the main focus of the review cycle. The team will have shared many experiences in working together and will feel a need to air some of these. The objective here is to improve performance, eliminating those processes and behaviours that do not support it. The results of the review should be formalized in some way so as to get commitment to improve performance in the future.

At the end of the operational cycle, it is important to re-examine the identity, the development and the support structure of the team. It may be necessary to reinforce some aspects of the identity, or some links with the organization and/or the external environment. The team leader needs to evaluate how the team has been supported by the organization and how the external networks have facilitated its performance. Then, if necessary, she must propose changes.

The review cycle determines the need for major shifts in focus of direction, composition and rules. Changes in the strategic environment, market shifts, competitive reactions, new economic opportunities may have caused shifts to which the team will now have to respond. If taking charge at this stage, an MCL may well want to review the output of existing teams, begin a process to force teams themselves into review in face of a new mission and vision.

When problems are structural rather than procedural, the team leader may need to propose a new purpose or direction for the team, and/or basically new composition of membership. If problems are coming from outside the team, the team leader may need to redesign the identity and/or the environmental support of the team. In any of these cases, it is advisable that the team restart with a new kick-off cycle before meeting the regular challenges derived from its mission.

Conclusion

Winning teams are the result of mastering several key processes and cycles. A team is a delicate social organism that follows certain stages in a continuous process. That process can take two different routes. It can follow a constructive route that strengthens the team, or a destructive one that destroys it. A start-up team needs a leader who knows how to design team structure that enables constructive engagement. When the MCL encounters process problems, she has to be able to identify and correct them before they pass into a destructive cycle. This becomes particularly challenging when the MCT is intensely involved in fighting the competition or themselves. Diverting that intensity into constructive processes can convert a losing team into a winning one.

Performance Measurement – Balancing the Scorecard

It will be of little value spending six months building a Balanced Scorecard that will probably be out of date on the first day of implementation. So we must get the scorecard 80 per cent right, operationalize it quickly, learn rapidly, and, over time, create more robust metrics that can be shared enterprise-wide.

– John Quail, 'BT Worldwide'[1]

Out of the Industrial Age and into the Twenty-first Century

The increasingly competitive environment of the new economy has radically changed perceptions on how company performance is gauged. For better or for worse, traditional measures – such as earnings per share and dividend policy – have been swept aside. Spurred by the demand for a change in business organization and practices, companies are waking up to the idea that such change requires a whole new system for measuring performance. New business models cannot rely solely on traditional, centuries-old accounting methods. The realization that business models encompass both tangible and intangible assets – such as information and relationship capital – has inspired management and academics to work out better methods of capturing and measuring such things.

Firms now widely accept the fact that traditional performance-measurement systems must be redesigned. They are rethinking the linkages from company performance to incentive compensation plans as well. However, companies generally lack a common internal understanding of the meaning of performance measurement. Without this common definition, companies cannot identify the areas of performance most critical to developing meaningful incentive plans. For a mission critical leader (MCL) performance measurement is defined as the process of quantifying action in the context of a *Window of Effectiveness* (where the impact of resource-allocation decisions are measured) and of a *Window of Efficiency* (where the economy of resource allocation used to achieve change is measured).

Because the tenure for the mission critical leader and team is limited, while the tenure for the business is long term, we must differentiate between measures for the business and incentives for the leader and her team. Then we must provide linkages that couple company performance with that of the MCL's performance. For businesses, quarterly and year-end results have been monitored and reported with traditional control systems. However, these old-economy systems seldom take into account the very distinct periods of an MCL's tenure – the Windows of Effectiveness and Efficiency. Obviously, results from the first window will differ greatly from those in the second. The first window often involves resource-allocation decisions that certainly will not have an immediate positive return and may even cause bottom-line results to dip. In effect, the feedback of these decisions is delayed.

Resolving Two Perspectives: The Company and the Mission Critical Leader

In this fast-moving economy, traditional approaches to performance measurement set leaders up for failure. As we all know when buying shares or bonds, we are warned that past performance is not an indicator of future earnings. Every financial package on the market comes with such a warning. Yet managers of old-economy businesses run on exactly the opposite assumption, taking decisions about the future with only historical data to guide them. Anyone who has studied this in depth will tell you that it's like driving a car using only the rear-view mirror to catch glimpses of where you've been. If you're driving very slowly, you won't run into too much trouble. But if you speed up to 150 km and more per hour, you are courting disaster. Moreover, because companies compete increasingly on knowledge and innovative capability – items that traditional accounting methods simply ignore – they are increasing the demand for more comprehensive measurement systems. Luckily, the very technology that has enabled change in business practices has brought solutions to information-system management. Technology is now readily available to track large quantities of data. Online electronic systems are able to monitor every facet of the business constantly.

Bringing the two perspectives of company and leader together into one reporting system has been a challenge.[2] The old economy made things easier. Managers made decisions based on business models that were analysed by management accountants. It was the accountants' job to measure and report financial and non-financial measures that were

AT&T Canada: The Mission Critical Leader and 1,000 Days

In 1995, Bill Catucci was hired to serve for 3 years as AT&T Canada's CEO. He had no CEO track record. The company was losing $1 million a day and nearing a default on $700 million debt. Catucci began his first 180-day period (Window of Effectiveness) preparing the ground necessary for a successful development of the balanced scorecard.

He articulated his mission as 'The Right People, the Right Customers, the Right Products, and the Right Price'. In terms of the BSC, it meant the management had to:

- develop market-leading network-technology-product offerings;

- implement a customer-intimacy strategy to provide the best total solution;

- achieve sustained profitable growth.

The BSC was completed after 4 months, and then Catucci and his project leader introduced it to the other ten business units. Catucci made it a point to: describe AT&T Canada's mission, vision, values and strategy; answer questions; and be visible company-wide. As he said, 'They want to hear what's happening, they want to know what their future is, and when they hear it from the CEO, they really believe it.'

By 1998, the end of Catucci's 3-year tenure as CEO, AT&T Canada had a 32 per cent growth rate (28 per cent higher than the industry average); its customer accounts skyrocketed to over 750,000 customers in 1998 (up from 350,000 customers in 1995); and its revenue per employee rose by 36 per cent (from $273,000 in 1995 to over $370,000 in 1998). In 1999, it was sold for more than fourfold the $250 million required to keep it operating in 1995.

internal to the company. Traditionally, management accountants took responsibility for making both planning and control decisions. Companies such as Hansens and BTR were highly successful using this approach in the past. In fact, in many such companies general managers invariably had a management-accounting background and drove the business by financial controls. They took the roles of problem solver, scorekeeper and cheerleader. They provided everything within traditional financial measures, such as return on equity, return on investment and earning per share. These metrics were called lagging indicators because they reflected the past short-term results, presenting to a company a picture of where it stood. On the other hand, they used very few non-financial metrics, such as customer and employee satisfaction, though these might have provided companies with a *predictive* picture of their future, long-term performance.

Traditional financial metrics worked well as a standard for measuring company performance in the old economy. It worked primarily with multi-layered, command-and-control organizations, who manufactured and delivered standard products and services. Today's companies are flatter,

AT&T Canada

1999 Sales (million): $599.1
1-Year Sales Growth: 1117.7%

Website Address: http://www.attcanada.com

Stock Performance: August 1999–August 2000

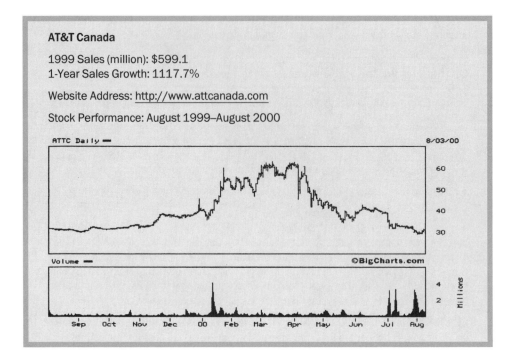

multi-functional organizations, which offer innovative products and services tailored to customers. The use of traditional metrics needlessly holds back these companies. Just as we have progressed from an industrial economy to an information economy, so too must our performance-measurement systems.

A Shift in Pace

Recently, there has been a mushrooming of techniques that address performance measurement – everything from ROM (see p. 134) to EVA (see p. 133). Several of these are briefly discussed in boxes throughout the chapter. The diffusion of these techniques was initially painfully slow (EVA first saw light of day 30 years ago) but is accelerating now in Europe. In 1996, 64 per cent of US businesses were designing new methods for incorporating non-financial data into their performance-measurement systems. Financial measures made up as little as 27 per cent of the metrics tracked by the 312 US organizations participating in an Institute of Management Accountants study. And 73 per cent of UK business leaders involved in a study expressed the belief that the needs of customers, employees, suppliers

SVA (shareholder value added) may very well become 'the global standard for measuring business performance' in a decade's time. The importance of shareholder value will grow not only with the globalization of capital markets, but also with the growth of involvement of individual shareholders.

The shareholder value method of measurement discounts future cash flow by the cost of capital. Shareholders' returns (dividends or appreciation in share price) are generated by these cash flows. While shareholder value is calculated by subtracting debt from corporate value and represents an absolute economic value, SVA is a forecast change in shareholder value. It is calculated with the following formula:

$$SVA = \frac{\text{(Present value of incremental cash flow before new investment)}}{\text{(Present value of investment in fixed and working capital)}^3}$$

and local-community members must also be met in order to best satisfy shareholders.[4] In 1999 Bain and Company reported that more than 55 per cent of all US companies and 45 per cent of European firms had adopted the 'balanced scorecard' in some form or other. It confirms Diageo CEO (chief executive officer) John McGrath's assertion that what is second nature to managers in the US is on the increase in Europe. Indeed, even Jack Welch, CEO of General Electric, seems to be marching to the beat of new performance measurements:

> We always said that if you had three measurements to live by, they'd be employee satisfaction, customer satisfaction and cash flow. If you've got cash in the till at the end, the rest is all going to work. If you've got high customer satisfaction you are going to get market share. If you've got high employee satisfaction, you're going to get productivity. And if you've got cash you know it's all working.[5]

The most widely used system today is the 'balanced scorecard' and its various derivatives. Its application needs examination.

The Balanced Scorecard

The balanced scorecard (BSC) was created by Robert Kaplan and David Norton in 1992. Since then it and its derivatives have become on the most widely used frameworks for combining non-financial and financial measures (such as EVA (see p. 133)) into a simple report. In its simplest form, BSC translates a company's strategic objectives into a set of performance

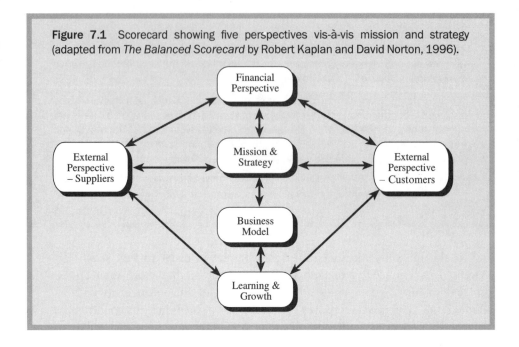

Figure 7.1 Scorecard showing five perspectives vis-à-vis mission and strategy (adapted from *The Balanced Scorecard* by Robert Kaplan and David Norton, 1996).

measurements. In Figure 7.1 it is broken down into five major perspectives of measurement: financial, external – customer and supplier – internal business process and learning and growth.

An effective BSC accomplishes six central points:

1   embodies the divisional strategy through cause-and-effect relationships;

2   effectively communicates strategy to direct reports and stakeholders by translating its strategy into performance targets;

3   guides the leader and employees to behave in alignment with overall company strategy;

4   links non-financial and financial measures in such a way that non-financial measures shed light on the company's financial performance in the future;

5   uses only a limited number of measurements that are most integral to a successful strategy;

6   emphasizes the costs and benefits brought to a company for its higher focus on financial or non-financial measures.

Using the five perspectives, the scorecard not only balances financial with non-financial measures, but resolves tension between metric objectives that are both short term and long term, external (customers, suppliers and share-holders) and internal (business processes, learning and growth). In short, it translates a division's mission and strategy into goals and measures.[6]

A generic model of the scorecard resolves several aspects of the leaders 1,000-day imperative. First, it deals with the apparent dichotomy found in the Windows of Effectiveness and Efficiency, the fact that they occur in successive periods and with clearly evolving objectives. Second, it addresses the issue of new business models: most scorecards in the past dealt only with old-economy models, hence were somewhat inflexible. Third, in order to gain momentum for successful implementation, the scorecard has to incorporate all the stakeholder targets of a leader's strategy. In other words, the scorecard isn't a two-stage process whereby it is developed and then sold to stakeholders. It is a one-stage process in which selling and development go together in order to get stakeholder commitment.

BT Worldwide: Building Speed into the Scorecard[7]

With the goal 'to be the most successful worldwide communications group', British Telecommunications (BT) plc set out to design a BSC system on Internet time. BT's new strategic framework gave it the strength necessary to enter the global arena, develop powerful strategic alliances and joint ventures, and reorganize into three customer-focused divisions (BT UK, BT Solutions and BT Worldwide). Central to the balanced scorecard's success is its flexibility: the scorecard can be changed at any time in response to the fast pace and unpredictability of the ecommerce industry. In addition, it is compatible with various other measurement systems of BT's partners, which enables the continual development of strong relationship capital.

Three core components of BT's BSC are its feedback mechanism, its strategic planning and implementation frameworks, and its 'facilitators'. BT's feedback mechanism is accelerated to keep up with the rapid pace of Internet time. As John Quail, director of quality for BT Worldwide, noted:

> In a market place as unpredictable and fast-moving as the Internet, competitive advantage will be gained by those companies who can learn and adapt quickly. The mechanisms for capturing what's going on in the Internet market place must be robust and constant, and we must have the capability to rapidly refine strategies and their implementations to meet market and customer requirement.

Driven by the need to make strategic planning and implementation as real time as possible, BT has a 'two speed' strategy: (1) under the annual cycle,

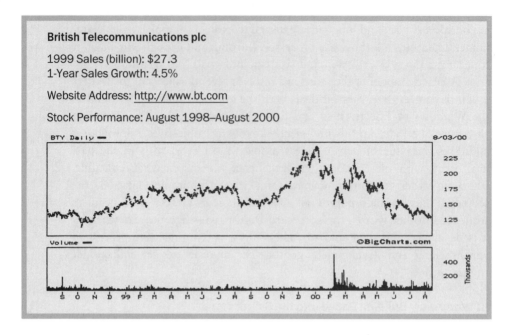

British Telecommunications plc

1999 Sales (billion): $27.3
1-Year Sales Growth: 4.5%

Website Address: http://www.bt.com

Stock Performance: August 1998–August 2000

BT makes adjustments to its vision, mission and overall strategy and (2) using the 'interim, fast-track' speed, BT can execute quick changes in response to the market. As a result, BT's scorecard is closely linked to market dynamics. It is developed quickly, with the idea in mind that it cannot be perfect and will have to have its metrics altered several times each year. Nothing is set in stone. As Quail said:

Step 1   Guidelines to developing a scorecard:

1. Obtain clarity, consensus and commitment *before* building a scorecard: 'Who are the stakeholders?', 'Who will resist and why?', 'What is the strategy for dealing with them?'

2. Review resources necessary for change: 'How much training will it take to educate the organization?', 'How much time do we have to implement?', 'How much will the existing system have to change?'

It will be of little value spending six months building a BSC that will probably be out of date on the first day of implementation. So we must get the scorecard 80 per cent right, operationalize it quickly, learn rapidly, and, over time, create more robust metrics that can be shared enterprise-wide.

Until the ecommerce industry becomes a bit more mature and develops standard definitions of such measurements as customer satisfaction and loyalty, BT plans to use the BSC's 'soul-searching' questions to guide it

ABC (activity-based costing) tracks the cost incurred by a company during the entire time it provides a product or service. ABC integrates what were once several activities – value analysis, process analysis, quality management and costing – into one analysis. It also does away with the old view of costs according to their individual operations. Instead, it consolidates costs into one measurement derived from the entire organizational process for providing a good or service.

Activity-based costing refines a company's costing system by viewing single activities (events, tasks, or units of work with shared goals) as the core sources of cost. It measures the costs to complete individual activities and the costs of products and services are based on the costs required to create them. ABC is used by companies to create ABM (activity-based management) under which managers use information generated by ABC to meet customer needs and increase profits through pricing, product mix, cost reduction and other types of decisions.

towards identifying its strategic objectives, targets and measures. ('To achieve our vision, how should we appear to our customers?' and 'How will we sustain our ability to change and improve?')

In addition, BT has developed a means for defining success in partners who have their own strategic-measurement models. Rather than force its scorecard on its partners, BT has developed a scorecard that is compatible with other measurement systems. When development of a BSC is requested by a joint-venture-management team, BT 'facilitators' respond to help its partners' senior-management teams create their own scorecard. The facilitators are sensitive to the fact that cultural differences play an important role in how the joint-venture-scorecard measures are understood, managed and reported. As Quail observed:

> In some Asian societies it is regarded as a sign of weakness to declare that one of your chosen suppliers underperforms, and thus managers would attempt to score the supplier quite highly. Yet in other cultures it is acceptable to be critical of suppliers. For any organization wanting comparable scores across regions, which we do not do, this has to be borne in mind.

BT has a global problem, and is using the BSC to try and resolve those issues. Working in Internet time means having to redefine the measures on an ongoing basis. Quail clearly recognizes relationship capital as a primary resource, he takes into account the fact that relationships that exist in Europe are quite different to those in Asia. The issue of relationship capital is important to BT, and new metrics must address this.

An MCL cannot afford to neglect the BSC for any length of time. As we have discovered, the linkage between internal activities outlined in the business model and activities of customers and suppliers in the external environment have become critical to success. Many of these linkages are physical; for example, data transfer through a B2B system have to be measured in the scorecard. Many linkages such as relationship capital are intangible things that make up an important part of the business model. These need to be articulated, measured and monitored.

Analysis of Linkages

Several authors have pointed out that linkages have to be established between measures of the scorecard and day-to-day implementation of strategy. That actually means establishing the *strength* of linkages between the business model and the measures of the scorecard. As the business model is redefined clearly, those linkages need to be reassessed. Take, for example, the IKEA model discussed in Chapter 4. In terms of a scorecard it starts to look like Figure 7.2.

The issue of linkage becomes important as the MCL introduces changes. She must have an understanding of what drives of the respective measures and whether the change strategy will actually influence the measure. For example, IKEA has a perceived problem with customer

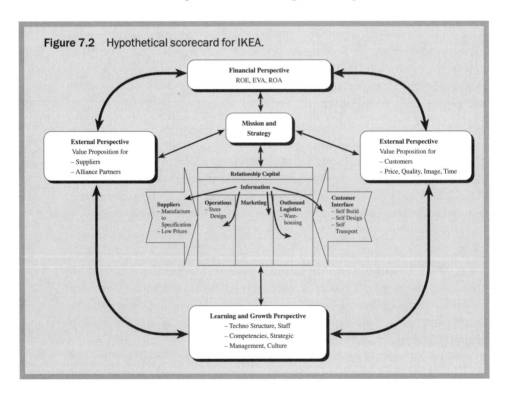

Figure 7.2   Hypothetical scorecard for IKEA.

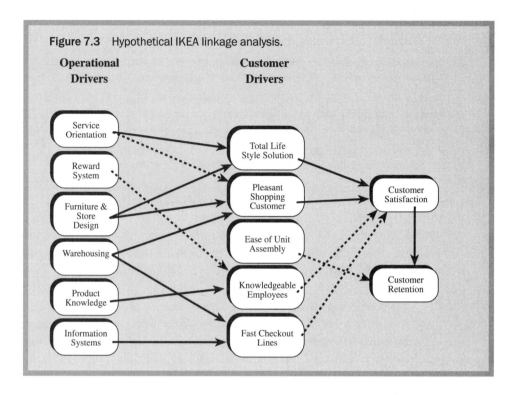

Figure 7.3 Hypothetical IKEA linkage analysis.

queues. There are masses of people moving through IKEA stores (220 million in 1999) and when they arrive at the till there is often a long tailback and subsequent wait to check out. The internal process and customer drivers can be outlined as in Figure 7.3.

What's important here is to identify where linkages are weak or strong. In this example, fast checkout lanes could be a weak link. However, IKEA's strong store design provides the setting for a very pleasant family event, and customers are not impatient to leave. Since there is strong linkage in the ease of assembly of its product units, IKEA would not be well advised to throw all its resources into shortening checkout queues. In fact, in July 2000 IKEA, which was planning the opening of twenty more stores in the UK, was boldly advertising its faults on television – long queues being one of them. An executive explained it like this, 'People have service expectations but IKEA isn't about service and it can be hellishly crowded. So we tackled the truth and told why IKEA is like it is.'[8]

Implementing the Scorecard

Once a leader has built momentum for a new scorecard it can be cascaded through her organization and embedded into its culture. Cascading is

Step 2   Guidelines to developing a scorecard:

3. Assess knowledge and ability: 'Have we the capability of doing this on our own?', 'Do we need some help?', 'Can we learn this through seminars or a consultant?'*

4. Test linkages: 'Are we focusing on the appropriate measures to get the responses we want?', 'Given the time constraint what's important and what do we leave for later?'

* Two good contacts: Randall H. Russell, Balanced Scorecard Collaborative rrussell@bscol.com and Lori Rockett, Emergence Consulting, Lori.Rockett@ emergenceconsulting.com

established through meetings, presentations, training and on-the-job training. Invariably there are people problems. Consultant Lori Rockett with the firm Emergence, that markets the BSC, puts it this way:

> Many times top management says, 'This scorecard looks great! We like it ... now make it work!' ... Putting the scorecard down on paper and defining its measures is not so tough. This is all done at a high level with the top-management team ... It is after 6–9 months when the 'rubber meets the road' and you hit real resistance ... It is conceptually strong and easy to learn, but very difficult to implement ... Many times the data is not there – systems do not currently support it. Which means radical change management ... And many times more training and better communication is needed, overcommunication in fact ... Many people lower in the organization do not even know about the scorecard ... this lack of communication and training leads to credibility problems for the new model.

Practice suggests that effective cascading will make a difference when it is implemented through the careful groundwork of a step-by-step programme:[9]

- Determine scorecard measures for next level in the cascade – At each level, people need to know what the scorecard means and how it will affect them.

- Verify that cascaded measures are at the appropriate levels – It's useless to discuss corporate financial targets with supervisors if they have no direct influence on the supervisor's unit.

- Establish and affirm linkages and alignment – Creating alignment between the mission critical team (MCT) and other divisions will require focused energies.

- Clarify targets – Record them and call for commitment.

- Establish summary measures – If early in the Window of Effectiveness define short-term measures; after that, identify expectations regarding overall results.

- Refine steps for gathering, reporting and reviewing results during implementation.

Kaplan and Norton work with a time-frame in which 16 weeks are required to implement a BSC, and 24 months for results to emerge. They say 'At the start of the third year, the initial strategy has been achieved and the corporate strategy requires updating.'[10] This means that provided the cascading process has been effective, the MCL should be able to exit this process successfully within the 1,000-day period. However, whether or not to link the scorecard to EVA remains a big decision for leadership.

EVA (economic value added)

A good Scotch whisky may be expensive to the consumer, but does it offer good returns to distillers? This is what John McGrath asked when he headed up IDV – International Distillers & Vintners. He wanted to know if good whisky actually created value for the company. His analysis of slow-distilling products – whisky, sherry and port – and fast-distilling products – vodka and liqueurs – revealed something management hadn't previously known: certain products were not only failing to create value for the company, they were actually destroying value. Management immediately started shifting funds to higher value-added brands and refocusing advertising expenditures in line with that knowledge.

That was 1993. Wind the clock forward to 1999, and we find John McGrath as CEO of Diageo PLC. A merger of GrandMet and Guinness, including McGrath's old division, IDV, had created Diageo. As part of the opening moves during his Window of Effectiveness, McGrath had introduced the question, 'Which parts of our business create value and which parts destroy it?' At the same time he changed the measurement system to include EVA – economic value added. EVA provides a system of measurement, evaluation and reward at all levels of the business based on value-creating ability. In effect, McGrath examined the business model and asked those people managing each of its activities to make decisions that would create value for shareholders and themselves. In exchange for good

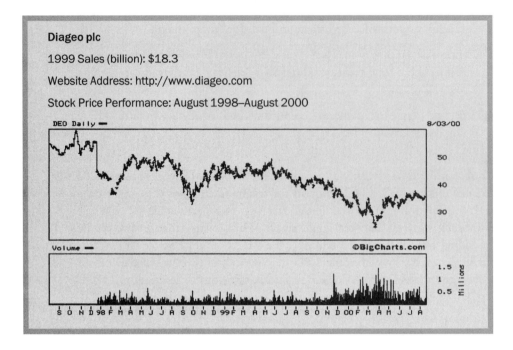

Diageo plc

1999 Sales (billion): $18.3

Website Address: http://www.diageo.com

Stock Price Performance: August 1998–August 2000

performance, McGrath's system offered huge bonuses. In a company of 85,000 employees and revenues of £14 billion, this was no mean feat. The award of bonuses is actually a thorny issue for large traditional corporations. New-economy companies don't have the problem, because they are small, run on an entrepreneurial basis, and lack the historical legacy that ties them to past incentive schemes. In new start-ups there are often unexpected handouts for good performance. Big established firms with entrenched remuneration and reward systems usually don't have that flexibility. McGrath therefore needed to tackle the incentive issue head-on.

ROM (return on management) is a non-quantitative financial figure that measures how much a company gets back for the time and energy of its managers. It is calculated as follows:

$$ROM = \frac{\text{productive organizational energy released}}{\text{management time and attention invested.}}$$

Companies use ROM to judge how well managers are choosing among various possible uses of their time and how well they are carrying out those choices. It answers the question: 'Are we getting the maximum payback from every hour of the day that we invest in implementing your business's strategy?'[11]

Diageo's performance-measurement system is based on several elements: short-term market expectations; a long perspective; and team-effort rewards and best-in-class grading. Short-term market expectations measure how a business performs over a 3-year period in view of market expectations. This provides a baseline for a bonus target – performing above the line improves the bonus.

The long-term perspective 'banks' two-thirds of a manager's bonus for several years to ensure that no end-game strategy was played that burnt out the business in the short term. 'Banking' is meant to ensure improved performance over the long term.

Because McGrath felt that his managers would not be able to affect change on their own, he grouped people into areas of accountability and rewarded them collectively for performance. This put a lot of pressure on the group to achieve the targeted measures.

Finally, the best-in-class measures rank Diageo against nineteen other companies – some of them direct competitors like Kellogg, Nestlé and Unilever – and other old-economy performers such as Gillette, Procter & Gamble and Coca-Cola. Incentives were tied to senior management's ability to put Diageo into the top of that group within 3 years.

Diageo is an interesting company because it has much in common with other large European companies. It was created by the merger of large players in one sector. Its product base is diverse, ranging from restaurant chains to Scotch whisky. It is global, stretching over 200 countries through a web of subsidiaries and agencies. It is good in some areas, terrible in others, and it needs to get up to speed. Some of its businesses have been flourishing for 100 years, but if John McGrath and his team don't get the change right, it may only survive another decade.

That McGrath chose EVA as his measurement instrument revealed a lot about the way he wanted to go. He needed to generate accountable value-creating action fast, and determined that EVA provided both the carrot and the stick. It incorporated the incentives and the controls to monitor performance on a day-to-day basis. He justified EVA in these terms, '... there is now evidence on both sides of the Atlantic that this approach to management works.'[12]

McGrath's linking of tight financial measures to team performance is fairly innovative. The importance of teams is emphasized in the literature[13] but few leaders are able to implement effective systems. Most prefer to gauge team effectiveness with non-financial measures such as learning, sharing and supportiveness. McGrath's system design contains crucial new performance-measurement structures that are process orientated and linked to compensation systems at the team level.

> **Step 3   Guidelines to developing a scorecard:**
>
> **5.** 'How do we link compensation to the scorecard?', 'What is the existing scheme and what would it take to change it?', 'What impact will using EVA targets have on profitability during the 1,000-day period?'
>
> **6.** Develop a time-frame for implementation. Give yourself 16+ weeks for implementation. Outline each stage of the process.

Despite McGrath's enthusiasm, the questions remain: Is EVA as good as he suggests? Is EVA so comprehensive that it can be implemented on its own and with no other supporting systems? And where does leadership fit in the overall system? Is EVA so geared to financial data that it blots out the importance of the leadership making it work? At the end of the day what interests us is why Diageo opted for EVA and can EVA be improved upon?

According to *Fortune Magazine*, EVA is 'today's hottest financial idea and getting hotter.'[14] EVA's measurement of company performance breaks from traditional methods by including a company's total cost of capital. In its simplest form, EVA poses the question: Does this business, product or service create value? It looks at this problem through the eyes of an investor. Its proponents say that it gives a better reflection of value than does traditional ROE (return on equity) or ROA (return on assets). They believe that these latter measures lead to overtly conservative or aggressive behaviour. In contrast to traditional measures, EVA examines the current period net income less the interest charge for using the firms capital. The formula is:

$$EVA = NOPAT - C\% \, (TC)$$

Which simply means that the economic value added (EVA) equals net operating profit after taxes (NOPAT) *minus* a percentage charge of the total capital of the company (TC). (If this description appears somewhat plodding, bear with me – the secret of EVA's implementation by John McGrath at Diageo was 'Simplify, simplify, simplify'.[15] (To wit: Martin Rafferty, Irish financial wizard and Chairman of United Drug, maintains that when it comes to corporate managers and company financial statements, most can't make head or tail of them!)

The charge on the capital assertion is important because it focuses management attention on the company's obligation to shareholders. It also provides an explicit mechanism to formalize the risk structure of the business, both in amount of capital and in cost of capital. For comparison, look at the example shown in Table 7.1 in which management needs to decide on a new investment to add to its existing business:

	Existing business	+	New investment	=	Results after investment
Income	230		170		400
Capital (equity)	1,000		1,000		2,000
ROE	23%		17%		20%

Table 7.1 Basic comparison of ROE versus earnings.

While earnings will grow with the new investment, ROE will decline. If performance measures are based on earnings, then there is every expectation that the investment will proceed. If performance is measured by ROE, then management will likely turn down this investment because it falls below the minimum average threshold – 23 per cent. In a company such as Volkswagen AG, the Financial Director Bruno Adelt says it is not that black and white, that management would study both perspectives before taking a decision. However, that opinion has not stopped Volkswagen from debating the move to EVA.

The issue is: Does the EVA perspective influence management's decision making? Let's say that the cost of capital is 15 per cent. The EVA perspective would then be as shown in Table 7.2:

	Existing business	+	New investment	=	Results after investment
Income	230		170		400
Capital (equity)	1,000		1,000		2,000
ROE	23%		17%		20%
Cost of capital	15%		15%		15%
Capital charge	150		150		300
EVA	80		20		100

Table 7.2 Basic comparison of ROE, earnings versus EVA.

Where EVA is linked to the incentive scheme, the recommendation would be to invest where value is added even when, as in this case, it is one-quarter of the earlier investment. Of course, where EVA is negative (i.e. value is being destroyed) investment is foolish. Moreover, where existing businesses reflect a negative EVA, management needs to take decisions about creating value or divesting. For example, McGrath found in one of the Diageo businesses, the highly profitable $1 billion Pillsbury food business, that 23% of its stock-keeping units (SKUs) in food-service business were not creating value. For various reasons these SKUs were 'necessary' to fill out a range of products or compete in a market space. 'In other words,' said McGrath, 'We didn't have a good food-service business. We had a good business dragged down by a quarter of its operations.'[16]

Problems for the Top-Management Team

In many respects the decision to link EVA to the compensation plan of a company is a tough one to make. Many companies encounter three significant drawbacks. The first is that the actual implementation calls for the total commitment of the top-management team. The TMT may be divided on the issue, signalling trouble in the future. The second barrier arises from the first; the implementation of EVA reveals that the company may have been destroying value in the past, not only in isolated areas as in the case of Diageo but across the board. This discovery puts the TMT in an extremely poor light, one that they hardly feel enthusiastic about. Lastly, EVA makes a strong assumption that most business models will simply fall into line behind its implementation without having to use additional measures. This is tantamount to saying that if we pay Raúl to score goals for Real Madrid then the other many skills of the team (e.g. defence and goalkeeping) will fall into place behind his performance and will have no need of separate measurement. Stern Stewart and others have seen the anomaly of this and have tried to fill it with the scorecard approach.

The term EVA is copyrighted to Stern Stewart & Co. In 1998, at least 300 companies worldwide were using Stern Stewart's EVA-based compensation system. Under an EVA-based compensation system, a formula is used to establish new targets each year, and leaders and managers receive higher bonuses the higher the EVA achieved. As with any new incentive plan, it is crucial to be aware of the fact that people may very well resist the linkage of their compensation to EVA. Thus, effective communication of the new system and proper timing of the roll-out is key to its success.

EVA has several clones in the 'economic profit model' by Copeland et al. and 'shareholder value creation' by Rappaport. These concepts have similar management processes for identifying an 'EP tree' or 'value map' used in breaking down the sources of economic profit into its various components. Such an understanding of how shareholder value is created allows managers to communicate this information to employees, assess their operating plans, and layout incentives.[17]

While EVA is now an increasingly popular financial-performance-measurement tool, its fundamentals date back to the start of capitalism. It removes obstacles put in the way by traditional accounting-based performance metrics, and challenges leaders to manage in a more effective manner by linking their interests directly to those of the shareholder. As a result, EVA allows leaders to look at their company in a whole new light.[18]

West Friburg Regional Bank[19]

West Friburg Regional Bank (WFRB) has 3,500 employees, 54 branches and $5.8 billion in assets. It generates a net income of $48 million. In 1998, WFRB had a budget-based management-incentive-compensation scheme that linked CEO and executive bonuses to three annual bank measurements: earnings, return on shareholders' equity and return on assets.

The scheme was an '80–120' incentive plan under which participants received bonuses for performance within a forty-point range of budgetary percentages. They did not receive a bonus if they performed at less than 80 per cent of budget and did not receive an additional bonus for performing at greater than 120 per cent of budget. However, their bonuses increased in value as their performance improved from 80 to 120 per cent of budget. The incentive plan had the characteristics described in Figure 7.4 with two 'go golfing points' – if performance fell below 80 per cent of budget (could mean permanent golfing) and if performance rose above 120 per cent of budget (golfing on sunny days only).

In late 1998, WFRB's new CEO, Michael Markham, believed the Bank was in urgent need of a redesigned financial-management system that encouraged decentralized decision making. After a decade of

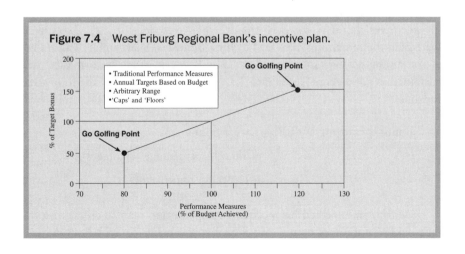

Figure 7.4   West Friburg Regional Bank's incentive plan.

acquisitions, WFRB was composed of nine affiliate banks. It lacked a uniform performance-measurement framework. He also thought that the bank needed line-of-business reporting that would emphasize performance in different operating units and reward managers accordingly. A model that measured performance and linked it to the compensation scheme would remove the 'shackles' of the traditional model, allowing employees to be more entrepreneurial and add more value to the firm. He asked himself: 'Is the organization ready for a new performance metric? Will employees understand EVA, since it is different from reported earnings? How will Wall Street react to this decision? And will the Board endorse a system that has the potential to pay out far larger incentive rewards to managers than other similar-sized banks are paying?'

After careful thought, Markham viewed the potential benefits resulting from an EVA financial management and compensation system as far outweighing the risks; so, in early 1999, he began working with a consultant to devise a new plan. The creation of the system was to take place in four phases over a time-frame of 1 year:

1   measurement of EVA at the corporate level;

2   design of EVA incentive plans at the corporate level;

3   measurement of EVA at major business units;

4   detailed EVA communication plans (internal and external) to the investor community.

After identifying the new EVA measurements for WFRB, the consultants designed an incentive plan that, unlike the old model, did not have predetermined caps and floors. Instead, it had a 'bonus bank' where WFRB placed negative awards for performance below expectations, and two-thirds of executives' bonuses for performance that exceeded targets. (Executives were paid the remaining one-third of their bonuses.) Such a plan was aimed at containing performance in bad years and ensuring that performance was sustained in good years (see Figure 7.5). It can be described by the following formula:

Bonus award for WFRB = Target bonus

+ Sharing percentage (change in EVA

− Expected improvement)

Markham expected his incentive compensation plan to create an estimated $196 million of cumulative EVA improvement for WFRB. However, while laying out the plan is one thing, actually implementing it is quite another. Markham was sure to come across great challenges in explaining the new model to WFRB and getting the company to buy into it. Without strong, universal commitment, the plan was sure to run into major difficulty. As Markham may already have noted, research suggests that CEO turnover is correlated with poor EVA performance.[20]

Though arguments for EVA are fairly convincing, it remains controversial. A recent *Wall Street Journal* article claimed that there was no evidence to support the Stern Stewart findings that EVA companies outperformed the market. Stern Stewart refuted the statement saying that the *WSJ* article was based on sloppy research that included

MVA (market value added) is another concept coined by Stern Stewart. It is a measurement of the net present value of a firm as calculated by subtracting the economic value of capital used by a firm from the firm's market value. Thus, it is the difference between the capital investors put into a company and the capital they would generate if the company were sold today. If we discount the present value of a firm's expected annual EVA, we have calculated its MVA. Some drawbacks of MVA are that it cannot be measured for companies that do not trade on the market and it cannot be calculated at the division, business unit, subsidiary, or product-line levels. It is the internal measure of EVA that makes up for this weakness of MVA's external emphasis.

companies that were not even EVA companies. Stern Stewart remains the major force in the consultancy market selling EVA and the linked compensation plan.

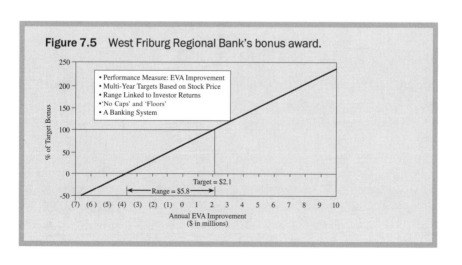

Figure 7.5   West Friburg Regional Bank's bonus award.

- Performance Measure: EVA Improvement
- Multi-Year Targets Based on Stock Price
- Range Linked to Investor Returns
- 'No Caps' and 'Floors'
- A Banking System

% of Target Bonus

Target = $2.1
Range = $5.8

Annual EVA Improvement
($ in millions)

Conclusion

The MCL has to have measurement systems that are accurate and demanding of her people. These systems have to provide incentive and clear sanctions even when things aren't going to plan. Implementation of a measurement system has to be swift. It must be initiated during the Window of Effectiveness. This chapter suggests that the scorecard system be used to focus energies on appropriate measures. This system, linked to a compensation plan of the EVA type, can provide the MCL with potent tools.

Leadership Architecture

Working in Internet time is a challenge to the mission critical leader (MCL). It means having to think fast and act more decisively than ever before. It means pressure to understand, articulate and promote the overall picture as quickly as possible. Can you imagine Michelangelo, Frank Lloyd Wright or Antoni Gaudi – the great Catalan architect – saying, 'Look I've got an idea for a building in my head. Just follow my instructions and it'll come together in the end.'

Yet, leadership in the new market place is often approached this way because getting up to speed is critical, sometimes before substantive issues have been addressed. The current assumption seems to be that you can be a great leader if only someone gives you something to lead about. Part of the blame for this state of affairs lies in leadership books which talk only about leadership, never about markets, products, production or anything else the leader must tackle. The other part of the blame lies in books on finance, marketing, production, and the like. These discuss balanced scorecard or marketing, but seldom mention leadership. Only in executive-development-leadership programmes do business issues overlap with leadership concerns. At the IESE–Michigan Global Programme for Management Development, we try to give an integrated view that ties leadership to areas like global marketing, finance, IT, etc. This chapter will give an overview of the thinking that goes into the development of leaders on such programmes.

With the rapid shift to a new economy, CEOs (chief executive officers) no longer retain the locus of architectural design and implementation at their levels. It has moved to mission critical leaders and teams at lower levels. Middle managers have become the architects of the new organization. They are now responsible for matching the pace of change to the creation of the architecture of a knowledge-based organization. They must take responsibility for the design and composition of social and systems architecture. As architects, MCLs must convert a vision into tangible and intangible benefits. This transformation engages the MCL in a delicate balancing act. James O'Toole, Head of the Aspen Institute and one of the most thoughtful writers on leadership, describes this balance as 'design, composition, tension, balance and harmony'. Achieving such delicate balance requires managing each of the following issues:

- the scaffolding of social architecture;

- vision and passion;

- power and patronage;

- product architecture;

- process support.

Diagrammatically these emerge as shown in Figure 8.1.

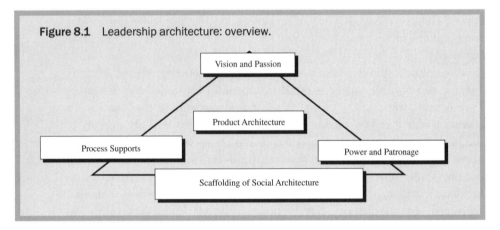

Figure 8.1   Leadership architecture: overview.

MCLs are like architects. They need to sketch out the big global picture and at the same time have an understanding of the fine detail. They need to develop an architectural overview that balances the ephemeral, a perspective of how the future will look, with the concrete. A mission critical team (MCT) needs a vision, a dream of how things should be, counterbalanced by a clear representation of the way things are.

Companies such as Motorola, General Electric (GE) and Shell are famous for their development of strong leaders. These companies have seen that social and systems architecture have to be sophisticated unifying forces within a business. CEO Jack Welch comments, '*The concept of an operating system with social architecture that shares learning is inbred in everybody that's here.*'[1] As the shift to knowledge-based organizations accelerates, social and systems architecture is changing fast. Mechanical bureaucratic models no longer function adequately within organizations. The role of the centre of the organization has been questioned as never before.

The Shift from Centrality of Control

In global businesses social and systems architecture typically came from the top of traditional firms, packaged as business systems and organizational models. Top management traditionally maintained the prerogative of control over these models. They did not surrender this prerogative lightly. For instance, let's look at John Deere & Company. Hans Becherer, CEO for more than 10 years, had been highly successful in maintaining the company as a leader in worldwide farm equipment. He had been rated as one of the US top leaders by headhunters Thomas Neef and James Citrin of Spencer Stuart.

Becherer's vision for the business was termed 'genuine value'. This vision supposedly captured the essence of service to the company's constituents and codified the John Deere way of doing things. Reinforced by a large global organization, the social architecture embedded continuous improvement, profitable growth and business innovation around the concept of 'genuine value'. When net income declined by 77 per cent in 1999, together with a 15 per cent drop in sales and revenues, Becherer appeared taken by surprise. Ironically, he declared that this was 'clear proof that our actions to create a new kind of company, one of greater depth, breadth and balance, are having the intended effect'. Big change was in the offing, and Becherer clearly felt a need to declare that he was in control.

In fact, top management often need to maintain a centralist control mythology, even when it's blatantly obvious that this is not the case. The central tenet of the control myth is believing that if you don't know about it then it can't be happening. Previously, of course, leaders could make assumptions about systems and social architecture because these concepts were well established, and supported by historical precedence. Now, terms such as customization, interconnectivity, networks, speed and commodization are fast replacing old concepts. New understanding and knowledge generates uncertainty as it replaces old knowledge. As a result, CEOs are having their task redefined. Ghoshall and Bartlett see this change as a movement from, '*Institutionalising control to embedding trust, from maintaining the status quo to leading changes. As opposed to being designers of strategy, (CEOs) take on the role of establishing a sense of purpose within the company*'.[2] *(Author's parentheses)*

The idea that only those at the top of the organization would know how to develop social and systems architecture is ludicrous. In fact, Ghoshal and Bartlett have suggested that blind faith in the old business models and philosophy is making many leaders not architects, but wreckers of their own operations. Large organizations simply cannot keep up with the pace of change. Says CEO Jack Welch, *'The idea that one person could run a $120 billion company that's in as many different businesses as we are in is outrageous!'*[3]

Think Global, Sink Local

Contrary to what you might expect, the Internet isn't democratizing the workplace as everyone predicted it would. It certainly hasn't necessarily created more freedom of action or thought. The paradox of the Internet age is that in the face of its almost limitless opportunity, bureaucratization of imagination is actually on the rise in large organizations. With new technologies and digital interactivity entering the workplace daily, the knee-jerk response of the organization has been to recoil from this development. In parallel with the development of the Internet, large corporations have implemented highly centralized business systems. Companies with global products, such as Coca-Cola and Benetton, have tried to create the illusion of global control that has become part of the ritual of growth, as though too much freedom, too much democracy, would kill the golden goose.

Coca-Cola discovered, as it reeled from one disaster – the hysterical reaction to its tainted product in Brussels to another, the planned boycott of its products by marginalized black employees – that going global can have serious repercussions if leadership ignores local concerns and mores. Douglas Daft, the new CEO of Coca-Cola, commented on the shift required of the business:

> (*We were*) generally moving towards consolidation and centralized control ... when we were 'going global' ... we knew that we had to centralize control to manage the expansion. The world, on the other hand, began moving in the 1990s in a different direction, demanding greater flexibility, responsiveness and local sensitivity, while we were further centralizing decision-making and standardizing our practices, moving further away from our traditional multi-local approach. We were operating as a big, slow, insulated, sometimes even insensitive 'global' company; and we were doing it in a new era when nimbleness, speed, transparency and local sensitivity had become absolutely essential to success.' (Author's italics)

European companies too have a history of centralization that leaves them out of touch with local sensitivities. The Italian clothing group

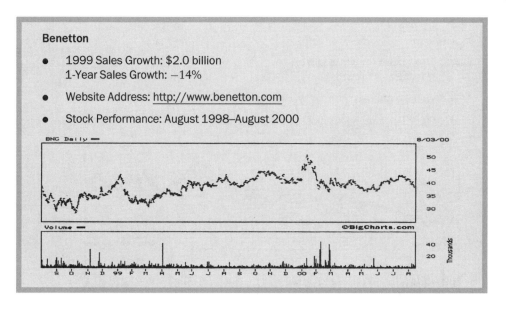

Benetton

- 1999 Sales Growth: $2.0 billion
  1-Year Sales Growth: −14%

- Website Address: http://www.benetton.com

- Stock Performance: August 1998–August 2000

Benetton built a successful global brand with a series of advertisements that became progressively more controversial during the 1990s. Each new ad campaign would provoke an avalanche of protest from a different sector of the community. From headquarters outside of Venice, Benetton's creative director, Oliviero Toscani, declared that the mission of advertising was not to provide a showcase for products, but to convey the meaning and imagery associated with the brand name.

In the US, the reaction of consumers was evident. A booming business in the early 1990s, Benetton slowly saw its revenues in the US shrink to 5 per cent of its total global income. Franchisees in the world's largest market were caught in the downward spiral. Toscani's final advertising effort for Benetton was a death-penalty protest in the US that sympathetically presented inmates on death row. The ads caused outraged families of the criminals' victims to picket US stores. Big clients such as Sears terminated contracts to distribute Benetton products throughout its 850 stores.

Toscani departed, muttering about elderly US marketing executives who clung to obsolete ideas. Benetton's US business was in tatters. Its competitors, GAP and Old Navy, were reaping the benefits of Benetton's lack of local sensibility. Clearly, creating local sensitivity requires careful scaffolding of social architecture.

Organizations like Wal-Mart have learned to create sensitivity locally. *'We needed to push more decision making and authority down to the country level, because errors that were being made were the result of people not making decisions rather than making poor decisions,'* said

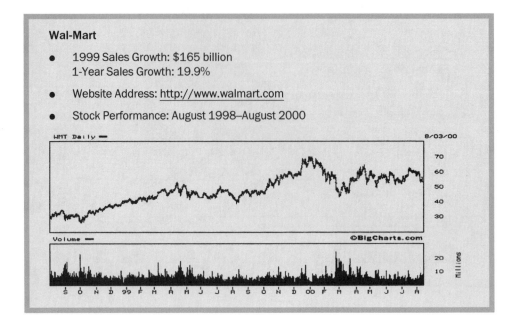

Wal-Mart

- 1999 Sales Growth: $165 billion
  1-Year Sales Growth: 19.9%

- Website Address: http://www.walmart.com

- Stock Performance: August 1998–August 2000

John Menzer, who had served as CFO before he was named as international President and CEO. He went on: '*Some of the decisions relating to customer service and programs could have been made in country as opposed to waiting for corporate approval.*' To remedy the situation, Wal-Mart developed a corporate-governance plan which identifies and establishes what Menzer calls 'bandwidths of responsibility'. Thus, an executive in Korea or Argentina knows within the established bandwidth which decisions need to be made in country and which ones should involve communication with Bentonville.[4]

Social Architecture

'It's social architecture that makes the organization function and provides continuity after his [the CEO's] departure', says Jack Welch at GE. Warren Bennis, famous leadership author and Professor at the University of South California, has put it this way, '*Leaders must learn to develop a social architecture that encourages incredibly bright people to work together successfully and to deploy their own creativity.*' He maintains that successful social architecture builds a culture of respect, caring and trust. It gives people a chance to deploy their full talents.[5]

'Social architecture represents how managers spend time and allocate energy. Managerial time and energy become the factors that employees see most often. How managers spend time represents what managers think is important,' says human-resource guru Dave Ulrich.

Social architecture is the tangible and intangible behaviours that configure the shape of a living space for acceptable corporate behaviour. It is time related and therefore short lived. It comprises a web of values and beliefs, of tacit knowledge, of the nods and winks that grow mutual respect, of acknowledgements of mutual dependence between team members; all of which bind us to others with whom we work.

Scaffolding a Social Architecture

Most global businesses do not have the social structure to deal with mission critical assignments. As creative as Benetton was in production and advertising in Italy, it showed insensitivity in the US, one of its most crucial extremities. Moreover, since the concept of social architecture is still illusive, Benetton must work almost intuitively to develop its own. Those who have divined the process, including Intel, Hewlett Packard and Wal-Mart, have no fear that other companies will commandeer the wisdom. They know that if competitors don't have the structure, they likely don't comprehend the concept either.

Social architecture somehow seems the lesser for having to be defined. Trying to create it is not unlike trapping Barcelona nightclub smoke in a bag in order to create the same atmosphere at home. You believe you will get it right if you take home the bag, and release its contents. Unfortunately, the result you'll get will be little more than the smell of stale beer and cigarette smoke in your house. Canned atmosphere won't win you any points with your friends, anyway. Most will suspect that you just can't be bothered to experience the real thing.

Facilitation at Work

A unique social architecture can be developed by focusing on deliverables such as training and development, knowledge management and work conditions. However, there are aspects, such as spontaneous cooperation and accumulating tacit knowledge, that the MCL can facilitate but not control in the workplace. Her facilitations in these areas generate a scaffolding process which the organization uses to build capacity within a social architecture. The basic rudiments of scaffolding are:

- Skill formation that revolves around the development of technical skills and people skills (primarily how to work in teams). Because many bright and talented folk fall in love with their own ideas, they are often amazed that they may have to work through them with someone else. Initially, many people have difficulty developing meaningful face-to-face relationships in high-performance teams. They enter the team as individuals and generally feel more comfortable with electronic relationships. They may have forgotten how valuable teamwork can be.

- Spontaneity that is self-generating. Skill training can never produce spontaneity. Spontaneity suggests an unconstrained and unstudied manner or behaviour that arises from natural inclination or impulse. It enables an individual to cooperate within the team without fear. Most organizations suffocate spontaneity. As Warren Bennis observed, deploying creativity in a spontaneous environment is neither forced nor tedious. It provides an opportunity to grow an idea into something bigger, better and more feasible.

- Knowledge, mainly tacit, because most explicit knowledge has been captured by knowledge-management systems. Explicit knowledge systems will never capture the most valuable knowledge in successful social architecture. Most of that knowledge is tacit, transient and accessible, given the right architecture.

While the process of facilitating scaffolding may seem fuzzy, it is actually comprised of practical actions that allow the MCL to develop the process over time. For instance, a particular action can focus team members on markets and customer needs, thus building the capability of a team. A successful series of facilitations creates social architecture and systems that change employee behaviour.

Table 8.1 illustrates the MCL actions needed to get scaffolding erected.

So What Happened to Culture?

Culture is a greatly overworked concept and has had a chequered history. Managers may have read volumes of descriptive analysis of it, but encounter difficulty in actually tackling culture and changing it. Ghost stories of failed culture-change attempts now paper the office walls of human-resource managers. Often, it comprises the mantra behind which implementation failure hides. How many times don't we hear 'We couldn't do it because the culture got in the way'?

Culture probably still exists in the broader framework of large

The focus	The actions	The questions
Articulation	Consistently driving home the vision and strategy in order to create a shared mindset. 'Walking the talk' is the behaviour required.	Do we believe and share in the vision?
Speed	Searching ways of bringing products and services to market in less time.	How long is the time to money cycle? Can we do it faster? Can we bring product-concept freeze any closer to market introduction?
Connectivity	Making sure that everyone (including customers) and everything is interconnected and information flowing freely.	How well are we connected? Who's in the loop, who's out and why? How is spontaneity occurring in this free flow?
Knowledge	Implementing systems adapted to support the learning processes.	How do we learn around here? How do we get better at this?
Accountability	Measuring and evaluating progress.	Who is making all this happen? How do we reward them?

Table 8.1 Leadership architecture: focussing action.

organizations, mainly as a set of indecipherable labels that explain little and provide less in this Internet age. The culture myth promised a renaissance within traditional organizations that has never been delivered. Now, with the advent of social architecture, the question arises as to whether it is simply a replacement for the old jaded concept of culture.

Social architecture is different, however. It can focus on time pacing rather than event pacing, a trend that Kathleen Eisenhardt endorses (Eisenhardt and Brown 1998). Traditionally, companies have reacted to events such as technology shifts, competitor moves and customer demands. Event management has taught managers how to pace themselves to achieve stability and predictability in planning. On the other hand, time management is calendar driven. It is regular, rhythmic and proactive, and has a powerful psychological impact – it creates a relentless sense of urgency around deadlines and common goals.

The MCL faces the problem of creating a social architecture in a very limited domain – here, living space pertains only to those who live within it or have contact with it. Social architecture is tangible, it is about design and composition, and it creates a unit's capability. As it develops, social architecture encompasses both internal and external networks, eventually taking in outside stakeholders such as customers and suppliers.

Vision

Every MCL has a unique vision of the future. That vision is highly complex, emotional and even spiritual. The fulfilment of the vision can produce constructive tension in the organization through the interplay of creativity and knowledge. Knowledge accumulated through experience and learning is, by definition, obsolete. It is deepened and stretched through creativity which upends the assumptions and foundations of that knowledge. This stretching creates a tension between the probable and the possible. Out of the tension of *the possible*, a vision arises. It involves an attractive state of being, sometime in the future.

Cogent visions generate a tension that gives meaning to the people who share them. A problem arises in the business when the vision is articulated in a trite way. A leader may have a genuine sense of the vision, but may articulate it badly. Articulation and communication can be weak areas for an MCL. Simply stating that an organization is going to be Number 1 or 2 is no longer adequate to motivate a team. People have heard this kind of tired rhetoric too many times for it to have any cogency.

Fear of Complexity

The tension of a vision can move mountains. However, powerful visions require powerful and specific articulation and communication. A vision is unlikely to move anything or anyone if it is articulated in platitudes such as 'We must try harder' or 'The customer is Number 1'. These are the work of mediocre marketing departments, not of a leader's mind. A vision statement that sounds as if it has been produced for halfwits will simply annoy its audience. Often, the statement has evolved out of a team's perceived need to keep communications simple. But simple straightforward communication is never trite. In fact, when skillfully developed, it can make the most complex issues comprehensible. One has only to look at the motivational power of great texts such as the Bible and the Koran to realize that ordinary people can develop formidable powers of articulation when inspired by great ideas. Audiences are equally able to deal with complex visions when are presented articulately. Martin Luther King's 'I have a dream' in Washington or Mandela's 'It is an ideal for which I am prepared to die' Rivonia trial speech reflect the triumphant communication of a resounding theme. Like Douglas McArthur's 'I will return' speech, their themes are idealistic and uncompromising. An MCL needs to understand that visions must be communicated so as to enthral people.

A Guide to Vision Creation[6]

Table 8.2 poses some useful questions when thinking about a vision for a mission critical unit.

Creating a Pasion for the Vision

When an individual or team have spontaneously generated creative tension around a vision, they have a sense of ownership and start to feel a passion for that vision. If there is one thing that differentiates traditional business

The big themes	What are the real issues to be addressed by the unit? The Benetton factor? Is the vision so distant from the market that customers won't understand it?
Stakeholders	What individuals and organizations have a stake in the future of the unit? How many of them will be included in the sharing exercise?
Early-warning signals	What early-warning signals might have been detected in the external environment that forewarns substantial change? What trends do they indicate?
Major events	What future events could happen, both inside and outside our unit, that would have a big impact on us, and how likely are they to occur? How would the unit survive under these conditions?
Influence	How much leverage does the unit have? What would it take for the new unit to influence the course of events and how could that leverage be applied?
Alternatives	What options could be available to us, and what might their consequences be? Of the alternative futures that might occur for our unit and its environment, which are more likely to be favourable to our survival and success? How do we follow these up?
Resources	What future resources might be available, and what would we have to do to secure them?
What if . . .	What could happen if we continue on our present path without any changes?

Table 8.2   Guide to vision creation.

Vision and Values

A guide used by GE leaders (always with unyielding integrity), who:

- create a clear, simple, reality-based, customer-focused vision and are able to communicate it straightforwardly to all constituencies;

- reach, set aggressive targets, recognize and reward progress, while understanding accountability and commitment;

- have a passion for excellence, hate bureaucracy and all the nonsense that comes with it;

- have the self-confidence to empower others and behave in a boundaryless fashion, believe in and are committed to work-out as a means of empowerment, are open to ideas for anywhere;

- have the capacity and comfort to develop global brains and global sensitivity when building diverse and global teams;

- have enormous energy and the ability to energize and invigorate others, stimulate and relish change, not be frightened or paralysed by it, see change as an opportunity, not a threat;

- possess a mindset that drives quality, cost and speed for a competitive advantage.

from mission critical units, it is this sense of passion. Unlike their staid counterparts, mission critical units have emotional attachment to their visions, their ideas and, eventually, their output. Through constant articulation of the vision the team gains increased understanding and passion. Unlike its subjective romantic counterpart, this objective passion can be communicated and defended on an intellectual level.

Power

As one of the new regional directors of the UK's National Health Services (NHS), Bernard Harris had a lot going for him – a successful career in pathology, experience in the US and strong support from London. At his first meeting with direct reports, he spoke of changing the region, of developing high motivational levels and increased resources from friends in high places. All in all, people were impressed as they returned to their offices.

During separate meetings with each individual Harris exuded charm, wit and intelligence. He seemed to understand people's problems and reassured them that they would be able to sort them out. As people compared impressions over lunch and coffee, they agreed that they could imagine change taking place under this new regional head.

In the first few months, change did indeed take place. New resources were provided in some areas. Conditions improved in others. On reflection, most people felt that things were getting done – though not as fast as they had first expected. But they felt that this was due, at least in part, to the organizational sluggishness of the NHS.

Harris had initially required all direct reports to meet with him collectively on Monday mornings, but as the months went by more and more people found reasons not to go. Part of the problem lay in the fact that Harris was struggling to keep up with ongoing demands and problems. He did not take time to deal with dwindling attendance at the meetings. He simply shifted the meeting schedule to once a fortnight then, after declining attendance set in once again, to once a month. People now felt that the meetings achieved little that they could not do on a face-to-face basis themselves.

Harris began spending less and less time in his office and had started to attend more and more meetings in London. Soon he was on several important committees, one of which reported directly to the Minister. Back in the region, things started to feel exactly as they had felt before Bernard Harris's arrival.

Like many intelligent charismatic people, Harris believes that transformation is accomplished through personal power and influence – the extrinsic forces. Leaders often charm people into believing that single-handedly they can defeat the demons of bureaucracy. Just as often, they run out of energy. They have no vision that can be shared. Team members are essentially left waiting for action on the part of the leader. Action can be long in arriving, once the leader becomes bogged down in a morass of tasks for which he is solely responsible. Had Harris been able to share a vision – allowing those around him to help create, adapt and nurture it – he would have had more chance of making it happen. Inevitably Harris's meetings with individuals became known as 'sofa sessions' – where you would tell your therapist all your problems, leave and nothing would happen until the next meeting.

By sharing his vision with those around him Harris would have seen his original creation disappearing. That is one of the implications of empowerment. However, this is also the nature of the power of transformation; imagery of the vision is always disappearing as it receives the feedback of its realization. In other words, as a vision takes the form of a product or service the original visionary is given direct feedback on how that vision is being implemented. In the process the vision is diluted. Only someone who has no power to implement can nurture a vision without having feedback.

Looking at it from another perspective, Harris could have been successful if he had shared the vision. Sharing the vision would have increased tension and hence the force of the implementation. To Harris this would have meant losing his own vision, when he shared it with others, but gaining a new reality far greater than he could have achieved on his own. The new reality would have been a collectively owned one, nurtured and delivered by the team.

Power of Transformation
If vision is created out of the clash of creativity on accumulated knowledge, then power is the energy created by that clash. That energy enables us to transform imagery into reality. The power of transformation combines extrinsic forces such as personality (charisma), authority and access, with the intrinsic tension of the vision. To sustain the vision, a leader must balance extrinsic and intrinsic forces. When either extrinsic or intrinsic force overpowers, momentum is lost. For instance, the Benetton fracas in the US represents a global-brand vision run amok. The intrinsic force of that vision was not appropriately balanced by the extrinsic force of franchisees in the US. Power is inevitably lost in such situations, and vision cannot be transformed into a reality – in this case, increased revenues.

By the same token, if the vision is weak, then the power is inherently weak, in which case a leader might resort to coercive or utility power. Coercive power plays on the fears of both leader and follower. Utility power plays on materialism, the belief that there's something in it for both leader and follower. In a society that is becoming increasingly democratic, neither coercive nor utility power move long-term constituents, unless rewards or sanctions are enormous.

Table 8.3 outlines some points to factor into your understanding of power formed by shared vision.

Patronage
In the Internet age we think of individuals as free agents. The free-agent concept plays to the trend of increased attention to the individualism of both customers and employees. However, it ignores patronage, a vital aspect of MCL success. Imperatives cannot be successfully completed if the MCL remains a remote figure, isolated from sources of power and influence in the environment. The great architect Michelangelo needed Lorenzo de Medici, as Jack Welch needed Reg Jones, to achieve great work. Gaudi constructed extraordinary buildings under the patronage of José Guell. Sir Colin Marshall turned British Airways around under the patronage of Lord King. Jesse Jackson was nurtured and inspired as a leader by Martin Luther King.

	Concept issues	Deliverables
Vision tension	Does this vision have sufficient tension to persuade others to follow? In other words, will it move them?	Is it well articulated? Where is it articulated – notepad, flipchart, email? How would it be best delivered – presentation or report?
Shared ownership	Is there shared acceptance of the vision? With whom is it shared and do they own it? What behaviours indicated sharedness?	What is the best forum for sharing? How will we create maximum openness? Is the vision teachable? Is facilitation required? By outsiders or insiders?
Motivation	What is the personal agenda of the MCL – ambition, altruism? What is the motivation of the others? Does the MCL and others have sufficient demonstrated integrity to sustain the vision?	Have all motivations been discussed? Is there a consistency among the team's motivations to transform the vision into a reality?
Influence/ Resources	Is the team able to marshal the resources necessary for delivery? Is the team able to influence gatekeepers to resources? Has the team made contact with those able to influence the outcome?	Have the major stakeholders been identified? What are the objectives and deadlines for doing so?
Feedback	How does the reality match the vision? What needs to change – the reality or the vision? What feedback mechanisms are in place – are they sufficiently candid to make a difference.	How many town-hall meetings have been held?

Table 8.3   Power and shared vision.

Teradyne Corporation, a small Boston start-up in the 1960s, had grown into a $1.5 billion business by 1999. Its success lay in manufacturing high-price-tag equipment for testing circuit boards, telephone networks and semiconductor chips. Although its product

*could cost as much as $2 million a unit, Teradyne dominated its
market.*

*The problem for Teradyne's management was that someone within
the firm had come up with a new, low-cost technology that would sell
at one-quarter of the cost of the old technology. Though not yet as
good as the old, the new technology was extremely promising.
However, with so much vested interest in the old technology management believed that the new product had little chance of surviving
beyond the drawing board. Alex d'Arbeloff, CEO of Teradyne, didn't
accept that line of thinking and decided that a new approach was
called for.*

*D'Arbeloff had served on the boards of several start-ups in the past,
and decided that the new product should be treated as a start-up, not
as a division of an existing business. The product was called 'Integra'
and its leader was Marc Levine. Instead of moving through the divisional budgetary process, Levine was to treat the business as a start-up
and appoint his senior management as its Board of Directors. In this
way, Integra bypassed all the bureaucratic hassles that usually apply to
an R&D project.*

*As a business Integra could recruit top talent from the outside.
Levine felt that 'A divisional project never has the best people on it'. It
was free to develop outside suppliers without risking bad blood with
Teladyne's current network. At the end of the day, it could take
technological risks without having to worry about existing customers.
'A division is always pressed to do the next logical thing – and make it
compatible with the existing line' said Edward Rojas, a Teradyne VP.*

*With d'Arbeloff's patronage Levine was able to originate a whole
new business process for the start-up Integra. His brief was simple 'Be
aggressive on the technology, do something no one else has done.'
Treating this business as a start-up with venture capital helped
d'Arbeloff focus on Levine's efforts to churn out a viable product fast.
Within 18 months of the start-up, Integra had sold 250 units,
generated $150 million in revenues and sailed into profitability.*

As illustrated above, a patron can provide protection and access to
resources. Companies such as 3M and Royal Dutch/Shell try to systemize
this patronage. Since 1996 Shell has tried to change the way mission critical
units get off the ground through the GameChanger programme. The
programme not only allocates resources to jump-start innovative projects,
it also makes sure that the project matures under the patronage of an

appropriate senior executive. An MCL is wise to seek out a patron early in her process.

Patronage also assumes commitment on the part of senior executives. That commitment can be assessed in terms of three criteria:

- Dedication of senior executives to the vision and shared goals of the MCL, and a willingness to invest resources.

- Involvement of senior executives in the form of direct, hands-on feedback. Executives meet often with team members to shape the perception that there is commitment at the top.

- Outcomes (current results and future expansion plans) – they know them and are conscious of potential consequences.

Understanding Product Architecture

As Martin Blake looked over the boardroom table at his two guests, he wondered how this whole thing would turn out. He had heard about their company, Directolite.com, from a friend. They were working on a solution to a problem that had stumped the telecommunications industry to date – how to get sufficient bank width into offices and homes without having to install dedicated optic-fibre line. This had become known as the 'last mile' problem. Blake looked at the two people in front of him, and felt skeptical about their ability to come up with a solution.

The telecommunications industry had invested millions in trying to solve this problem without success. Now he had Jim Lear and Tony Fox telling him that they had the solution. Jim was a computer engineer whose last three jobs had been with dotcoms that had folded unceremoniously. Tony was only 29, but his CV described his experience as '20 years of passionate involvement in the IT world'. He had a hairdo from hell and rings hanging from several parts of his body. He had worked in numerous dotcoms, some had failed, some still existed. As they talked, a surprising thing happened: Blake began to suspect that they had solved the problem. He was going to have to swing a deal with them fast.

Jim, the one without the rings, was saying 'You see, we don't have the big picture like you folks. That's why we need you. You've got the distribution and the network, haven't you?' Tony, the one with the rings, nodded in encouragement.

Jim and Tony lacked more than distribution logistics, they lacked the experience to put this thing together globally. Blake had completed similar assignments before, admittedly none as disruptive as this technology, however. He was beginning to feel that if the project worked, it could turn telecommunications on its head. He would need to work at light speed to put together a proposal to his Board, then a plan to get this product launched.

Nowhere has Internet time been more evident than in the development and launching of new products and services. In the past, companies had a clear development path that looked something like the one in Figure 8.2.

The stages of the model are conveniently sequential. Moreover, managers came to understand the rhythm of successful product launch through years of trial and error. The problem we have seen with companies such as Yahoo, Microsoft and Netscape is that these companies often address many processes simultaneously, sometimes without even knowing what the eventual outcome will look like. Their model looks more like the one in Figure 8.3.

What has happened is that the traditional 'concept freeze' milestone has moved very close to the 'market introduction' milestone. This leaves a great deal of uncertainty as to the precise detail of the final product which, in turn, means that concept and product development have to be tightly linked activities, not sequential ones. In fact, they have to occur simultaneously. In order to achieve this, an MCL has to take into account the ability of the team to manage the joint evolution of technology and its application context. This is called 'technology integration' by Marco Iansiti and Allan McCormack. Its purpose is to capture rich knowledge of the product, user

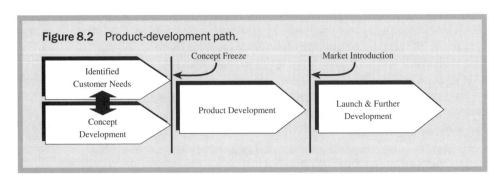

Figure 8.2   Product-development path.

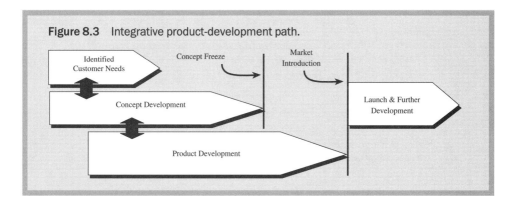

Figure 8.3   Integrative product-development path.

and production environment, and use it to guide product choices. Technology integration is also driven by product architecture.[7]

For a business organization, the vision will always focus on the tangible and intangible products and/or services. The MCL must understand the product or service launch in the context of existing and past products. If she is able to utilize the existing brand architecture, she can shorten the time to market substantially. Brand gurus David Aaker and Erich Joachimsthaler[8] believe that undertaking a brand-architecture audit is essential to understanding where a product or service fits in. Such an audit must include the factors shown in Table 8.4.

Process Architecture

John Raab faced an uphill task in managing the small division of CRC, a large chemical business of which he had assumed control. The industry was in the doldrums, revenues had sagged 15 per cent in the previous year. In addition, the specialized chemical the division man-ufactured seemed up against a bleak future. Staff morale was low and the company was struggling to break even on current contracts, even while fighting for work that would be marginally profitable.

The boom years for chemicals were really over. Price-cutting dominated the intense competition that had become normal in the industry. Because companies needed contracts to cover their overheads, pricing often fell below costs. For CRC, the priorities were to get the contract, then try to break even by maintaining scrupulous efficiency on the job. This was not easy given the motivational state of employees. For years they had been well paid. The company's

Brand portfolio	Includes all the brands and subbrands attached to product-market offerings. A non-trivial task when there are many brands.
Portfolio roles	Taking a systems view to the roles performed by each brand within the portfolio. Believing that brands exist in silos can be dangerous when allocating resources.
Product-Market context roles	Analysing how a set of brands combines to describe an offering in a particular product-market context.
Brand-portfolio structure	Understanding the relationship between different brands, the logic of that structure in terms of grouping, hierarchy and range.
Portfolio graphics	The pattern of visual representations across brands and contexts. Often limited to the logo but sometimes extremely complex.

Table 8.4   Product architecture: brand audit.

relationship with the union had been easy. Now profits had dried up as the company fought for survival. Now, its relationship with the union was difficult.

Raab knew that motivational speeches were unlikely to make much difference. Short-term motivation was not going to solve the problems of the company in the medium term anyway. What he needed was a complete rethink of how the company was operating. He called his senior team together for a weekend retreat.

Raab shared his vision for the future with the team, then got down to work on his view of the current reality. It was obvious that the company's antiquated financial systems were not responsive enough for a business that needed to know on a daily basis how it was doing. The fact that management had a rough idea of the company's financial position at the end of each week, and an accurate one a week after the end of the month, was not good enough for Raab. A business fighting for survival needed to have its pulse taken every day he said, and the management team agreed. Over the rest of the weekend they worked on the concept of a financial reporting system that would give them a perfect view of the business each day.

Things are seldom easy, however. A further 4 months was needed to get the system up and running on a number of pilot sites. A simple *on-site system, it gave supervisors quick access via a terminal to daily performance. With the help of a clerical assistant, data was updated every evening. In the morning meeting, staff would check to see how they were doing. The daily meeting was a simple idea that Raab had picked up on a visit to a local motor plant. Providing a daily forum for focusing on progress and work problems made a lot of sense to Raab. Soon, he had his local managers trained and ready to handle the daily workout session.*

Soon projects starting running at 80% of their projected costs and several of them promised to bring in profits. Raab had managed to tie a reporting system to the motivational system of his employees. Once they became aware of how they were doing on a daily basis, they started working with much greater intensity, bringing down costs, and getting projects to break even. In a sense employees had now taken on the responsibility for survival themselves.

What was important for this business was being able to learn and implement new processes that locked into the financial system. Ford's quality meetings or GE's workout processes are not conceptually complex. In fact, one might say that they are very simple and easy to understand. The hitch comes in trying to implement them. This usually involves unlearning old processes and replacing them with new ones.

Having a process architecture is like deciding to monitor your heart and your running times when training for a marathon. It isn't good enough simply to have a vision of yourself crossing the line. It isn't good enough just to have the motivation to get up each morning and take a 10-kilometre run. You need a monitoring system to check performance on a regular basis. Understanding the system and how it plugs into the organization is important, because poor systems can undermine an MCT.

Most managers are good at focusing on work processes. Because operations have been their main focus for years, few experienced individuals rise through the organization without understanding day-to-day work processes. The problems for them are getting a broader perspective, and learning and implementing new processes. To break through these problems, many companies are implementing approaches such as Six Sigma. Six Sigma is a quest for quality. It micromanages work processes starting at a point outside the company: customers. It asks a simple question, what are the critical success factors for the customer? It then works backwards into the organization to tackle the problem internally.

Leadership processes	Work processes	Behavioural processes	Change processes
Direction-setting processes	Clear goals for operational and strategic performance	Clear approaches to communication, decision making and learning	Rationale for direction and path of change.
Negotiating and selling processes	Agreements and support on resources	Gaining acceptance of approaches to communication, decision making and learning	Convincing others that change is needed and that proposed changes are correct.
Monitoring and control processes	How well are we doing?	Current behaviours match desired approaches?	Critical milestones reached and planned changes implemented?

Table 8.5   Process architecture.

Process architecture describes the weave of formal processes that prescribe and measure inputs and results of the MCT. In its simplest form, the process architecture reflects the weave shown in Table 8.5.

Conclusion

A leader needs to have a broader repertoire. He needs to be the architect of his organization. That will require being able to articulate the overarching vision of the business, as well as to get down to the detail of actually transforming that vision into a reality.

A Concluding Achievement

Much has been written about managing your career in the Internet age. Most new books advise you to keep updating your skills and moving on. Very little is said about closing off your existing job, however. This advice is generally based on the assumption that you will leave a job and never look back. However, the mission critical leader (MCL) does not approach her career as an accumulation of jobs. She considers every career move in the context of an overall career path. Within that context, there are very specific issues that she must address as she enters the achievement and conclusion phase of an assignment.

In each job, she works within a 1,000-day imperative. As that starts to close, in anywhere from 700 to 1,000+ days, the MCL needs to prepare the ground for a successful exit. Nitin Nohria and James Champy[1] have discussed the issue of successfully leaving the job in some detail. They emphasize that a leader must be prepared to exit gracefully, whether or not her tenure has been successful. They mention John Scully at Apple and Mikhael Gorbachev as leaders who did not see the signs and who, as a result, become sources of pessimism within the organization. This unhappy ending can be avoided by preparing for the end of a project from its start. An MCL enters an assignment knowing for certain that she will be leaving the job some time down the road. She does not regard her exit in the same way as we often regard death – 'as though it were no more than an unfounded rumour', in Aldous Huxley's words. She regards it as an event to be factored into the overall job strategy.

In exiting gracefully there are several factors that the MCL needs to tend.

Relationship Capital

During this assignment the MCL has invested in relationship capital and should not contemplate cutting this off. Even when moving to another company or industry the MCL wants to leave relationship capital in a condition which will allow her to call on the network in the future. That means leaving all the stakeholders with an understanding of the reasons for her exit, and information on how to contact her.

Successor

Early on in the assignment the MCL will have identified and nurtured one, if not several, potential successors. She will have given this person or group special guidance and coaching, especially during the second half of the 1,000 days. In grooming this person, the MCL is preparing a viable internal candidate that she can offer the organization on her exit. This will be particularly valuable in organizations where appointments are only made internally.

Finding and nurturing a successor who is completely different from oneself is a challenge. The unsung hero in General Electric's (GE) success over the past 20 years is Reginald Jones, a former CEO (chief executive officer). Jones was a successful CEO. By the time he stepped down, he had built GE into a formidable force. During the last 2 years of his tenure he dedicated himself to developing candidates for his job. Jones was a chain-smoking, golf-playing accountant from Stoke-on-Trent. His selection methods involved tough weekends away with him, playing golf, talking strategy, drinking and basically 'seeing how the candidates got through the test'. This may seem very old world, but it allowed Jones to hand over the reins to Jack Welch and happily leave the stage. The record speaks for itself.

Headhunters and HR departments produce a barrage of tests and reports to back their candidates for leadership. The MCL will certainly consider these numbers in her final decision. But she will ultimately make her decision based on her knowledge and experience of the candidate, the organization and the assignment.

When the organization has been passing through a particularly difficult stage of merger or downsizing, employees start to suffer from survivor syndrome – a strong sense of disorientation and insecurity about their own ongoing tenure. It would be naive to think that the MCL doesn't pass through this as well. Her disorientation and insecurity may manifest itself most clearly in what Michael Watkins and Dan Ciampo[2] call successor syndrome. When this occurs, the MCL begins to react to the insecure environment. She wonders, 'Will there be another assignment for me after this one?' and 'How will I perform in a new position?' At this point, she may begin to withdraw her support from her successors, leaving them afloat without a mentor. She may begin to cling ever more firmly to her own position, believing that nobody could perform the job as well as she. The belief that she is unique and irreplaceable can blindside an MCL near the end of the assignment.

The Measures

The MCL has to ensure that the measures and measurement system used during her tenure reflect the progress of the team. These may be her only surviving legacy of the mission, and they have no value unless people are able to understand and work independently with them after she walks out the door. As we saw in Chapter 4, Al 'Chainsaw' Dunlap made a huge impact on Sunbeam. The share price soared 80 per cent during his *Window of Effectiveness*. However, everything came crashing down after he left the company. Some reports stated that accounting methods used during his tenure were questionable. No leader should find himself in the position of opening a new Window of Effectiveness with claims and counter-claims about his previous tenure ringing in the air. A leader's credibility is seriously damaged when people hear rumours like 'I hear that he was up to some funny business on his last assignment.'

Are Careers Dead?

Fashion would have us believe that the career is dead. If having a career means passing years in mind-numbing organizational incarceration, then we can be grateful that it is dead. Most of us have a secret dread of being trapped into spending our lives in the company of the living dead. Indeed, this dread may have germinated as we watched out parents navigate their work lives. In the not-so-distant past, people accepted their roles as organizational entities. Given the turbulent economic and political histories of the last century, many people felt compelled to take on a sentence of lifetime servitude with a large organization in exchange for the comparative security it offered. The comfort derived from having someone or something looking after you overshadowed the fact that the big organization was a killer of creativity and intellectual stimulation. A sense of obligation drove some people – they felt a duty to family or friends. Others felt loyalty to an organization that provided stability and a predictable career path.

The new market place has changed all that. Companies no longer reciprocate employee loyalty. They restructure almost constantly, though not necessarily out of machiavellian expediency. The reality is that in response to the economy, organizations are being forced to take on new forms. So too careers are taking new shapes to fit the new organizations. Businesses change form rapidly through mergers and acquisitions, downsizing, and even break-up. The negative impact of this on employees is that they are unlikely to serenely sit through entire careers in a single organization. The positive impact is that there are many more opportunities in the market place.

The new economy is also creating virtual, or near-virtual organizations in which the need for solid internal structure gradually disappears. Increasing customization is also flattening structure. The philosophy of business-process reengineering was geared to bringing the organization nearer to the customers. But now customers themselves are starting to drive the structure. Customization has forced stuffy organizations to go outside to customers and to become acquainted with them and their needs.

Career Prisoners

Highly talented people often create prisons for themselves through poor career-management skills. A curriculum vitae that should be affording real satisfaction after 10 or 15 years of hard work may instead seem like a ball and chain. If your career has become more a hindrance than an achievement, the problem may be that you have not paid attention to the depth and scope of the assignments you've undertaken during your career.

Debra Whitely, an old student of mine, had completed her under-graduate work in the UK and Italy. She had followed this with an MBA in France. Since she was also fluent in several languages she naturally gravitated to a job in international marketing with a large consulting firm. And so it was, and the years came to pass. Fifteen years later Whitely had worked in four companies, and now held the senior position of International Marketing Director. At this point, she wanted to break out and do something different. However, her CV bound her as squarely to marketing as if she were chained to a wall. She could only move in a limited way in her career search, but she was eventually yanked back into an international marketing function. Worse, her income had reached such a high level that it became impossible for any prospective employer to see Whitely doing anything different for the same cash.

To most people her job was exciting. She travelled to some of the most exotic spots on the globe, was highly paid, kept an apartment in the city and a house down on the coast. But that's not how Whitely saw it. She felt the future prospects were mostly limited to what had gone before, that life had become boring and lacked passion. The wheels were fast coming off and though she knew it, she couldn't read the signs. Like a prisoner, she had lost control of her most limited resource: time. She had a young family, which put tremendous pressure on her because she felt herself growing increasingly remote from family life. In fact, she seemed incapable of applying to her private life the criteria she used at work. At home she struggled with simple things like problem definition, prioritization and resolution.

There are a lot of people like Whitely still around. They are talented and hard working. They believe that if they throw all their efforts into the job they're currently doing, they will reap the pay-off later on. They are mistaken. In a modern society where there was a balance in the interrelationship of service and trust, such conviction was well placed. But we have ceased to believe in the omni-benevolence of organizations in post-modern society. We know that organizations no longer retain responsibility for the careers of the individuals who work for them. Organization and career have now been separated without much thought as to where the responsibility for individual career management lies. Moreover, private and business life have completely subsumed each other – there is no separation between the two. Whitely had truly imprisoned herself; she could only break out through drastic action. She explored the idea of starting her own business, but decided that she didn't have the resources. Eventually, she took on a new assignment unrelated to international marketing at a reduced salary. This position gave her the flexibility to balance her life, but at the cost of an income that had taken years to achieve. The sacrifices and compromises Whitely made were really the result of not managing her career in the earlier years.

Career Management

Now that organizations are taking a back seat in the career-development process, individuals must take full responsibility for their own career management. For an MCL, this means formulating a career strategy that enables her career to take shape over time. In hindsight, a career should be seen as a series of loosely interrelated work activities, undertaken with an overriding objective in mind. Ideally, it will be viewed with a sense of satisfaction. A career strategy sets the MCL on the path to ultimately achieving that sense of satisfaction.

Personal Mission

One of the primary elements of permanence for an MCL should be an overall personal mission. A mission is the glue that holds and shapes the varied succession of assignments together as a career. Without personal mission, a career has little meaning. A career mission is a source of motivation and eventually satisfaction; it is part of getting a life.

A manager who does not track meaning in his assignment, who does not have a clear personal mission can lose his bearings in the frenetic corporate dealings of the new market place. José Jiménez is a good example of this. After deregulation of the economy in Spain, most banks had been involved in a succession of mergers that essentially rationalized the whole sector. During that time, I visited José Jiménez, a senior manager in one of the largest banks. He had spent most of his professional life working for two banks in the sector and had risen to seniority in his current job at the second bank. He had been devastated by a recent takeover of the bank (euphemistically called a merger) that had left him without a job. Though his separation package left him fairly well off, he felt disappointed by the organization and let down by colleagues who had failed to protect him or find him a new role. His plans were unclear, though he saw himself forced into self-employment, probably in consultancy.

I felt sympathetic toward Jiménez, but also believed that he had made some basic mistakes. First, he allowed the bank to manage his career. He had assumed, wrongly as it turned out, that his jobs would continue undisturbed until his retirement. Instead, he became a victim of waning career development and promotion systems. In the new economy, the tacit understanding in a job situation is that the MCL will take full responsibility for his own competitiveness, as well as the team's and, ultimately, the business's. In return, the company offers, not the dependence relationship of previous years, but rather the power of employability. Employability means being able to operate as a free agent in the market place but, by the same token, having to carry the responsibility for doing so.

Jiménez did not apply mission critical values to his career. His jobs had little interrelationship, and, as a result, his career had little shape. He did not think in terms of the 1,000-day imperative; therefore, he was not used to opening and closing assignments in a controlled way. Needless to say, he was inadequately prepared for dealing with this highly emotional change. If Jiménez had been able to view his career mission as separate from his existing job, he would not have been as emotionally devastated by the closure of this job assignment.

Chris Bartlett of Harvard believes that when an MCL with her own focused mission joins a company such as McKinsey, 3i or Intel – companies that foster strong missions – she positions herself in a community of purpose in which she can share knowledge and other resources. She does so without precise knowledge of how she will benefit, but confident of collective gain. She, in turn, contributes to the collective company mission. When she exits, she takes stock of the knowledge and experience she's gained with as much diligence as she tallies the stock options or separation benefits that she has earned. Then she moves on to the next assignment, realigning her mission as she goes.

Staying Too Long

Jiménez had made another basic mistake. He had not given thought to a message buried within the statistics of executive tenure: approximately 50 per cent of senior executives will be out of their jobs within 5 years.[3] The risk of failure for a manager climbs precipitously in the second 1,000-day period. Even if an executive survives the first 1,000 days more or less in one piece, he may find that his survival is due more to woolly performance measures within the organization than to performance itself. The second 1,000-day period will reveal a more complete picture of achievements and shortcomings. Jiménez worked for a bank with inadequate result measurements. At lower levels in management, Jiménez had managed to blur performance with activity and involvement. Higher up he ran into trouble as he simply became more exposed to direct scrutiny.

Taking on or hoping to take on a second term is fraught with danger. Some indicators of this are shown in Table 9.1.

Business mission/strategy drift	Unlikelihood of getting it clearly focused again, especially if you haven't got it right the first time.
Career drift	A second term is an action replay often seen as an attempt to make up for things not done. This usually fails. Unless you are Jack Welch, you are probably going to have some difficulty rejuvenating yourself.
Frustrated subordinates	Failure to identify successor.
Reduced learning	Ability to see learning opportunities declining.
Innovation droop	Lack of new ideas, especially if the first wave worked.
Stale social architecture	Ritualistic behaviours even if membership changes – people start to know what the boss wants.

Table 9.1   Dangers of staying too long.

Career Strategy

Being an MCL means forming some ideas of how to develop a credible track record. A history of wise choice of assignments and appropriate departure does not alone guarantee success. Conversely, being passionately involved in a project that fails shouldn't mean the end of opportunities, provided one can recover, regroup and emerge wiser from the experience. In the context of the 1,000-day imperative, a track record should be viewed in its entirety, successes and failures balanced against reflective consideration of what value was carried forward from an experience.

Each mission critical assignment forms a single *tessera* of the mosaic that makes up a career. If you look closely at a mosaic you will find it is made up of hundreds, sometimes thousands, of *tesserae*. Those little blocks of different colours combine to form a whole image. The *tesserae* will be grouped together by colour and form to give a certain shape or impression, much as assignments are grouped together at different phases of the MCL's personal development, and add to the overall image of a fulfilled satisfying career.

Career Scaffolding

To create such a mosaic requires more than just a personal mission. It requires a conscious development of a career scaffold. Imagine that your career mosaic is being constructed on the wall of a building that you admire. Your alma mater, your old school or even your home. The wall is all of 20 metres high. Initially you will be able to cluster groups of tesserae near the base of the wall but eventually you are going to have to erect a scaffolding which will allow you to get up to the 10-metre mark and then the 20-metre mark. When you are working on the scaffolding you will be fairly high up, but by this time the image will be a lot clearer because you have completed the basic foundations of the mosaic. Each day you will come to work and hopefully wonder at the beauty of the lower sections of the mosaic before climbing up from level to level on the scaffolding to work on the current section.

A career scaffold serves several purposes. Once the pattern becomes clearer at a lower level the MCL erects another slightly higher level and starts work based on the experience and learning at the previous level. Reaching higher levels is not possible without a reflection on what has gone before. More importantly, being able to establish a level of abstraction makes going higher easier. Often what we learn from an experience is fairly mundane and obvious unless we can abstract it and give that learning broader application. Like the story of the electrical engineer who, when asked at his retirement party what he had learnt from his long career in electricity, replied 'Don't work on electrical equipment with your hands wet.' Having gained the experience, the MCL moves learning to a conceptual level.

Developing an impressive track record of mission critical projects is only meaningful if a leader is able to learn from her experiences. As Larry Huston, Director of Innovation and Knowledge at Procter & Gamble says, 'High performance innovators are "high bandwidth" people. They know a lot about many different areas. They know the literature, they know the cutting edge and build diaries and mechanisms to stay in touch. They are knowledge driven, not technique and trick driven. They believe that knowledge drives creativity, that creativity without knowledge is fantasy.'[4] What most HR managers forget when looking at curriculum vitae is that a historical perspective is a reasonable perspective, but not necessarily a good indicator of future behaviour. A curriculum vitae is only good if it can demonstrate that the person has an ability to make serendipitous connections between learnt experiences.

Brilliant ideas do not just happen; they are a result of long, conscious and subconscious reflection on problems. This is where career scaffolding comes in. A career scaffold allows an iterative reflective process that abstracts tangible hands-on experience in order to create knowledge that is applicable to future activity. This is knowledge creation at its softest, most implicit or intangible. It can make the difference between someone who moves from experience to incomprehensible experience and someone who carries knowledge and wisdom away from every experience. Once he has acquired experience an MCL must search for serendipitous connections between different levels of its scaffolding.

An MCL can trawl through meaningful constructs with the possibility of new discoveries only if learning is not a passive unemotional process for him. People often pay lip-service to the adage 'We learn from our mistakes.' In fact, most of us are unable to truly learn from our mistakes unless we (1) apply ourselves to learning from the experience, or (2) make a mistake so huge that learning becomes blatantly obvious. When driving at full speed, you only need to put the gears into reverse once to know that this is not a wise practice.

Learning and Knowledge Acquisition

Scratch the surface in many successful companies and you will find arrogance, and a belief that there is nothing new to be learnt, that the organization has all the knowledge it needs. This kind of thinking can lead to expensive mistakes. It might be why Novell's CEO Raymond

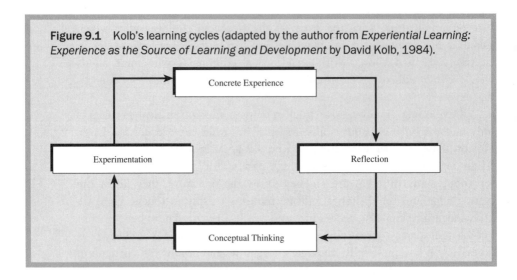

Figure 9.1   Kolb's learning cycles (adapted by the author from *Experiential Learning: Experience as the Source of Learning and Development* by David Kolb, 1984).

Noorda decided to pay $1.4 billion for WordPerfect, then allow his management to run roughshod over WordPerfect's culture and management, resulting in a haemorrhaging of managerial and technical talent. In less than 1,000 days Noorda offloaded WordPerfect for $124 million – 10 per cent of its original price.[5]

Sumantra Ghoshal and Chris Bartlett at Harvard say that when the solution to a recurring problem is 'try harder' there is usually something wrong, not with the execution, but with the terms of the solution. Applying attention may not be sufficient to learn from experience. As Kolb has shown (Figure 9.1), learning from experience is not a natural process for many people. Some people are able to reflect on concrete experience, others learn from abstract concepts.

Each person actually develops her own learning style. Some styles will include the ability to reflect and learn from an experience of failure. Kolb's learning cycles demonstrate that learning is really a cyclical process. The experience occurs, then is followed by a reflection phase. This includes the process of formulating abstract concepts, then experimenting with these concepts. Of course, personal viewpoint tends to emphasize particular aspects. It is unusual for someone to be strong in all aspects.

The search for a new business model is based on a process of learning and knowledge acquisition. By systematically moving through a process one is likely to hit on serendipitous connections that give insights into new opportunities.

Looking back is only one part of the story; it's going forward to the next assignment that is the second part, and the greater challenge. Here the MCL applies the learning of the past. Interestingly, the larger the track record, the more learning the individual brings, the more difficult it becomes to think about the next assignment. Reaching a certain level in the organization brings with it increased complexity of assignment.

The Stretched Assignment Equals Burn-out

Global companies are stretching the capabilities of their managers to unprecedented lengths in order to get value-added return. How long can the average general manager last in such a capacity? And when he has been used up, will anyone want to take his place?

When Ken Dovey and I started researching whether MCLs were being pushed to a point of burn-out back in 1999, we found little to be optimistic about. We posed the following questions: Would the economy of the new millennium create, on the one hand, a mature group of managers who were disillusioned about business and who wanted out as soon as possible? On the other, would it create a young talented group who no longer wanted to work for the big organization? The results of this discussion would obviously have implications for the development of MCLs.

We found general managers whose jobs had been stretched to such an extent that they faced serious threat of burn-out. They were constantly on the move, spending one or two days in the office and the rest on an airplane, moving from location to location. Short-term pressure was as ubiquitous as their collective optimism in the belief that things would come right. For many of them, accolades received in the past for successful assignments had convinced them of their own invincibility. Burn-out manifested itself in different ways: serious disorientation at times, irritability, personal-relationship disruption and so on. Many saw the complications of present assignments as short-term phenomena though there was little indication from the organization that this was the case.

For years the traditional route into senior management, at a company we shall call, Hitech Cars in Germany, had been through sales, marketing and for some general management of a country division. Many of the company's most successful managers had come that route, taking 20 years or more to climb into the top levels of the organization. In this respect, Hitech had always been a conservative organization though not terribly different from its competitors, Ford, General Motors (GM) and Volkswagen.

Jürgen Wind fitted the mould of the average general manager. Wind had initially been exposed to brand management working for a competitor. He had moved to Hitech in the late 1970s. There, he had climbed through several marketing and sales positions including a stint in head office. Currently, he served as General Manager of Hitech's Middle East operation where he was entirely responsible for business in the region. His charge included marketing, distribution, support and administration in fifteen different centres.

By the late 1990s things were changing. Hitech's results lagged behind its competitors. Its core business was fuzzy. Organizationally, it had become unwieldy as the sectors rationalized along global lines. Management decided to act fast. The parts division was spun off into a separate entity while global-business divisions were formed to deal with increasing competitive pressure. Jürgen Wind was not left untouched in the rapid change process. As global divisions based on product lines were formed, each country's general manager had a more ambiguous role. In so far as legislation in the Middle East differed from Germany, there would always be a need for a country manager, but the role had become very limited. The decision was taken to give Wind responsibility for the business in Europe and Africa – thus forming an EMEA structure – Europe, Middle East and Africa.

Suddenly Wind found himself with an organization that covered half the world in alien markets that promised much but were extremely different. Hitech's volumes were comparable with its two main rivals, but, like them, had still shown no substantial return for its efforts. These companies were in for the long term but most of them were haemorrhaging cash.

Wind's success in the Middle East had been based on in-depth knowledge of the products and markets. He had developed an executive cadre that handled the day-to-day running of the business. He had then positioned himself so that he could become involved in any part of the business immediately if there was a need for his involvement. His overarching role was to form the strategy of the business and make sure the various divisions were moving in the right direction.

Now he found himself building up air miles as he moved from one centre to the next. Many of his executive cadre were now assigned to far-flung destinations – Hong Kong, Hamburg and Istanbul. He found himself unable to focus on any one issue long enough to deal with it efficiently. His own performance fell. The fact that the team below him moved around as quickly and often as he did only added to his problems. Senior management at Hitech sympathized, but most of them privately thought that Wind was not up to the job. Of course, no one stopped to consider that they had never been dealt an assignment as broad as Wind's.

The story of Jürgen Wind is not unusual. Competent general managers are being stretched as a matter of course in new flat global businesses. Many of them are long-time loyal retainers whose careers have been built within these organizations. Senior management depends on their loyalty to get the job done. But loyalty is rapidly waning as a motivating factor. Downsizing in the 1990s ensured that there was only a small group of people who remained loyal to the business. There is little likelihood of that stock being replenished. Some companies – Motorola, for instance – have become so alarmed by loss of faith in the organization that they have developed a checklist to guide individual behaviour (see textbox).

Motorola's Individual Dignity Entitlement

- Do you have a substantive, meaningful job that contributes to the success of Motorola?

- Do you know the on-the-job behaviours and have the knowledge base to be successful?

- Has the training been identified and been made available to continuously upgrade your skills?

- Do you have a personal career plan, and is it exciting, achievable and being acted on?

- Do you receive candid, positive or negative, feedback at least every 30 days that is helpful in improving or achieving your personal career plan?

- Is there appropriate sensitivity to your personal circumstances, gender and/or cultural heritage so that issues do not detract from your personal career plan?

- 1999 Sales: $30.9 billion
  1-Year Sales Growth: 5.2%

- Website Address: http://www.mot.com

- Stock Performance August 1998–August 2000

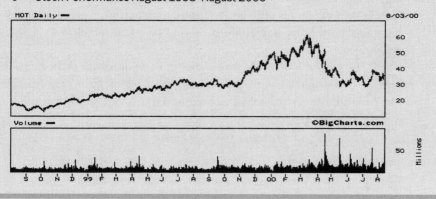

Traditional-economy career stories like these have become more and more familiar. The new economy creates constant change, a rolling over of every competency every 1,000 days or less. 'My résumé is a disaster. Eleven companies in 25 years ... but I have had to learn to live with a murky business identity,' says successful 'virtual CEO' Randy Komisar.[6] Komisar has kept moving after each assignment and built strong marketable knowledge. In mission critical organizations, such CVs will become the norm. Organizations and CVs will move in the same direction.

Exit Strategies

The difference between Jürgen Wind and Randy Komisar is the way they look at the end of an assignment. With the shorter duration of leadership tenure, articulating an exit strategy, however vague that might be, becomes necessary for leaving the job as succinctly as possible. Wind never thinks along these lines, Komisar always does. Acknowledging that the assignment at hand is relatively short lived and that there is an assignment after it just makes sense. Burying your head in the sand and relying on the organization to look after you is part of the old-economy routine – and it's no longer working.

When Bernard Merric took over at HP's BCD division it looked like there was very little to be done. The division had worldwide responsibility for large-format printers and had been increasing revenues by something like 25 per cent for some years. *'Some people thought I would take my mountain bike and go up into the mountains, but a job like this is not like that,'* he says, *'there is always something to do, problems to be solved, strategy to be redefined.'*

The division's earlier success had created cohesion within a high-performance team. Merric had his work cut out for him in getting the team back to basics and focused on new objectives. Merric's main focus during his tenure was on market orientation, continued product innovation, and time-to-market issues. By day 500, he was seeing the results he was looking for. He then swung his attention to identifying, nurturing and empowering a successor, so that by day 1,000 he would be transitioning out to his next assignment.

'The second half of my tenure was to make sure that there was a team in place that would ensure the competitiveness and viability of the business.' Merric exited from the job and became HP's Vice-President for Retailer Relations in the Optics Group.

Successful exit strategies work, is illustrated by the points in Table 9.2.

The Next Assignment

One thing that Whitely, José Jiménez, Randy Komisar and Jürgen Wind have in common is the problem of deciding on the next assignment. Each

Results orientation	They create an appropriate tension for closure on a period and assignment.
Successor orientated	They focus on succession.
People development	Employees feel there is room for them (space is being made).
Future orientation	They allow the MCL to leave the business in good condition and ready for a successor.
Career strategy	They keep the MCL moving.
Rejuvenation	They provide opportunities for reevaluation and adding value to personal worth.

Table 9.2   The positive side of exit strategies.

one wants to make the right decision, but is faced with a complex set of criteria that all MCLs face in this situation:

- **Personal mission** – If you look beyond the actual assignment, does it move in the right direction or is it simply locked in a cul-de-sac of wait and see. Komisar might simply wait for something to turn up, while Wind would probably search hard for something suitable.

- **Challenge and learning** – is there sufficient substance in this assignment to provide stretch room for the manager. Will it exploit accumulated knowledge, and ensure personal growth? As Jack Welch says, 'The new psychological contract is that jobs at GE are the best in the world for people who are willing to compete.'

- **Lifestyle and values** – is this where I/we want to live and spend our leisure hours? Does the job mesh with our personal values? Edgar Schein designed a questionnaire some years ago that provided a perspective on career anchors. Career anchors are basically the set of values that peg you to careers – things like a passion for technology, your need for security or desire to be a general manager. Over the past decade, the career anchors of my MBA students at IESE have been transforming into lifestyle anchors. Ten years ago, the anchor biased towards general management, but, today, people are more conscious of leading a well-rounded life. What I see is that they have as much passion and intensity for their work, but they want to ensure that they work in the place they want to live with and with people with whom they like to spend time.

- **Remuneration** – what is the package; are there incentives and what about having to bail out if someone you don't get on with acquires the business? Money is important, but being offered less shouldn't prevent one from taking on an assignment which has long-term benefits in learning and skills expansion.

- **Mission critical team** – are there sufficiently talented people in there for you to go in alone or are you going to take some of your cohorts with you. What are the ethical issues involved here? What happens if you leave your previous assignment seriously debilitated by poaching your old team?

- **Resources** – does the assignment require operating on such limited resources that the chances of success are significantly reduced? Obviously, many organizations are strapped for resources, which is why they are looking for an MCL. They hope she will be able to raise resources. The MCL needs to weigh up the existing potential resources and decide on how realistic expectations are.

The Hunted Head

Leaving career management in the hands of headhunters may be tempting. Headhunters or executive-search consultants play an ever-increasing role in the career-management process as companies step back from that responsibility. In fact, as more and more companies turn to headhunters to find suitable leadership material, the MCL may begin to develop relationships with several headhunters. Looking at a new assignment through the eyes of a more objective appraiser is always helpful. The MCL must ensure that, in taking on a relationship, she does not cede control or responsibility for personal development.

Headhunting

Objectively, how does the organization recruit people, then retain them through the development process until they reach general management or MCL level? Recruitment and retention are being pursued by new-economy businesses through a combination of headhunting and financial incentive. The difficulty of attracting executive talent ranks high on most CEOs' problem lists. Getting the best and the brightest on the payroll can turn into a major crisis for companies. As new-economy businesses have come up against problems – such as distribution logistics or IT management – they have turned to poaching capable people from established organizations. Many of the candidates can bring a dozen years or more of experience in a functional area to the poacher. Accordingly, they lure them away with enormous incentives – sign-on fees, stock options or restrictions and production bonuses are commonplace. In fact they are often remunerated beyond their wildest dreams.

The only ones caught unawares by this shift are the organizations whence they come. Amazon set out specifically to headhunt senior executives from Wal-Mart. Not surprisingly, Wal-mart retaliated legally to prevent the exodus of distribution executives on the basis that Amazon had stolen not only personnel, but years and years of development capital.

There is no doubt that part of the ongoing change in organization involves more and more outsourcing of HR duties. This often involves creating a close relationship with a headhunter who will then take charge of company recruitment. As a matter of course, many fast-growing companies nurture strategic relationships with several headhunters. Without these relationships, such companies would never be able to satisfy their executive needs.

The headhunting industry has grown exponentially as the 1,000-day imperative takes hold. According to Hunt-Scalon Advisors, surveyors of the industry, total revenues for the industry were an enormous $8.3 billion in 1999, up from $3 billion in 1993. If ever there was an indicator of the growth levels of mobility, it is this statistic.

Using the services of headhunters has several implications for the business:

- To enter the fray – and headhunt. Sometimes the issue is not *whether* to headhunt, but how best to manage it. What has made entering the fray more complex is the fact that in the new economy headhunters are changing their approach. They are joining forces with venture-capital managers. In this process they put good ideas together with finance and good people. 'Now having the attention of a first-rate recruiter is as critical to making a company successful as good technology is,' says Kathryn Gould, who moved from old-style headhunting into venture capital in Silicon Valley.[7]

- To develop insider-promotion policies – this can damage employee loyalty and create unhappiness within.

- To absorb the higher costs – headhunters take time, anything up to 6 months and they cost something like one-third of a first-year salary.

- To deal with disparity between newcomer and old-timer salaries – sign-on and incentive bonuses can effectively raise salaries exorbitantly.

- To avoid retaliation from the scalped organization – most headhunters operate under a code of conduct that keeps recently placed employees off limits for anything up to 2 years. It usually bars client employees from being tapped in searches performed for a competitor.

- To keep company secrets from moving.

The Pressure for Creative Destruction

Sixty years ago Joseph Schumpeter came up with the idea of 'creative destruction', the economic process of constant innovation that destroys old functions while introducing the new.[8] The 1,000-day imperative requires that MCLs submit themselves to this same process, effectively destroying and recreating themselves through constant new knowledge acquisition and through retraining.

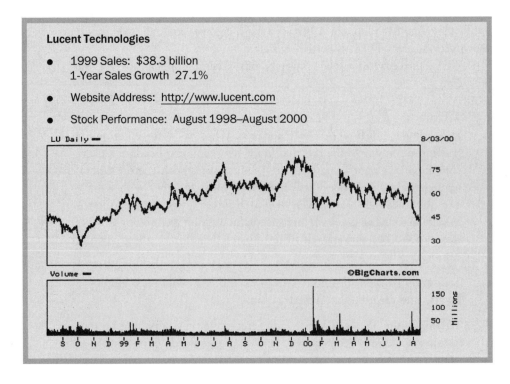

Lucent Technologies

- 1999 Sales: $38.3 billion
  1-Year Sales Growth 27.1%

- Website Address: http://www.lucent.com

- Stock Performance: August 1998–August 2000

Although under the present circumstances it seems counterintuitive, some organizations are still investing heavily in people in lower levels of the organization in order to keep them highly competitive, employable and loyal. Surveys show best practice companies investing an expected 14 days of training each year at an average cost of $7,300 per employee.[9] For instance, Lucent Technologies Inc. believe in almost non-stop training for its people. Apart from mentoring programmes, employees are offered a plethora of external courses including degree courses for further development. Says one employee, 'These opportunities tell me that there's a future for me at Lucent ... my motivation level is higher; I feel more confident and secure knowing that I'm investing in myself ... and Lucent gets a person with more skills, who's very driven and who can be more valuable to the company.'

What does this indicate? For one thing, that the HR departments themselves are confused by the trend to the new economy. The role of HR, and training and development in particular, has gone through some rapid transformations recently. In the movement towards corporate universities, training resources have been concentrated. The idea is that the corporate university nurtures and guards the specialised knowledge and skills that provide competitive advantage. The 'university' can outsource all other training needs to service providers. Unfortunately, the service provider may often provide the specialized knowledge and skills, while the 'university' provides mundane skills training. Confusion over appropriate functions will persist for some time, however, until 'universities' themselves become mission critical. However, many organizations are outsourcing the whole function of development on the basis that they are unlikely to improve on the plethora of programmes offered in the market place.

Conclusion

This chapter started with the closing of an MCL's assignment. The close was also the beginning of a new assignment. For that reason the MCL has to close each assignment as positively as possible. She has to leave relationship capital, measures and a successor in place, in order to walk away from the job. An MCL must be able to do this at least ten times in a career. We looked at people like Randy Komisar, the 'Virtual CEO', who worked about eleven assignments in 24 years. By that time, of course, the MCL is looking back on a substantial career. Careers are currently shape-shifting as fast as organizations. The MCL needs to think accordingly. Using the mosaic metaphor, a career that develops in a variety of different areas becomes more successful over time as its mission and character become clearer.

Concluding Observations

It is no coincidence that an architectural metaphor is used in this book. Between the dream of what could be achieved and the achievable, the mission critical leader (MCL) works as the architect who builds a bridge connecting the present to the future. That bridge is made up of practical step-by-step stages that lead to recognized excellence. Like the great architects Michelangelo and Antoni Gaudi, the MCL will participate in only one stage of the total construction. That stage is limited to a 1,000-day period. Accepting that as a premise of the mission critical leadership model throws leadership itself into a different light.

This book does not claim to be a panacea for all the problems a leader can encounter. Clearly, there are issues that remain unresearched, messy and unresolved. These become a challenge, not only for researchers, but for managers taking on mission critical leadership:

1. The ongoing process of globalization and increasing competitiveness supports the idea that all organizations will eventually go mission critical. What happens, then, to businesses that do not speed up? In Europe there are many medium-sized businesses that have chosen to ignore the new economy – can they survive? Their positions are tenuous, because they choose not to follow guidelines that are rapidly becoming *de rigueur*. For instance, MCLs with established track records are likely to gravitate to those companies that currently offer substantial financial rewards. Resultantly, the strong get stronger and the weak start to disappear. As an example, in Catalonia, a region which has been very prosperous in European terms, family businesses have always dominated. As many of those businesses struggle with new-economy competitors, strong family control may be crippling their competitive abilities – they neither attract nor hold any MCLs.

2. As MCLs in middle-management positions continue to take responsibility for the delivery of the business mission and model, there is a change in the balance of power. MCLs are becoming more like athletes or movie stars. Their ability to turn a division fast gives them tremendous negotiating power. This shift was triggered by

the break in the old-economy tacit employer–employee contract which previously held leaders in a master–servant relationship. The swing continues under the process of continued globalization. This has spawned a set of individuals who bear professional allegiance to no one other than themselves. If a mission critical leader and team have no long-term commitment to the organization, then what are the prospects of organizations in their present form existing much longer?

3   Applying mission critical-leadership principles to managers already well into their 1,000-day tenure but not yet showing anticipated results raises a serious problem. Do they attempt to start again in the present assignment along the lines suggested by Gabarro and Watkins (Ciampa and Watkins 1999), or do they cut their losses and move to another assignment? This problem is not easily resolved. Given all the indications that tenure will still be restricted to 1,000 days, choosing a path of perseverance is inherently risky. A leader is very likely to get bogged down, underachieve and exit with little to show for it. Yet, if the leader exits early he may have to field accusations that he lacks persistence. If, in addition, he has put no successor in place, he definitely will not enjoy a graceful exit. The very idea of 'long term' is anathema in the new economy. The pressure is on MCLs to deliver in the short term. However, brownie points are awarded to leaders who master the art of balancing short-term demand with bottom-line results to produce long-term sustainability for the business. The rough rule of thumb is to leave a business in a condition in which a successor can prosper and do better than oneself. How do we reward those MCLs who are good at this? EVA (economic value added) tries to cover this but assumes continued employment in the organization. Once you walk away you lose your 'banked' bonus.

4   As an MCL builds and develops a strong mission critical team (MCT) members will feel a strong allegiance to the leader rather than to the organization. When exiting from an assignment, the MCL runs into serious ethical problems if tempted to take the team with him. A rush of resignations that large can seriously undermine the assignment and the business itself. This is a long-term objection yet to be measured.

5   The long, long-term project in an MCL's life is his career. Responding to the swing from paternal-biased tacit contracts, MCLs have to manage their own careers. What are the limits to this idea, in view of demographic trends that show people living longer than ever before? Is the prospect of completing mission critical assignments until the age of 60 or 70 all that attractive? Or

do MCLs move to different arenas – non-profit, non-business assignments where they can apply their abilities indefinitely and constructively?

6   Having given up many non-mission critical functions, do human-resource (HR) managers have a future in the new economy? How, beyond assisting in the recruitment of MCLs, can HR management guide an organization to provide ongoing, challenging assignments for its employees? Ongoing learning remains under the umbrella of the organization. To wield influence in that area, HR must have upward influence to the TMT (top-management team) and to MCLs themselves. That would suggest that the HR function will have to become mission critical in order to survive.

This book addresses companies in which the potential for change exists. I am constantly reminded that not all organizations are able to adopt mission critical leadership because they have become too slow, rigid and generally calcified to take on anything so dramatic. Hopefully, these organizations will become the real challenge for future MCLs. The survival of some of our major institutions are threatened if they don't.

Notes

Chapter 1: Introduction to Mission Critical Leadership

1   Jupiter Communications, 'Online Banking Penetration in Europe, Total Accounts, 1999–2003,' January 2000.

2   Online Banking–Big Opportunity and Big Risk,' *Deutschebank Alex. Brown Report* 3 January 2000.

3   James O'Toole, *Leadership A to Z: A Guide For the Appropriately Ambitious* (San Francisco, CA: Jossey-Bass Publishers, 1999).

4   'Comstellar Launches With Innovative Business Model and Premier Management Team; Architects of Tomorrow's Communication Technologies,' *PR Newswire Europe Limited* 11 July 2000.

5   Quentin Hardy, 'Balancing the Need for Speed With a Respect for HP's Past,' *Forbes Magazine* 13 December 1999.

6   Louise Kehoe, 'The Americas: Reinventing Company of Inventors,' *Financial Times (London)* 16 November 1999.

7   See, for example: John Kotter and James Heskett, *Corporate Culture and Performance.* (New York: Free Press, 1992); John Kotter, *The General Managers.* (New York: Free Press, 1982); and John Kotter, *Leading Change* (Boston, MA: Harvard Business School Press, 1996).

8   Peter Sinton 'Icons of Invention; Business Leaders See Bright Future for the Region,' *The San Francisco Chronicle* 29 December 1999.

9   Michael Cusumano and David Yoffie, *Competing on Internet Time: Lessons From Netscape and Its Battle With Microsoft* (New York: Free Press, 1998).

10   Jeff Bailey, 'Second Helping: Star Rescuers Take on Waste Management and End Up Tarnished – Trio's First Effort to Salvage Ailing Trash Giant Flops; Now, They Try Again – Neglected Books, an III CEO,' *The Wall Street Journal* 29 February 2000.

11   Peter DeLisi, 'A Modern-Day Tragedy: The Digital Equipment Story,' *Journal of Management Inquiry* June 1998.

12   Chester Barnard, *The Functions of the Executive* (Cambridge, MA: Harvard University Press, 1968).

13   'Changing of the Guard,' *Chain Store Age* March 2000.

14   Dean Foust, David Rocks and Mark L. Clifford, 'Is Douglas Daft the Real Thing?' *Business Week* 20 December 1999.

15   Jon Ashworth, 'Airline Crews May Live to Miss Ayling,' *The Times (London)* 26 April 2000.

Chapter 2: Mission Critical Leadership in Action

1   John Gabarro, 'When a New Manager Takes Charge,' *Harvard Business Review* May/June 1985.
2   Dan Ciampa, and Michael Watkins, *Right From the Start* (Boston, MA: Harvard Business School Press, 1999).
3   Peter Ferdinand Drucker, *Management Challenges for the 21st Century* (New York: HarperBusiness, 1999).
4   Jane Robins, 'Media: the First 100 Days of Greg Dyke,' *The Independent (London)* 11 July 2000.
5   Opp. cit.
6   Alex Berenson, 'In Silicon Valley, Loyalty Means Paying a High Price; Cultural Strengths Help Offset Loss of Paper Wealth,' *The New York Times* 28 May 2000.
7   Alessandra Galloni, 'UK: Hunt for BA Boss Takes Off This Week,' *Reuters English News Services* 13 March 2000.
8   Alessandra Galloni, 'UK: Newsmaker-BA's Ayling – Right Strategy, Wrong Man?' *Reuters English News Service* 10 March 2000.
9   Christopher Bartlett and Ashish Nanda, 'Intel Corp.: Leveraging Capabilities for Strategic Renewal,' *Harvard Business School Case No. 394141* 9 March 1994.

Chapter 3: Reassessment and Alignment of the Business Models

1   'Comstellar Launches with Innovative Business Model and Premier Management Team; Architects of Tomorrow's Communication Technologies,' *PR Newswire Europe Limited* 11 July 2000.
2   Michael Lewis, *The New New Thing: A Silicon Valley Story* (New York: W. W. Norton, 2000).
3   *Chemical Market Reporter* (Schell Publishing Company, 17 April 2000).
4   Pankaj Ghemawat, David Collis, Gary Pisano and Jan Rivkin, *Strategy and the Business Landscape: Text and Cases* (Reading, MA: Addison-Wesley, 1999); James Davis and Barry Cushing, *Accounting Information Systems: A Book of Readings with Cases* (Reading, MA: Addison-Wesley, 1980); Robert Kaplan and Anthony Atkinson, *Advanced Management Accounting.* (Upper Saddle River, NJ: Prentice Hall, 1998).
5   Michael Porter, *Competitive Advantage: Creating and Sustaining Superior Performance* (New York: Free Press, 1985).
6   Martin Puris, *Comeback: How Seven Straight-Shooting CEOs Turned Around Troubled Companies* (New York: Times Business, 1999).

Chapter 4: Relationship Capital

1   Carl Shapiro and Hal Varian, *Information Rules: A Strategic Guide to the Network Economy* (Boston, MA: Harvard Business School Press, 1999).
2   Jeffrey Pfeffer and Robert Sutton, *The Knowing-Doing Gap: How Smart*

Companies Turn Knowledge into Action (Boston, MA: Harvard Business School Press, 2000).

3   Carl Shapiro and Hal Varian, *Information Rules.*

4   Peter Ferdinand Drucker, *Management Challenges for the 21st Century* (New York: HarperBusiness, 1999).

5   Nitin Nohria and Sumantra Ghoshal, *The Differentiated Network* (San Francisco, CA: Jossey-Bass, 1997).

Chapter 5: Winning Teams

1   Margot Cairnes, *Approaching the Corporate Heart: Breaking Through to New Horizons of Personal and Professional Success* (Sydney: Simon & Schuster, 1998).

2   Jon Katzenbach, *Teams at the Top: Unleashing the Potential of Both Teams and Individual Leaders* (Boston, MA: Harvard Business School Press, 1998).

3   David Pottruck and Terry Pearce, *Clicks and Mortar: Passion-Driven Growth in an Internet-Driven World* (San Francisco: Jossey-Bass Publishers, 2000).

4   Ibid.

5   Louisa Wah, 'Creating an Outstanding Leadership Team,' *Management Review* February 2000.

6   Daniel Goleman, 'What Makes a Leader?' *Harvard Business Review* November/December 1998.

7   Darren McCabe and David Knights, '"What Happens when the Phone Goes Wild?": Staff, Stress and Spaces for Escape in a BPR Telephone Banking Work Regime', *The Journal of Management Studies* March 1998.

Chapter 6: Teams, Task Forces, and Tantrums: Getting Mission Critical Teams Working

1   Clayton Christensen, *The Innovators Dilemma* (Boston, MA: Harvard Business School Press, 1997).

2   Gary Hamel, 'Bringing Silicon Valley Inside,' *Harvard Business Review* September/October 1999.

3   J. Bailey, 'Honeywell's Team Approach to New-Product Development.' In *Time-Based Competition*, ed. J. D. Blackburn (Homewood, IL: Business One Irwin, 1991).

4   Meredith Belbin, *Beyond the Team* (Boston, MA: Butterworth-Heinemann, 2000) and Meredith Belbin, *Management Teams: Why They Succeed or Fail* (London: Heinemann, 1981).

5   B. Davids, 'Creating Culture Change Through Action Learning Processes – General Electric and Beyond' (presentation, June 2000).

6   B. W. Tuckman, 'Development Sequence in Small Groups,' *Psychological Bulletin* 1965.

7   Jeffrey Pfeffer and Robert Sutton, *The Knowing-Doing Gap: How Smart Companies Turn Knowledge Into Action* (Boston, MA: Harvard Business School Press, 2000).

8   Ibid.

Chapter 7: Performance Measurement – Balancing the Scorecard

1   James Creelman, 'British Telecommunications Worldwide: Building a Scorecard on Internet Time,' *The Balanced Scorecard Report* May/June 2000.

2   This case is adapted from the original entitled 'AT&T Canada: A New Strategic Governance System Quadruples Market Value,' *Balanced Scorecard Report* January–February 2000.

3   Alfred Rappaport, *Creating Shareholder Value: A Guide For Managers and Investors* (New York: Free Press, 1998).

4   Andy Neely, *Measuring Business Performance* (London: *The Economist* in Association with Profile Books, 1998).

5   Ibid.

6   Robert Simons, Antonio Dávila and Robert Kaplan, *Performance Measurement and Control Systems for Implementing Strategy: Text and Cases* (Upper Saddle River, NJ: Prentice Hall, 2000).

7   This case is adapted from the original by Creelman, 'British Telecommunications Worldwide.'

8   *The Times* 7 July 2000.

9   William Schiemann and John Lingle, *Bullseye!: Hitting Your Strategic Targets Through High-Impact Measurement* (New York: Free Press, 1999).

10 Robert Kaplan and David Norton, *The Balanced Scorecard: Translating Strategy Into Action* (Boston, MA: Harvard Business School Press, 1996).

11 Robert Simons and Antonio Dávila, 'How High Is Your Return on Management?' *Harvard Business Review* January/February 1998.

12 'Mastering Management,' *Financial Times* December 1998.

13 *Harvard Business Review on Measuring Corporate Performance* (Boston, MA: Harvard Business School Press, 1998).

14 Al Ehrbar, *EVA: Three Real Keys to Creating Wealth* (New York: John Wiley & Sons, 1998).

15 John McGrath, 'Tracking Down Value,' *FT Mastering Management Review* December 1998.

16 'Mastering Management,' *Financial Times* December 1998.

17 Al Ehrbar, 'EVA: Measure Performance,' *Strategy and Leadership* May/June 1999 and Kenneth Lehn and Anil Makhija, 'EVA and MVA: As Performance Measures and Signals for Strategic Change,' *Strategy and Leadership* May/June 1996.

18 Opp. cit.

19 Charles Kantor, 'Restructuring Performance Measurement and Incentive Compensation Plans for Shareholder Wealth Creation' (Winter 2000 [unpublished paper]).

20 Kenneth Lehn and Anil Makhija, 'EVA and MVA: As Performance Measures and Signals for Strategic Change,' *Strategy and Leadership* May/June 1996.

Chapter 8: Leadership Architecture

1   Matt Murray, 'Last Conglomerate: Can the House that Jack Built Stand When He Goes?' *The Wall Street Journal* 13 April 2000.

2   Sumatra Ghoshal and Chris Bartlett, 'A New Manifesto for Management,' *Sloan Management Review*, Spring 1999.

3   Ibid.

4   Mike Troy, 'Global Group Ready for New Growth Phase,' *Dsn Retailing Today* 5 June 2000.

5   Warren Bennis, 'Recreating the Company,' *Executive Excellence* September 1999.

6   Burt Nanus, *The Leader's Edge: The Seven Keys to Leadership in a Turbulent World* (Chicago: Contemporary Books, 1989).

7   Marco Iansiti and Michael McCormack, *Technology Development and Integration: An Empirical Study of the Interaction Between Applied Science and Product Development* (Boston, MA: Harvard Business School, 1992).

8   David Aaker and Erich Joachimsthaler, *Brand Leadership* (New York: Free Press, 2000).

Chapter 9: A Concluding Achievement

1   Nitin Nohria and James Champy, *The Arc of Ambition* (Cambridge, MA: Perseus Press, 2000).

2   Michael Watkins and Dan Ciampo, *Right from the Start* (Cambridge, MA: Harvard Business School Press, 1999).

3   C. M. Farkas and S. Wetlaner, 'The Way Chief Executive Officers Lead,' *Harvard Business Review on Leadership* (Boston, MA: Harvard Business School Press, 1998).

4   C. McCrae, 'Mini Cases in Brand Reality,' *Journal of Marketing Management* 1999.

5   M. J. Krol, L. A. Toombs and P. Wright, 'Napoleon's Tragic March Home From Moscow: Lessons in Hubris,' *The Academy of Management Executive* February 2000.

6   Randy Komisar, 'Goodbye Career, Hello Success,' *Harvard Business Review* March/April 2000.

7   Henry Goldblatt, 'Staying Smart/Managing Companies and Careers in the New Economy,' *Fortune Magazine* 16 August 1999.

8   Joseph Schumpeter, *Essays: On Entrepreneurs, Innovations, Business Cycles, and the Evolution of Capitalism* (New Brunswick, NJ: Transaction Publishers, 1989).

9   S. Watson, 'Train to Retain,' *Computerworld* 28 June 1999.

Bibliography

Aaker, David and Erich Joachimsthaler. 2000. *Brand Leadership*. New York: Free Press.

Allen, Jeffrey. 1995. *The Career Trap: Breaking through the Barrier to Get the Job You Really Want*. New York: AMACOM.

Allen, Robert. 1996. 'Human Resources Champions.' *Human Resource Planning*.

Ashworth, Jon. 2000. 'Airline Crews May Live to Miss Ayling.' *The Times (London)* (26 April).

'AT&T Canada: A New Strategic Governance System Quadruples Market Value.' *Balanced Scorecard Report* (January–February 2000).

Bailey, J. 1991. 'Honeywell's Team Approach to New-Product Development.' In *Time-Based Competition*, ed. J. D. Blackburn. Homewood, IL: Business One Irwin.

Bailey, Jeff. 2000. 'Second Helping: Star Rescuers Take on Waste Management and End up Tarnished.' *The Wall Street Journal* (29 February).

Baker, Wayne. 1994. *Networking Smart: How to Build Relationships for Personal and Organizational Success*. New York: McGraw-Hill.

Balu, Rekha. 2000. 'Exit Strategies: Turn out the Lights – This Job is Over! But before You Head off to Make a Fresh Start, You Need to Make a Smart Finish. Quitting Right Can Be a Great Career Move. Meet Five People Who Learned How to Quit Smart.' *Fast Company* (1 April).

Barchan, Margareta. 1999. 'Measuring Success.' *Strategy and Leadership* (May/June).

Barnard, Chester. 1968. *The Functions of the Executive*. Cambridge, MA: Harvard University Press.

Bartlett, Christopher and Ashish Nanda. 1994. 'Intel Corp.: Leveraging Capabilities for Strategic Renewal.' *Harvard Business School Case No. 394141* (9 March).

Battey, Jim. 2000. 'Careers by the Numbers.' *InfoWorld* (29 May).

Beer, Michael. 1988. 'Leading Change.' *Harvard Business School Case No. 9-488-037*. Boston, MA: Harvard Business School Publishing.

Beer, Michael and Nitin Nohria. 2000. 'Cracking the Code of Change.' *Harvard Business Review* (May/June).

Belbin, Meredith. 1981. *Management Teams: Why They Succeed or Fail*. London: Heinemann.

———. 2000. *Beyond the Team*. Boston, MA: Butterworth-Heinemann.

Bennis, Warren. 1999. 'Recreating the Company.' *Executive Excellence* (September).

Bennis, Warren and Burt Nanus. 1985. *Leaders: The Strategies for Taking Charge*. New York: Harper & Row.

Berenson, Alex. 2000. 'In Silicon Valley, Loyalty Means Paying a High Price; Cultural Strengths Help Affect Loss of Paper Wealth.' *The New York Times* (28 May).

Boulton, Richard, Barry Libert and Steve Samek. 2000. *Cracking the Value Code: How Successful Businesses Are Creating Wealth in the New Economy*. New York: HarperBusiness.

Brannick, Michael, Eduardo Salas and Carolyn Prince, eds. 1997. *Team Performance Assessment and Measurement: Theory, Methods, and Applications*. Mahwah, NJ: Lawrence Erlbaum Associates, 1997.

Brindle, Margaret and Lisa Mainiero. 2000. *Managing Power Through Lateral Networking*. Westport, CT: Quorum.

Brousseau, Kenneth, Michael Driver, Kristina Eneroth and Rikard Larsson. 1996. 'Career Pandemonium: Realigning Organizations and Individuals.' *The Academy of Management Executive* (November).

Brown, Shona and Kathleen Eisenhardt. 1995. 'Product Development: Past Research, Present Findings, and Future Directions.' *Academy of Management Review*.

——. 1998. *Competing on the Edge: Strategy as Structured Chaos*. Boston, MA: Harvard Business School Press.

Burt, Nanus. 1989. *The Leader's Edge: The Seven Keys to Leadership in a Turbulent World*. Chicago: Contemporary Books.

'Business Poses New Challengers for IT Architectures.' *Informationweek* (7 February 2000).

Cairnes, Margot. 1998. *Approaching the Corporate Heart: Breaking Through to New Horizons of Personal and Professional Success*. Sydney: Simon & Schuster.

Cardona, Pablo and Paddy Miller. 2000. 'The Art of Creating and Sustaining Winning Teams.' Technical note. Barcelona: IESE.

Champy, James and Nitin Nohria. 2000. *The Arc of Ambition: Defining the Leadership Journey*. Cambridge, MA: Perseus Books.

Chang, Richard and Mark Morgan. 2000. *Performance Scorecards: Measuring the Right Things in the Real World*. San Francisco, CA: Jossey-Bass Publishers.

'Changing of the Guard.' *Chain Store Age* (March 2000).

Chapman, Elwood and Sharon Lund O'Neil. 2000. *Leadership: Essential Steps Every Manager Needs to Know*. Upper Saddle River, NJ: Prentice Hall.

Chemical Market Reporter, Schell Publishing Company (17 April 2000).

Chowdhury, Subir, ed. 2000. *Management 21C: Someday We'll Manage This Way*. London: Financial Times Management.

Christensen, Clayton. 1997. *The Innovators Dilemma*. Boston, MA: Harvard Business School Press.

Ciampa, Dan and Michael Watkins. 1999. *Right from the Start: Taking Charge in a New Leadership Role*. Boston, MA: Harvard Business School Press.

Clark, Kim and Takahiro Fujimoto. 1991. *Product Development Performance: Strategy, Organization, and Management in the World Auto Industry*. Boston, MA: Harvard Business School Press.

Clegg, Stewart, Cynthia Hardy and Walter Nord, eds. 1999. *Managing Organizations: Current Issues*. London: Sage.

Cohen, W. M. and Levinthal, D. A. 1990. 'Absorptive Capacity: A New Perspective on Learning and Innovation.' *Administrative Science Quarterly* 35, 128–152.

'Comstellar Launches With Innovative Business Model and Premier Management Team; Architects of Tomorrow's Communication Technologies.' *PR Newswire Europe Limited* (11 July 2000).

Creelman, James. 2000. British Telecommunications Worldwide: Building a Scorecard on Internet Time.' *The Balanced Scorecard Report* (May/June).

Curtis, Keith. 1994. *From Management Goal Setting to Organizational Results: Transforming Strategies into Action.* Westport, CT: Quorum Books.

Cusumano, Michael and David Yoffie. 1998. *Competing on Internet Time: Lessons From Netscape and Its Battle With Microsoft.* New York: Free Press.

Daily, Catherine. 1995. 'An Empirical Examination of the Relationship Between CEOs and Directors.' *The Journal of Business Strategies* (Spring).

Davids, B. 2000. 'Creating Culture Change Through Action Learning Processes – General Electric and Beyond.' Presentation (June).

Davis, James and Barry Cushing. 1980. *Accounting Information Systems: A Book of Readings with Cases.* Reading, MA: Addison-Wesley.

DeLisi, Peter. 1998. 'A Modern-Day Tragedy: The Digital Equipment Story.' *Journal of Management Inquiry* (June).

Dess, Gregory and Joseph Picken. 1999. *Beyond Productivity: How Leading Companies Achieve Superior Performance by Leveraging Their Human Capital.* New York: AMACOM.

Dougherty, D. 1992. 'Interpretative Barriers to Successful Product Innovation in Large Firms.' *Organization Science.*

Dovey, Kenneth. 1997. PhD thesis, University of Technology, Sydney.

Drucker, Peter Ferdinand. 1999. *Management Challenges for the 21st Century.* New York: HarperBusiness.

Earley, Christopher. 1997. *Face, Harmony, and Social Structure: An Analysis of Organizational Behavior across Cultures.* New York: Oxford University Press.

Ehrbar, Al. 1998. *EVA: Three Real Keys to Creating Wealth.* New York: John Wiley & Sons.

——. 1999. 'EVA: Measure Performance.' *Strategy and Leadership* (May/June).

Eisenhardt, Kathleen and Shona Brown. 1998. 'Time Pacing: Competing in Markets That Won't Stand Still.' *Harvard Business Review* (March/April).

Enos, Darryl. 2000. *Performance Improvement – Making It Happen.* Boca Raton, FL: St Lucía Press.

'EVA & MVA as Performance Measures and Signals for Strategic Change.'

Evand, Philip and Thomas Wurster. 1997. 'Strategy and the New Economics of Information.' *Harvard Business Review* (September/October).

——. 1999. 'Getting Real about Virtual Commerce.' *Harvard Business Review* (November/December).

——. 2000. *Blown to Bits: How the New Economics of Information Transforms Strategy.* Boston, MA: Harvard Business School Press.

Farkas, C. M. and S. Wetlaner 1998. 'The Way Chief Executive Officers Lead.' *Harvard Business Review on Leadership.* Boston, MA: Harvard Business School Press.

Finkelstein, Sydney and Donald Hambrick. 1996. *Strategic Leadership: Top Executives and Their Effects on Organizations*. Minneapolis/St Paul: West Publishing Company.

Floyd, Steven and Bill Woolridge. 1998. 'Knowledge Creation and Social Networks in Corporate Entrepreneurship: The Renewal of Organizational Capability.' *Entrepreneurship Theory and Practice* (Spring).

Foust, Dean, David Rocks and Mark Clifford. 1999. 'Is Douglas Daft the Real Thing?' *Business Week* (20 December).

Friedman, Raymond and David Krackhardt. 1997. 'Social Capital and Career Mobility.' *The Journal of Applied Behavioral Science* (September).

Fruin, Mark, ed. 1998. *Networks, Markets, and the Pacific Rim: Studies in Strategy*. New York: Oxford University Press.

Gabarro, John. 1985. 'When a New Manager Takes Charge.' *Harvard Business Review* (May/June).

——. 1987. *The Dynamics of Taking Charge*. Boston, MA: Harvard Business School Press.

Galloni, Alessandra. 2000a. 'UK: Newsmaker-BA's Ayling – Right Strategy, Wrong Man?' *Reuters English News Service* (10 March).

——. 2000b. 'UK: Hunt for BA Boss Takes off This Week.' *Reuters English News Services* (13 March).

Garten, Jeffrey, ed. 2000. *World View: Global Strategies for the New Economy*. Boston, MA: Harvard Business School Press.

Gautschi, Ted. 2000. 'In This New Era, What Matters Most?' *Design News* (19 June).

Ghemawat, Pankaj, David Collis, Gary Pisano and Jan Rivkin. 1999. *Strategy and the Business Landscape: Text and Cases*. Reading, MA: Addison-Wesley.

Ghoshal, Sumantra and Bartlett, Chris 1999. 'A New Manifesto for Management.' *Sloan Management Review* (Spring).

Gibson, James, John Ivancevich and James Donnelly Jr. 2000. *Organizations: Behavior, Structure, Processes*. Boston, MA: Irwin/McGraw-Hill.

Gini, Al. 2000. *My Job, My Self: Work and the Creation of the Modern Individual*. New York: Routledge.

'Global Leader Focuses on Customer Needs.' *Business Korea* (December 1999).

Goff, Leslie. 2000. 'Anatomy of An E-Commerce Organization.' *Computerworld* (29 May).

Goldblatt, Henry. 1999. 'Staying Smart/Managing Companies and Careers in the New Economy.' *Fortune Magazine* (16 August).

Goleman, Daniel. 1998. 'What Makes a Leader?' *Harvard Business Review* (November/December).

——. 2000. 'Leadership that Gets Results.' *Harvard Business Review* (March/April).

Gormley, William Jr and David Weimer. 1999. *Organizational Report Cards*. Cambridge, MA: Harvard University Press.

Graham, Francis and Clare Minchington. 2000. 'Value-Based Management in Practice.' *Management Accounting* (February).

Gulati, Ranjay, Nitin Nohria and Akbar Zaheer. 2000. 'Strategic Networks.' *Strategic Management Journal* 21, 203–215.

Gustavsen, Bjorn. 1998. 'From Experiments to Network Building: Trends in the Use of Research for Reconstructing Working Life.' *Human Relations* (March).

Hamel, Gary. 1999. 'Bringing Silicon Valley Inside.' *Harvard Business Review* (September/October).

Hambrick, Donald. 1995. 'Fragmentation and the Other Problems CEOs Have with Their to.' *California Management Review* (Spring).

Hambrick, Donald and Gregory D. S. Fukutomi. 1991. 'The Seasons of a CEO's Tenure.' *Academy of Management* (October).

Hambrick, Donald, David Nadler and Michael Tushman, eds. 1998. *Navigating Change: How CEOs, Top Teams, and Boards Steer Transformation.* Boston, MA: Harvard Business School Press.

Hammonds, Keith and Ann Therese. 1998. 'The Daddy Trap.' *Business Week* (21 September).

Hardy, Quentin. 1999. 'Balancing the Need for Speed With a Respect for HP's Past.' *Forbes Magazine* (13 December).

Harrison, Roy. 1998. Move with the Goal Posts.' *People Management* (22 January).

Harvard Business School. 1998. *Harvard Business Review on Measuring Corporate Performance.* Boston, MA: Harvard Business School Press.

Harvard Business School. 1999. *Harvard Business Review on Breakthrough Thinking.* Boston, MA: Harvard Business School Press.

Heenan, David and Warren Bennis. 1999. *Co-Leaders: The Power of Great Partnerships.* New York: John Wiley.

Helgesen, Sally. 1995. *Web of Inclusion: A New Architecture for Building Great Organizations.* New York: Currency/Doubleday.

Hesselbein, Frances and Paul Cohen, eds. 1999. *Leader to Leader: Enduring Insights on Leadership from the Drucker Foundation's Award-Winning Journal.* San Francisco: Jossey-Bass.

Hesselbein, Frances, Marshall Goldsmith and Iain Somerville, eds. 1999. *Leading Beyond the Walls.* San Francisco: CA: Jossey-Bass.

Hodgetts, Richard. 1998. *Measures of Quality and High Performance: Simple Tools and Lessons Learned from America's Most Successful Corporations.* New York: AMACOM.

Hope, Tony and Jeremy Hope. 1996. *Transforming the Bottom Line: Managing Performance with the Real Numbers.* Boston, MA: Harvard Business School Press.

Iansiti, Marco and Michael McCormack. 1992. *Technology Development and Integration: An Empirical Study of the Interaction Between Applied Science and Product Development.* Boston, MA: Harvard Business School.

'Innovations Fuel DHL's Perishables Service.' *Logistics Management and Distribution Report* (October 1999).

Jacoby, Sanford. 1999. 'Are Career Jobs Headed for Extinction.' *California Management Review* (Fall).

Jarillo, José. 1988 'On Strategic Networks.' *Strategic Management Journal* (January/February).

——. 1993. *Strategic Networks: Creating the Borderless Organization.* Boston, MA: Butterworth-Heinemann.

Kamp, Di. 1999 *The 21st Century Manager: Future-Focused Skills for the Next Millennium*. London: Kogan Page.

Kantor, Charles. 2000. 'Restructuring Performance Measurement and Incentive Compensation Plans for Shareholder Wealth Creation.' (Winter [unpublished paper]).

Kaplan, Robert and David Norton. 1996a. *The Balanced Scorecard: Translating Strategy Into Action*. Boston, MA: Harvard Business School Press.

——. 1996b. 'Strategic Learning and the Balanced Scorecard.' *Strategy and Leadership* (September/October).

Kaplan, Robert and Anthony Atkinson. 1998. *Advanced Management Accounting*. Upper Saddle River, NJ: Prentice Hall.

Katzenbach, Jon. 1998a. *Teams at the Top: Unleashing the Potential of Both Teams and Individual Leaders*. Boston, MA: Harvard Business School Press.

——, ed. 1998b. *The Work of Teams*. Boston, MA: Harvard Business School Press.

Katzenbach, Jon and D. K. Smith. 1993. 'The Discipline of Teams.' *Harvard Business Review* (March/April).

Kehoe, Louise. 1999. 'The Americas: Reinventing Company of Inventors.' *Financial Times (London)* (16 November).

Kemp, Ted. 2000. 'Fixing the IT-Marketing Disconnect – When Teams Don't Talk.' *Internetweek* (10 July).

Kirkman, Bradley and Bensen Rosen. 2000. 'Powering up Teams.' *Organizational Dynamics* (Winter).

Kolb, David. 1984. *Experiential Learning: Experience as the Source of Learning and Development*. Englewood Cliffs, NJ: Prentice-Hall.

Komisar, Randy. 2000. 'Goodbye Career, Hello Success.' *Harvard Business Review* (March/April).

Komisar, Randy and Kent Lineback. 2000. *The Monk and the Riddle: The Education of a Silicon Valley Entrepreneur*. Boston, MA: Harvard Business School Press.

Kotter, John. 1982. *The General Managers*. New York: Free Press.

——. 1996. *Leading Change*. Boston, MA: Harvard Business School Press.

——. 1999. *On What Leaders Really Do*. Boston, MA: Harvard Business School Press.

Kotter, John and James Heskett. 1992. *Corporate Culture and Performance*. New York: Free Press.

Krackhardt, David and Jeffrey Hanson. 1993. 'Informal Networks: The Company.' *Harvard Business Review* (July/August).

Krol, M. J., L. A. Toombs and P. Wright. 2000. 'Napoleon's Tragic March fome From Moscow: Lessons in Hubris.' *The Academy of Management Executive* (February).

LaLonde, Bernard. 2000. 'The "Gap Creep".' *Supply Chain Management Review* (Winter).

Leenders, Roger and Shaul Gabbay, eds. 1999. *Corporate Social Capital and Liability*. Boston, MA: Kluwer Academic.

Lehn, Kenneth and Anil Makhija. 1996. 'EVA and MVA: As Performance Measures and Signals for Strategic Change.' *Strategy and Leadership* (May/June).

Lewis, Michael. 2000. *The New New Thing: A Silicon Valley Story*. New York: W. W. Norton.

'Lifelong Learning.' *Electronics Times* (26 June 2000).

McCabe, Darren and David Knights. 1998. '"What Happens when the Phone Goes Wild?": Staff, Stress and Spaces for Escape in a BPR Telephone Banking Work Regime.' *The Journal of Management Studies* (March).

McCrae, C. 1999. 'Mini Cases in Brand Reality.' *Journal of Marketing Management*.

McDermott, Lynda, Nolan Brawley and William Waite. 1998. *World-Class Teams: Working Across Borders*. New York: J. Wiley.

McGrath, John. 1998. 'Tracking Down Value.' *FT Mastering Management Review* (December).

'Mastering Management.' *Financial Times* (December 1998).

Miller, William. 1999. 'Building the Ultimate Resource.' *Management Review* (January).

Minton, Anna. 2000. 'Companies and Finance: UK: Hamleys out to Purge the Past.' *Financial Times (London)* (16 June).

'Mitchell International Announces Reorganization From Divisional to Functional Structure; Restructure Made to Better Serve Its Customers; Accommodate Accelerated Rate of Growth, and Form New International and E-Business Groups.' *PR Newswire* (10 May 2000).

Moses, Barbara. 1997. *Career Intelligence: Mastering the New Work and Personal Realities*. Toronto: Stoddart.

Murray, Matt. 2000. 'Last Conglomerate: Can the House that Jack Built Stand When He Goes?' *The Wall Street Journal* (13 April).

Nadler, David and Janet Spencer. 1998. *Executive Teams*. San Francisco, CA: Jossey-Bass Publishers.

Nash, Susan. 1999. *Turning Team Performance Inside Out: Team Types and Temperaments for High-Impact Results*. Palo Alto, CA: Davies-Black Publishers.

Nee, Eric. 2000. 'Hewlett Packard's New Evangelist.' *Fortune Magazine* (10 January).

Neely, Andy. 1998. *Measuring Business Performance*. London: *The Economist* in Association with Profile Books.

'Netergy Networks Unveils Expanded Strategy for Enabling Converged Voice and Data Services.' *Business Wire* (13 July 2000).

Nohria, Nitin and Sumantra Ghoshal. 1997. *The Differentiated Network: Organizing Multinational Corporations for Value Creation*. San Francisco, CA: Jossey-Bass Publishers.

Normann, Richard and Rafael Ramirez. 1993. 'From Value Chain to Value Constellation: Designing Interactive Strategies.' *Harvard Business Review* (July/August).

Olve, Nils-Göran, Jan Roy and Magnus Wetter. 1999. *Performance Drivers: A Practical Guide to Using the Balanced Scorecard*. New York: J. Wiley.

'100 Ways to Get Ahead In Your Career; Master These Secrets To Success, Suggested By Our Editors, Readers, and Vendors, And Your Career Will Soar. And Check www.designnews.com, Where You Will Find Regular Updates On These Topics.' *Design News* (3 July 2000).

'Online Banking – Big Opportunity and Big Risk.' *Deutschebank Alex. Brown Report* (3 January 2000).

Ostroff, Frank. 1999. *Horizontal Organization: What the Organization of the Future Looks Like and How It Delivers Value to Customers*. New York: Oxford University Press.

O'Toole, James. 1999. *Leadership A to Z: A Guide For the Appropriately Ambitious*. San Francisco, CA: Jossey-Bass Publishers.

——. 2000. 'Silicon Valley Needs Leadership – Silicon Valley Needs to Build a Legacy that Lasts, so that San Francisco Doesn't End up in 2050 Looking like Detroit in 2000.' *Information Week* (10 April).

Pasmore, William. 1994. *Creating Strategic Change: Designing the Flexible, High-Performing Organization*. New York: Wiley.

Perry, Lee, Randall Stott and Norman Smallwood. 1993. *Real-Time Strategy: Improvising Team-Based Planning for a Fast-Changing World*. New York: Wiley.

Pfeffer, Jeffrey and Robert Sutton. 2000. *The Knowing-Doing Gap: How Smart Companies Turn Knowledge into Action*. Boston, MA: Harvard Business School Press.

Phillips, Richard. 1999. *The Heart of an Executive: Lessons on Leadership from the Life of King David*. New York: Doubleday.

Porter, Michael. 1985. *Competitive Advantage: Creating and Sustaining Superior Performance*. New York: Free Press.

Pottruck, David and Terry Pearce. 2000. *Clicks and Mortar: Passion-Driven Growth in an Internet-Driven World*. San Francisco, CA: Jossey-Bass Publishers.

Puris, Martin. 1999. *Comeback: How Seven Straight-Shooting CEOs Turned Around Troubled Companies*. New York: Times Business.

Quinn, Mills and Bruce Friesen. 2000. 'Emerging Business Realities: Organizing for Value in a Wired World (part two).' *Consulting to Management* (May).

Rappaport, Alfred. 1998. *Creating Shareholder Value: A Guide for Managers and Investors*. New York: Free Press.

Rayport, Jeffrey and John Sviokla. 1995. 'Exploiting the Virtual Value Chain.' *Harvard Business Review* (November/December).

Richter, Frank-Jürgen. 1999. *Business Networks in Asia: Promises, Doubts, and Perspectives*. Westport, CT: Quorum Books.

——. 2000. *Strategic Networks: The Art of Japanese Interfirm Cooperation*. New York: International Business Press.

Risher, Howard, ed. 1999. *Aligning Pay and Results: Compensation Strategies that Work from the Boardroom to the Shop Floor*. New York: AMACOM.

Robins, Jane. 2000. 'Media: the First 100 Days of Greg Dyke.' *The Independent (London)* (11 July).

Rodríguez-Porras, J. M. 1988. *El Factor Humano en la Empresa*. Madrid, Spain: Ed. Deusto.

Romney, Marshall and Paul John Steinbart. 2000. *Accounting Information Systems*. Upper Saddle River, NJ: Prentice Hall.

Schiemann, William and John Lingle. 1999. *Bullseye!: Hitting Your Strategic Targets Through High-Impact Measurement*. New York: Free Press.

Schmickrath, Don. 2000. 'How Do Caterpillars Learn to Fly? Transforming Supply Chains at Hewlett-Packard.' *Supply Chain Management Review* (Winter).

Schumpeter, Joseph. 1989. *Essays: On Entrepreneurs, Innovations, Business Cycles, and the Evolution of Capitalism.* New Brunswick, NJ: Transaction Publishers.

Shapiro, Carl and Hal Varian. 1999. *Information Rules: A Strategic Guide to the Network Economy.* Boston, MA: Harvard Business School Press.

Shapiro, Eileen. 2000. 'Managing in the Cappuccino Economy.' *Harvard Business Review* (March/April).

Sheridan, John. 2000. 'Now It's a Job for the CEO.' *Industry Week* (20 March).

Sikorski, Douglas and Thomas Menkhoff. 2000. 'Internationalisation of Asian Business.' *Singapore Management Review* 22(1).

Simon, William. 1997. *Beyond the Numbers: How Leading Companies Measure and Drive Success.* New York: Van Nostrand Reinhold.

Simons, Robert and Antonio Dávila. 1998. 'How High Is Your Return on Management?' *Harvard Business Review* (January/February).

Simons, Robert, Antonio Dávila and Robert Kaplan. 2000. *Performance Measurement and Control Systems for Implementing Strategy: Text and Cases.* Upper Saddle River, NJ: Prentice Hall.

Simonsen, Peggy. 1997. *Promoting a Development Culture in Your Organization: Using Career Development as a Change Agent.* Palo Alto, CA: Davies-Black Publishers.

——. 2000. *Career Compass: Navigating Your Career Strategically in the New Century.* Palo Alto, CA: Davies-Black Publishers.

Sinton, Peter. 1999. 'Icons of Invention; Business Leaders See Bright Future for the Region.' *The San Francisco Chronicle* (29 December).

'60 HR Predictions for 2008.' *Workforce* (January 1998).

Snow, Charles, Raymond Miles and Henry Coleman Jr. 1992. 'Managing 21st Century Network Organizations.' *Organizational Dynamics* (Winter).

Spears, Larry, ed. 1998. *Insights on Leadership: Service, Stewardship, Spirit, and Servant-Leadership.* New York: Wiley.

Spekman, Robert, Lynn Isabella and Thomas MacAvoy. 2000. *Alliance Competence: Maximizing the Value of Your Partnerships.* New York: Wiley.

'Sterling Commerce Creates Single Global Organization to Meet Expanding E-Business Requirement.' *PR Newswire* (9 May 2000).

Tapsell, Sherrill. 1999. 'Hire Today Gone Tomorrow.' *New Zealand Management* (March).

Tesoro, Ferdinand and Jack Tootson. 2000. *Implementing Global Performance Measurement Systems: A Cookbook Approach.* San Francisco, CA: Jossey-Bass/Pfeiffer.

Threat, Holly. 1999. 'Measurement is Free.' *Strategy and Leadership* (May/June).

The Times (7 July 2000).

Tolbert, Pamela, Gerald Salancik, David Krackhardt and Steven Andrews. 1995. 'Review – Wanted: A Good Network Theory of Organization.' *Administrative Science Quarterly* (June).

Townley, Gemma. 2000. 'Innovative Start-ups Stealing a March on Traditional Structures.' *Management Accounting* (May).

Townsend, Patrick and Joan Gebhardt. 1997. *Five-Star Leadership: The Art and Strategy of Creating Leaders at Every Level.* New York: Wiley.

Troy, Mike. 2000 'Global Group Ready for New Growth Phase.' *Dsn Retailing Today* (5 June).

Tuckman, B. W. 1965. 'Development Sequence in Small Groups.' *Psychological Bulletin.*

Ulrich, David. 1997. *Human Resource Champions: The Next Agenda For Adding Value and Delivering Results.* Boston, MA: Harvard Business School Press.

———, ed. 1998. *Delivering Results: A New Mandate for Human Resource Professionals.* Boston, MA: Harvard Business School Press.

Ulrich, David, Jack Zenger and Norman Smallwood. 1999. *Results-Based Leadership.* Boston, MA: Harvard Business School Press.

Urban, Sabine, ed. 1998. *From Alliance Practices to Alliance Capitalism: New Strategies for Management and Partnership.* Wiesbaden: Gabler.

Vancil, Richard. 1987. *Passing the Baton: Managing the Process of CEO Succession.* Boston, MA: Harvard Business School Press.

Vicere, Albert and Robert Fulmer. 1998. *Leadership by Design.* Boston, MA: Harvard Business School Press.

Voss, Bristol Lane. 2000. 'Blown to Bits: How the New Economics of Information Transforms Strategy.' *The Journal of Business Strategy* (January/February).

Wah, Louisa. 2000. 'Creating an Outstanding Leadership Team.' *Management Review* (February).

Walsh, J. P. 1995. 'Managerial and Organizational Cognition: Notes from a Trip down Memory Lane.' *Organization Science.*

Wasserman, Stanley and Katherine Faust. 1994. *Social Network Analysis: Methods and Applications.* New York: Cambridge University Press.

Watson S. 1999. 'Train to Retain.' *Computerworld* (28 June).

'Wescam Announces Organizational Changes to Strengthen Customer Focus.' *Business Wire* (29 June 2000).

Yoffie, David and Michael Cusumano. 1999. 'Judo Strategy: The Competitive Dynamics of Internet Time.' *Harvard Business Review* (January/February).

Zigon, Jack. n.d. 'Measuring the Hard Stuff: Teams and Other Hard-to-Measure Work.' http://www.zigonperf.com/hardstuff.htm

Zwell, Michael and Robert Ressler. 2000. 'Powering the Human Drivers of Financial Performance.' *Strategic Finance* (May).

Index

1000 Day Imperative 7, 10
3M 158
Activity Based Costing 129
Amazon.com 12, 34, 48, 54
America Online 12
Amro ABN 5
Apple 12, 69
AT & T 123–124

Bain and Company 125
Balanced Score Card 125–133
Bank One 20
Barclays Bank 5, 24
Barnes & Noble 60
BBC 29
Bennetton 146–147, 149, 156
BMW 20, 75
Boo.com 12, 34
Border's Group 20
British Airways 10, 20, 37–41
British Petroleum 10, 20, 24
British Telecom 127–130
BTR 123
Bureaucratization of imagination 146
Burn out 175
Business Model 127, 133
    And the Internet 58
    Reassessing and alignment 34, 47–61
    Redefining 42
Bvlgari 12, 56–57

Calico Commerce 33
Career:
    Management 169–170
    Prisoners 168
    Strategy 172
Castells 83, 88
Centrality of Control 145

Charles Schwab 12
Chrysler 15
Cisco 6, 60
Citibank 5
Coca Cola 10, 20, 135, 146
Compaq 57
Compensation 138, 139
Comstellar 6, 47
Core Competency 57
Creative destruction 182
Customer Interface 53

Danisco 63
Dell 12, 35, 48, 50–52
Deutschebank 5
Diageo 125, 133–136, 138
Digital Equipment Company 15
Dow Chemical 48
Dunlop Slazenger 79

EasyJet 12
EBay 12
Economic Value Added 124, 133–141
Enso-Stora 21, 36
External Capital 66

Fear of Complexity 152
FedEx 53
Finanzauto 21, 43
First mover strategy 58
Fortis 5

General Electric 125, 143, 154
General Motors 59
Globally distributed teams 80–81, 99
    video conferencing 100
Grandmet 133
Guinness 133

Hansens 123
Headhunters 180
Henkel 27
Hewlett Packard 6, 8, 12, 21, 29–30, 35, 74, 84, 99, 149
Human capital 66
Human resource management and MCL 187

IBM 3, 12
ICI 3
IKEA 54–56, 130–131
Inbound Logistics 54
Information 51-52
Intel 12, 42, 149
Intellectual capital 66

JC Penny 32
Jobs & departure, exit strategy 165, 178
John Deere & Co 145

Knowledge:
  Based organization 143
  Management 66–67
  Systems 150
Knowledge of acquisition 174

Lastminute.com 12
Leadership Architecture 8, 17–19, 143–164
  Carly Fiorina 10
Learning cycles 174
London Stock Exchange 12

Managing Expectations 33
Market Value Added 141
Merrill Lynch 58
Mission critical teams
  Action-learning 112
  Best practice 107
  Characteristics 90
  Composition 108
  Criteria for selection 94–95
  Diversity 108
  Failure 103–104, 118
  High performance 86
  Innovation 110
  Key elements 105–106

Mavericks 95, 99
Measures 93
Mission 92
Outsiders 86
Problems 108
Risk and rewards 86, 93, 98
Special skills 95–96
Team leadership 94
Training 111
Motorola 143

Napster 1
NASA 3
Nestlé 135
Netscape 160
Networks 166
  Density 77–78
  Structure 76–77
  Advice 74–75
  Communication 73–74, 76
  Management of 71
  Trust 75–76
  Virtual 68–71
Nokia 6, 12

Patronage 156
Performance Measurement 121, 135
Phillips 11
Polarcup 36
Power 154–156
Preussag 60
Price Online 59
Process Architecture 161–164
Procter & Gamble 1, 2, 24, 135
Product Architecture 159

Qualcomm 12

Reckitt Benkiser 71
Relationship Capital 18, 44, 52, 63–82, 127, 129, 165
  Carly Fiorina 10
Resource Allocation Decision 122
Return on Assets 136
Return on Equity 136–137
Return on management 134
Rover 75
Royal Dutch Shell 3, 143, 158